Springer Studies in the History of Economic Thought

This series offers an outlet for research in the history of economic thought. It features scholarly studies on important theoretical developments and great economic thinkers that have contributed to the evolution of the economic discipline.

The series welcomes proposals for research monographs, edited volumes and handbooks from a variety of disciplines that seek to study the history of economic thinking and help to arrive at a better understanding of modern economics. Relevant topics include, but are not limited to, various schools of thought, important pioneers and thinkers, ancient and medieval economic thought, mercantilism, cameralism and physiocracy, classical and neoclassical economics, historical, institutional and evolutionary economics, socialism and Marxism, Keynesian, Sraffian and Austrian economics, econometrics and mathematical studies as well as economic methodology and the link between economic history and history of economic thought.

More information about this series at http://www.springer.com/series/16457

Ola Innset

Reinventing Liberalism

The Politics, Philosophy and Economics of Early Neoliberalism (1920-1947)

Springer

Ola Innset
National Library of Norway
Oslo, Norway

ISSN 2662-6098 ISSN 2662-6101 (electronic)
Springer Studies in the History of Economic Thought
ISBN 978-3-030-38884-3 ISBN 978-3-030-38885-0 (eBook)
https://doi.org/10.1007/978-3-030-38885-0

This Springer imprint is published by the registered company Springer Nature Switzerland AG
The registered company address is: Gewerbestrasse 11, 6330 Cham, Switzerland

Preface

This book is based on my Ph.D. thesis "Reinventing Liberalism—Early Neoliberalism in Context (1920–1947)", defended at the European University Institute in Florence in September 2017. I am very grateful to the editors of the Springer series on the History of Economic Thought for offering me the opportunity to publish the thesis as a book.

Over the six years that I have now worked on the topic of early neoliberalism, I have benefitted enormously from the help and advice of countless scholars. One of my favourite things about academia is how you can just e-mail almost any scholar anywhere in the world and receive thoughtful responses and offers to meet up in person. For their advice, comments and tips along the way, I would especially like to thank Philip Mirowski, Simon Reid-Henry, Edward Nik-Khah, Tiago Mata, Ann Thomson, Robert Lepenies, Simon Jackson, Naoko Shimazu, Hans-Michael Trautwein and Jennifer Burns, none of whom are in any way responsible for the contents of this book.

I have benefitted greatly from a number of research seminars, workshops and conferences held at the European University Institute during my time there from 2013 to 2017, both at the Department of History and Civilization, but also in the Department of Law. I would especially like to thank the participants of the interdisciplinary working group on neoliberalism, and the workshop "Why Neoliberalism?", which I co-organized in 2015 and 2016 with Julia Rone and Liam McHugh-Russell.

I would also like to thank the History Department at Stanford University for having me as a guest researcher in 2014 and the corresponding department at the University of Oslo for allowing me the same privilege in 2016 and 2017. My work would have been impossible without very helpful archivists at the Hoover Institution, Yale University Library, Het Liberaal Archief in Gent, Friedrich Naumann Stiftung in Gummersbach, King's College Archives at Cambridge, the LSE Archives, the Rubenstein Library at Duke University and Riksarkivet in Oslo.

I would like to thank my second reader Youssef Cassis, and especially my supervisor Lucy Riall, who expressed enthusiasm for my project at a time when it was badly needed, and who has used her experience as a historian in guiding me towards completion of the Ph.D. programme. Huge thanks are owed also to my external advisor João Rodrigues, who has shared his expertise in a most generous way and advised me through several re-writes of the thesis. Marie-Laure Salles-Djelic was the last member of the examining board and provided excellent advice and criticisms for which I am most thankful.

Funding for this project was provided by the Norwegian Research Council, project nr. 231807. Various archival trips and conference participations were financed by Torleif Dahls legat for historisk forskning, Borgermester Christies legat, the Department of History and Civilization at the European University Institute, the Institute for New Economic Thinking, the History of Economics Society and the European Society for the History of Economic Thought.

Lastly, I would like to thank Dorothy Hahn, without whose efforts both in 1947 and in 2015–2016, this thesis would not exist. She was the secretary of the Mont Pelerin Conference in 1947 and agreed to let me interview her in her home in Cambridge twice during the work on the thesis. I am very grateful to her.

I dedicate this book to my whole family, near and far, and especially to my wonderful wife, Elizabeth Morris Innset, and our daughter Astrid.

Moss, Norway
October 2019

Ola Innset

Contents

List of Figures

Chapter 1
Introduction

> … the scope of the liberal tradition expanded during the middle decades of the twentieth century such that it came to be seen by many as the constitutive ideology of the West. This capacious (and deeply confusing) understanding of liberalism was a product of the ideological wars fought against "totalitarianism" and assorted developments in the social sciences. Today we both inherit and inhabit it.
>
> Duncan Bell, "What is liberalism?" (2014)

What is the relationship between politics and the economy? Between democracy and the market? What *is* the economy and how are we to relate to it as a body politic? These questions should be of great interest to us in a time where loosely defined entities like "the market" or "the economy" appear in political discourse with great frequency, but lesser clarity. These questions were the main interest also of a group of 37 European and American intellectuals who gathered in the Swiss mountain village of Mont Pèlerin from April 1st to April 10th in the year 1947. The group was handpicked by Friedrich von Hayek,[1] an Austrian émigré economist who had recently experienced great success with his 1944 book *The Road to Serfdom*. They met to discuss liberalism and how to change it. This book tells the story of that ten-day meeting in 1947 and engages with the questions and ideas that animated Hayek and his fellow travellers.

[1]In the following, I will mainly use the aristocratic "von" only the first time I refer to European thinkers with that or other aristocratic prepositions in their surnames. Hayek himself used his name both with and without the "von" interchangeably after leaving Austria.

O. Innset, *Reinventing Liberalism*, Springer Studies in the History of Economic Thought,
https://doi.org/10.1007/978-3-030-38885-0_1

Neoliberalism

Several scholars and commentators attempting to understand more recent developments, such as the 2007/2008 financial crisis, austerity policies and the rise of New Public Management, have written about these issues under the rubric of *neoliberalism*. In recent years, the academic discourse surrounding neoliberalism has come under severe criticism, due to the many incompatible definitions and usages of the word (Wacquant 2011; Springer 2012; Flew 2014; Venugopal 2015). Neoliberalism is indeed the concept that permeates also this work, which unlike most treatises on the subject primarily falls under the category of intellectual history.

The reason for this choice is twofold. The first reason is simple: At the Walter Lippmann Colloquium in Paris, 1938, the group of thinkers who are the subject of this book, themselves decided to name their intellectual and political project *neoliberalism* (Jones 2012, 31). The word was suggested by the German economist Alexander von Rüstow (1885–1963), and François Denord has written retrospectively that "To be 'neoliberal' was supposed to imply the recognition that 'laissez-faire' economics was not enough and that, in the name of liberalism, a modern economic policy was needed" (Mirowski and Plehwe 2009, 48). I will argue in this book that neoliberalism was indeed an attack on the ideals of laissez-faire, but that it was also an attack on various forms of social liberalism. The 1938 meeting included several of the same people as the one in 1947, including Hayek, who my research shows played an important role intellectually and organizationally also for the 1938 meeting. In many ways, the Lippmann Colloquium was a failed, pre-war attempt at doing what the 1947 meeting did: establish an international organization for the development and spread of neoliberal ideas. Part I of this book uses the interwar years' socialist calculation debates, the 1938 meeting in Paris, the rise of fascism and the Second World War to map out the contacts between various thinkers who would meet at Mont Pèlerin[2] in 1947 and the ideas they developed in dialogue with each other and their opponents.

My second reason for using the word neoliberalism is that I consider it an apt term to describe the efforts of these thinkers. Several of them would self-identify as neoliberals up until the 1950s (Friedman 1951) but the term gradually faded, ceding ground to terms like "libertarianism" and "classical liberalism". This development might be a considered a reason to refrain from using the original label, but I will argue that the name neoliberalism is highly appropriate to describe the intellectual and political project which was instigated first in 1938, and then fully in 1947. When neoliberalism was chosen over other options such as "individualism" and "positive liberalism" (Jones 2012, 35), the participants of the Lippmann Colloquium also spoke of this new creed as a *retour* to liberalism (Audier 2008, 350). As we will see, many of the actors involved in the neoliberal project were conflicted about the degree of newness involved in their creed. While they did come to advocate a return

[2] The place in Switzerland is spelt with an accent over the first "e", but the organization uses an Americanized version when referring to itself. Consequently, I will be writing of The Mont Pelerin Society which had its first meeting at Mont Pèlerin.

to a past, liberal wisdom, my research shows that in their internal discussions, they were very clear about the need to *reform* and *change* liberalism, and update it to a new historical context. These tensions are apparent in their published work as well, although less obvious than in the minutes of the 1947 meeting. At Mont Pèlerin, the early neoliberals were actively debating the many problems of liberalism and how to turn it into a creed capable of fighting the political battles of a modern world.

As an intellectual historian, my aim with this book is to study the historical roots of an ideology and a political project which was once called neoliberalism. I will argue that although the protagonists themselves eventually disavowed this label, it is in fact a precise and historically accurate word to describe their project, precisely because their brand of liberalism amounted to something *new*. The how's and why's of this is the topic of this book, and much attention will be paid to situating neoliberalism in relation to other forms of liberalism, both synchronically and diachronically. Neoliberalism was both an intellectual and a political project. It arose in a very specific historical context in the 1920s, 30s and 40s, in debate and dialogue with socialism, fascism and the rise of mass politics. The question of the *impact* of both the neoliberal ideas and of the organization formed to promote them in 1947 is beyond the scope of this book. I do hope, however, that my work on the content and historical context of early neoliberalism will be useful for those in other fields, who see neoliberalism as a salient feature of social, political and economic life today.

It is important to stress right at the outset that the aim of this book is not to argue against neoliberalism, neither as an imagined whole, nor against any of the theories and positions espoused by the thinkers in question. A great number of journal articles and books that are devoted to understanding the political thought of neoliberalism also make their own arguments in relation to neoliberal positions. This could be considered a form of rational reconstruction, in the terminology coined by Richard Rorty, where the aim is to engage in a dialogue with past thinkers, and quite possibly also make arguments about the current validity of their claims (Rorty et al. 1984). These arguments can be based on perceived contradictions and weaknesses in neoliberal arguments; the ethical, political or philosophical positions of the scholars in questions; or some combination of the two. The economist João Rodrigues, for instance, has written that Friedrich Hayek's many comments on the importance of individuals' motivation and the moral makeup of a market society "contributes to undermine his claims that a market society can be neutral among different values" (Rodrigues 2013, 565). Writing of the same thinker, political theorist Andrew Gamble has claimed that Hayek's overall argument is "at its weakest" when he uses evolutionary arguments for a market-based society while at the same time discarding the traditions of socialism and "constructive rationalism" as mere "intellectual error" (Gamble 1996, 182). Another example of this approach to neoliberalism is Thomas Biebricher, who in his recent book *The Political Theory of Neoliberalism* shows a masterful understanding of neoliberal thought, and argues that "the problem does not lie with selective implementation, unfaithful to the spirit of the respective ideas *but the very ideas themselves*" (Biebricher 2018, 9). Impressive as all these critiques of neoliberalism are, they are still a different type of study than the one in question.

Additionally, there are of course a great number of scholars who write celebratory accounts of neoliberal thought and neoliberal thinkers, emphasizing the inventiveness of their arguments; the success of policies inspired by their thinking; their moral courage in staunchly defending the principles of individual liberty; and so on (Hartwell 1995; Zmirak 2001; Ebenstein 2003). The more intellectually advanced branch of this literature also moves beyond hagiography in criticizing some aspects of the theories in question, suggesting revisions and improvements (Caldwell 2004; Hardhaug Olsen 2015; Boettke 2019).

Rational reconstruction and the normative approach to political thought that it tends to entail is of course a wholly legitimate endeavour, and much of the secondary literature to which this book refers falls into this category. Even for those involved in what Rorty called historical reconstruction or intellectual history, the temptation to pass judgement over thinkers and theories that are so close to us in time and are believed by many to have greatly influenced our present conjuncture, can be tempting and hard to avoid. Daniel Stedman Jones writes already in the introduction to his history of neoliberalism, entitled *Masters of the Universe*, that "the initial appeal of neoliberal proposals led ultimately to a widespread acceptance by the 1980s of an overarching philosophy of free markets". He goes on to argue that "This was unnecessary" (Jones 2012, 5). These are not the types of claims this book seeks to make. It could be argued that the writing of the history of political thought is always a form of political thought in itself, something that could be exemplified by one of the fields' leading proponents, Quentin Skinner. Skinner's work in the history of political thought has sometimes entered into debates in contemporary political philosophy (Tully 1988; Edling and Mörkenstam 1995). The political project of neoliberalism is itself also a case in point, because as I will argue, it rested on a specific narrative of history and of the history of liberal thought in particular. These nuances and concerns notwithstanding, it is worth stating clearly at the very outset of this investigation that this book is *not* engaged in making normative arguments about what was wrong and what was right with early neoliberal thought. Rather, the aim is to advance our understanding of this body of thought through historical reconstruction and thorough *contextualization*—investigating the people, places and historical context out of which neoliberalism grew.

Methodology

Loosely inspired by the field of microhistory, I aim to make my subject manageable by centring investigations on one ten-day meeting in Switzerland in April 1947. Through a detailed focus on small events and developments, microhistory attempts to not only be exact and precise about these micro-events, but also to say something about their relation to larger developments, which can only be represented through generalizations that risk violating the ideals of precision and truthfulness that all historians aim to achieve (Levi 1991). Francesca Trivellato has introduced a separation between the original Italian tradition of microhistory, and later adaptations of microhistory in the Anglophone world. Despite not being a unified school of thought and never presenting a uniform or coherent theory about the relationship between the micro- and macroscales of analysis, Trivellato argues that Italian microhistory has been characterized by methodological reflexivity and attention to theory, whereas the Anglophone version has been more interested in narration (Trivellato 2011). The focus on micro-events in the Italian tradition has been used to question grand syntheses, and this is partly the motivation behind my decision to devote Part II of this book to a careful study of selected sessions from one ten-day meeting in 1947.

There are several competing, grand syntheses about neoliberalism. From Marxist writers like Gérard Duménil and Dominique Lévy, who claim that neoliberalism is an episode of the ongoing class struggle (Duménil and Lévy 2004), to Eamonn Butler of the Adam Smith Institute think tank, who refrains from using the label but nonetheless praises the influence of the thinkers in question as emancipatory against the threat of totalitarian tyranny (Butler 2015), and Foucauldian theorists like Wendy Brown, who see neoliberalism as a new form of political rationality, governing the formation of subjectivities in contemporary society (Brown 2015). Careful study of the micro-event that was the first meeting of the Mont Pelerin Society in 1947, will lead to revision of many of these syntheses, but the Anglophone notion of microhistory as a tool for narration certainly also plays a part in the choice of scale for Part II of this book. Through narration and attention to detail, we can arrive at a more truthful picture of this moment in time and place, and thus understand better the ideas that grew out of it. Coupled with a focus on the demographics and social background of the conference attendees, the aim is to arrive at a sort of cultural and social history of early neoliberal thought.

In the context of intellectual history, I would argue that this quasi-micro-historical approach can be helpful in order to achieve the elusive goal of *contextualizing* ideas, a goal of the field ever since the early interventions of Quentin Skinner and J.G.A. Pocock in the 1960s and the subsequent rise of the linguistics inspired methodology of the so-called Cambridge school. Disagreement persists as to what putting ideas in context actually means. Inspired by Ludwig Wittgenstein and analytical philosophy, Skinner and Pocock argued that political language had to be understood as speech acts, and that the job of the intellectual historian was to situate his or her object of study in relation to the wider discursive field of which they formed part, thus paying close attention to the authors intentions (Skinner 2002). This method has been widely accepted, but some have criticized the Cambridge school for focusing exclusively on classic texts. Scholars like Robert Darnton have argued instead for a "social history of ideas", one which includes texts from outside the canon of political thought, and even material objects like books, thus in some ways taking the contextual approach one step further (McMahon 2014, 16–17). This vibrant field is certainly an inspiration for my own work, and focussing on the first meeting of what was to become the Mont Pelerin Society gives the questions I am addressing in this book, and those that the participants themselves were addressing at the meeting, a more concrete, almost physical quality. It places these issues in time and space, allowing for an understanding of them that is less abstract than, for instance, a purely theoretical survey on neoliberalism and the epistemology of markets. In unpacking and contextualizing their arguments, I will bring attention also to matters like where in Switzerland the meeting was held, the social background of the participants, their excursions and even their meals. All with the aim of furthering our appreciation of who these people were and what sort of project they were engaged in. I would argue that this in many ways squares well with Skinner's insistence that the intellectual historian ought to understand what writers of classic texts were actually *doing* in writing what they did (Skinner 2002, 82).

The Mont Pelerin Society

Scholars with divergent opinions on the subject matter all agree that The Mont Pelerin Society has been central to neoliberalism. As early as 1945, Friedrich Hayek convinced the investor Anthony Fisher to set up a think tank as a better way of influencing politics than becoming an actual politician, and in 1949 Hayek described his goal of influencing intellectuals and public opinion more indirectly in the article "The Intellectuals and Socialism". In 1981, Fisher set up an organization called the ATLAS Network (Djelic 2014), and today it is an umbrella organization for no less than 496 think tanks and organizations in 98 countries all over the world (October 2019). David Harvey thus locates the intellectuals of the Mont Pelerin Society firmly at the beginning of his *A Brief History of Neoliberalism* (2005) (Harvey 2005, 19–22). For Harvey, the ideas developed by the members of the Mont Pelerin Society mainly served as justifications for the restoration of class power, which in Harvey's Marxist view is the essence of "neoliberalization" (Mirowski and Plehwe 2009, 20). Angus Burgin, an historian of the American Right, sees the work of the Mont Pelerin Society as central to what he calls "the reinvention of free markets after the Depression", which is the subtitle of his meticulously researched *The Great Persuasion* (2012). Similarly, the before-mentioned British historian Daniel Stedman Jones emphasizes the importance of the Mont Pelerin Society as a transatlantic meeting place for market-friendly, liberal economists from Europe and the US in his book *Masters of the Universe* (2012) (Jones 2012, 73–78). Both Burgin and Stedman Jones see neoliberalism mainly in opposition to the paradigm known as Keynesianism, and understand it as a set of economic policies concerning deregulation of financial markets, monetary policies inspired by monetarism, privatizations and a shrinking of the public sector in general. Harvey's class interests thus play only a minor part in these narratives of what Burgin calls "the spirit of an age" (Burgin 2012, 214).

We may call these two approaches to the study of neoliberalism and its history the "Marxist" and the "Policy" approach, respectively (Innset 2016). Philip Mirowski is amongst those who offer a somewhat different analysis of neoliberalism, one that is in fact centred even more on the Mont Pelerin Society. Mirowski's work in intellectual history draws on ideas from Michel Foucault's 1979 lectures on neoliberalism, Foucault (2008) and on methodology from Science and Technology Studies (STS) in defining neoliberalism simultaneously as a "thought collective" and a political movement (Mirowski 2013, 26). In a postface to the volume *The Road from Mont Pelerin*

(2009), co-edited with Dieter Plehwe, Mirowski locates the Mont Pelerin Society right at the centre of a complex structure of think tanks, lobby groups, fake ("astroturfed") grassroots organizations and loosely affiliated university faculties, who have wielded considerable influence over global politics in recent decades. Within what Mirowski identifies as the Neoliberal Thought Collective (a notion derived from Ludwig Fleck) (Mirowski and Plehwe 2009, 35) there are strands and opinions so divergent that it almost seems difficult to understand that they could actively work together. As we will see, there were at least three main strands of the early neoliberal movement: Austrian economics, German "ordoliberalism" and American Chicago-school economics. These could be divided into different subgroups, the list could be expanded, and some of the thinkers in question can also be said to alternate between the three different approaches. The very variety of ideas within the Mont Pelerin Society makes it difficult to discuss thinkers as diverse as, for instance, Milton Friedman and Friedrich Hayek under the same umbrella concept of neoliberalism. That, however, is exactly what I aim to do in this book, and the fact that both Friedman and Hayek were founding members of the Mont Pelerin Society is part of the rationale for such a cause of investigation. In his book about the 2008 financial crisis, *Never Let A Serious Crisis Go To Waste* (2013), Mirowski writes that "the MPS [The Mont Pèlerin Society] will serve as our Rosetta Stone: any idea or person with membership or strong ties to the organization will qualify as 'neoliberal'" (Mirowski 2013, 39). Mirowski thus uses the Mont Pelerin Society as a conceptual tool to overcome the problem of how to define neoliberalism.[3] It could perhaps be argued that this tool is stretched somewhat when Mirowski defines contemporary actors as "neoliberals" due to connections with organizations belonging to the ATLAS Network, but in the years that is the scope of this book, 1920–1947, the method certainly makes a lot of sense.

In his collection of essays on the history of German economic thought *Strategies of Economic Order* (1995), Keith Tribe argues in an article on the German Historical School that "Too often effort is devoted to gathering together contemporaries under some convenient label, seeking to minimise or ignore inconvenient difference. A more useful attitude of mind is to accept heterogeneity as a natural, rather than a pathological, condition; we should accept it for the insights that it can give us, rather than seek to abolish it" (Tribe 1995, 67). It should be clear that Tribe's important insistence that heterogeneity within economic and social thought is natural and gives rise to insights is not at odds with the approach of this book. On the contrary, internal differences are an important aspect of the notion of a thought collective. The key to understanding neoliberalism lies not in their many internal differences, but rather in what brought them together: a common political cause. Despite their many intellectual differences, the early neoliberals joined forces, something that points to the very political nature of their project.

[3]In the introduction to *The Road To Mont* Pélerin, Plehwe describes "the MPS network of organized neoliberal intellectuals ... as a litmus test for identifying the relevant actors" (Mirowski and Plehwe 2009, 4).

Reinventing Liberalism

While R.M. Hartwell, the official historian of the Mont Pelerin Society, discusses the work of the organization as a "revival of liberalism" (Hartwell 1995, xi), John Zmirak writes about "liberalism renewed" (Zmirak 2001, 78) and Pierre Dardot & Christian Laval have opted for the phrase "the reinvention of liberalism" (Dardot and Laval 2013, 49–74). This last term, "reinvention", is employed rather often in modern academic discussions, but to my knowledge, no one has yet to explain what is actually meant by it. It often appears to refer to a sort of transformation (Elliott 2013). The word "invention" suggests that something brand new is brought into being, but the prefix "re-"implies that it is in some ways also a repetition. I find that some of the ambiguities involved in using and deconstructing this phrase are useful for the study of neoliberalism. The thinkers discussed in this book sometimes referred to themselves as neoliberals, and I will show that they were consciously engaged in a project to change liberalism. The question then becomes: "what was new about their liberalism compared to other liberalisms available to them, and why did these thinkers, at that time, feel the need for a renewed creed?" In order to answer these questions we must know something about the history of liberalism prior to the period in question (1920–1947).

There are several competing histories of liberalism, and although Adam Smith (1723–1790) used the adjective *liberal* to refer to certain policies (Klein 2004), the word *liberalism* only entered political discourse in the early nineteenth century. This has led some scholars to date the birth of liberalism to the tumultuous years after the French revolution of 1789. Edmund Fawcett is one of these, noting how the first to adopt the term "liberal" openly in politics were the Spanish *liberales*, members of the Cortes in the early nineteenth century, and that the term subsequently "acquired a past" (Fawcett 2014, 8–9). One of the advantages of this narrative is that it brings forward liberalism's ambivalent relationship to democracy and suffrage. The many episodes of horrendous violence during the Jacobin terror in 1793–1794 were taken by French liberals as proof of the horrors democracy can lead to if the power of the masses is not curtailed and limited. The historian Andrew Jainchill has written of liberal intellectuals like Benjamin Constant (1767–1830) and Alexis de Tocqueville (1805–1859) that they constituted a "republican centre" in French, post-terror politics, critical of both the Jacobins and monarchical absolutism (Jainchill 2008, 2). As we will see, their reflections on the terror were to provide the blueprint for neoliberal critiques of socialism and theories of totalitarianism, where the root problem was seen to be mass democracy itself. Constant introduced a separation between "liberté des anciens" and "liberté des modernes" in 1816. His claim was that the excesses of the Jacobin revolutionaries had essentially been a result of Jean-Jacques Rousseau's (1712–1788) inability to understand that modern freedom could not be the same as that of the ancients. The "ancients" found freedom in active political participation, but Constant claimed that this was impossible in a modern world. According to Fawcett, the liberals argued that "Far-flung, mass society was putting that ancient ideal (direct democracy) out of reach" (Fawcett 2014, 42). Constant argued that for modern people like himself, freedom was in fact almost the opposite of political participation: it was to be found in protection from politics and society (Constant 1819). Jainchill writes:

> In their reflections on the French Revolution, liberal-minded thinkers criticized Jacobinism for believing that politics could remake a prior social reality, for assigning priority to the political rather than the social (…) Another important consequence of assigning priority to modern liberty was the view that representative government was superior to democracy (…) Liberals thus held representative government to be more than a substitute for democracy. It was a replacement of democracy that freed modern individuals rather than, as Rousseau had famously claimed, disempowered them. (Jainchill 2008, 13)

As we will see, the first liberals' constitutionalist critique of democracy and politics would be transposed by the neoliberals onto the domain of the economy.

It has, however, become more usual to begin the history of liberalism at a much earlier date than when the word was first in use. Duncan Bell notes that this only became a dominant view as late as the turn of the twentieth century (Bell 2014, 692), and Helen Rosenblatt argues that US hegemony during the Cold War turned liberalism into an American ideology of individual rights (Rosenblatt 2018). As we shall see, the intellectuals studied in this book played a certain part in this, inspiring later followers to construct grand narratives of the rise of freedom and what they would call "classical liberalism" (Conway 1998; James 2014; Butler 2015). These narratives are usually grounded in British history and stretch back at least to the Glorious Revolution of 1688 and the English Civil War (1642–1651). Eamonn Butler of the Adam Smith Institute even argues that liberalism was developed when Anglo-Saxons colonized Britain in the year 400 and then developed common law when invaded by Scandinavian Vikings in the year 800 (Butler 2015, 14). Ideas of a "social contract" and principles of religious toleration, individual freedom and political representation increasingly formed part of political discourse at the time, inspired by the works of thinkers like Jean Bodin (1530–1596), Thomas Hobbes (1588–1679) and especially John Locke (1632–1704). Duncan Bell notes that "contextualist" intellectual historians "have repeatedly questioned Locke's elevated status as a (or the) foundational liberal", and J.G.A. Pocock insists that although "elements were present which would in due course be assembled by means of this formula [liberalism] there was no system of doctrines corresponding to its later use" (Bell 2014, 688). Significantly, what was retrospectively dubbed "liberalism" was not anything resembling a unified political programme.

James L. Richardson has pointed to how issues of democracy, or what contemporary historians of political thought sometimes refer to as "popular sovereignty" (Bourke and Skinner 2016) was often the centre of controversy even in the pre-history of liberalism. In *Contending Liberalisms in World Politics*, Richardson calls liberalism's first phase "Elitism vs. democracy" and shows how, in the English Civil War, the popular group known as "The Levellers" stood against Army officers like Oliver Cromwell, who "defended the traditional principle that the vote was for those with a stake in the country". The Whig party (which effectively became The Liberal Party in the 1860s) supported a government of the people as opposed to absolutism (Bourke and Skinner 2016, 213) but there were rival interpretations of what "a government of the people" really meant and Richardson insists that The Whigs still rejected any form of what he calls democracy (Richardson 2001, 22).

Most of those fighting absolutism in England appealed to a doctrine of popular sovereignty (Sabbadini 2016, 165) but the interventions of The Levellers show what a contested concept it was. Some years later, Edmund Burke (1729–1797) would argue that "the people is the True Legislator", while also criticizing the French Revolution and arguing for strong constitutional restraints on the power of democracy (Bourke and Skinner 2016, 214).

Social Liberalism Versus Laissez-Faire

David Harvey equates neoliberalism with laissez-faire in *A Brief History of Neoliberalism* (Mirowski 2008) and even recent historical scholarship has argued that neoliberalism is a project to reinvent "free markets" (Burgin 2012). In journalism and public debate, the unfortunate conflation between neoliberalism and laissez-faire is still very common. On the opposite side, some scholars have recently begun arguing that since it is clear that early neoliberalism was *not* laissez-faire, but instead a project aiming to use modern states for liberal ends, early neoliberalism must have been a form of social liberalism (Nordbakken 2017). In my opinion, this too is a misunderstanding, and I will argue that neoliberalism was an explicit attack on both laissez-faire and social liberalism. After "Elitism vs. Democracy", Richardson calls the second phase of the history of liberalism "Laissez-faire versus Social Liberalism", and these were also the two main forms of liberalism available in the historical conjuncture neoliberalism grew out of. Richardson writes that "The cleavage was not articulated as one between elitism and egalitarianism but was readily recognized by contemporaries as such. (…) The central issue remained essentially the same: were liberal rights and freedoms to be genuinely extended to all?" (Richardson 2001, 32). The phrase *laissez-faire* translates to something like "let-do", and with the rise of political economy, this doctrine became a defining notion of elitist liberalism. Increasingly, debates regarding production and trade blended with political and philosophical debates. Bernhard Mandeville (1670–1733) had written his *Fable of the Bees*, in which he claimed that the self-interested actions of businessmen tended to be transposed into a common good, and Adam Smith would elaborate on this with his notion of the "invisible hand". These ideas were the basis upon which proponents of laissez-faire in the nineteenth century would argue against government "intervention" in what was perceived to be the affairs of businessmen. These were certainly privileged, white men with a "stake in the country" who were glad to be rid of monarchical absolutism, but less keen to expand suffrage and the scope of democratic power.

Utilitarians were a branch of liberals who wanted the goal of politics to be the maximum possible level of happiness. Due to the perceived benefits of so-called free trade, utilitarians originally cast their lot with laissez-faire. This changed around the time of the death of their founder, Jeremy Bentham (1748–1832) (Richardson 2001,

32) when the overall happiness level achieved by laissez-faire policies started being called into question.[4] Richardson writes:

> The reaction against laissez-faire prompted a new direction in liberal thought in Britain and Germany in the later nineteenth century and, to a much lesser extent, in France and the United States. This amounted to a major rethinking of liberalism in the light of the conservative and socialist critiques of laissez-faire. Accepting part of the critique, the social liberals (the English "new liberals") maintained that this did not mean an abandonment of liberalism but rather its reformulation. (Richardson 2001, 36)

Key thinkers in this endeavour were John Stuart Mill (1806–1873), Thomas Hill Green (1836–1882) and Leonard Hobhouse (1864–1929). They argued against government passivity in economic affairs and in favour of extensive social programmes and redistribution. At times, social liberalism would be hard to distinguish from socialism, and according to Richardson, "the same question arose in France of the Third Republic, where the boundaries between liberalism, radicalism and socialism were ill defined" (Richardson 2001, 38). These *new liberals* saw their more proactive policies as resulting from a belief in what they saw as liberal values, but also from new insights gained as to how liberty may be secured for more people. I will argue in this book that neoliberalism was neither laissez-faire nor social liberalism, but that it was framed as an explicit attack on both major strands of liberal thought available at the time. This is why the name *neoliberalism* is such a fitting one.

The Dual Argument

This double attack on both laissez-faire and social liberalism is neatly summed up in what I will call "the dual argument". I will make the case that this two-pronged argument was made by the most important actors in the network of early neoliberal thinkers. In his book *Liberalism—The Life of an Idea*, Edmund Fawcett identifies liberals in the 1930s and 40s as "antitotalitarians" (Fawcett 2014, 275). The thinkers he discusses under this rubric are Friedrich Hayek and Walter Lippmann, who indeed represented two of the most important intellectuals in the early neoliberal movement. But what did the neoliberals mean by "totalitarianism", and how did they change and *reinvent* the content of liberalism by employing this concept as liberalism's "Other"? William Davies has written that "neo-liberalism is the product of two crises, not one. The 1930s are as important to its genesis as the 1970s" (Davies 2009). This book is about the importance of the first of these crises: The Great Slump of the 1930s and the rise of dictatorships in Europe. The concept of totalitarianism, explaining both the Fascist, Nazi and Communist dictatorships in Italy, Germany and Russia, respectively, as a result of the same development, became crucial for US foreign

[4]One striking example is the Irish famine of (1845–1852), in which the population of this British colony sank by 25%. At the time, British politicians and administrators used the dogma of laissez-faire both to deny helping the Irish in any way, and even refrained from banning the ongoing export of much needed food from Ireland to England (Ross 2002, 224; Coogan 2012).

policy in the Cold War (Gleason 1995) but before that it was also an important starting point for early neoliberalism. A large part of the pretext for the first meeting of the Mont Pelerin Society was indeed the fight against totalitarianism, and several of the leading figures of the network had in the years before 1947 expounded theories claiming that totalitarianism was the result of "collectivism" and economic planning. The notion that economic planning led to totalitarianism did not, however, lead the neoliberals to advocate a position of laissez-faire, nor to claim that states had no role to play in economic affairs what so ever. On the contrary, the neoliberals presented their programme as an attack also on laissez-faire liberalism, which they claimed had proven futile in the face of the totalitarian danger.

My concept of "the dual argument" thus designates the combination of the claim that "economic planning" leads to totalitarianism, with the simultaneous assertion that "laissez-faire" would not be an adequate political programme to defeat "totalitarianism".[5] Almost all the early neoliberals would at some point between 1938 and 1944 write a book or paper including this dual argument. I will argue that a full appreciation of the tensions involved in the dual argument is something of a key to understanding early neoliberal thought.

Part I of this book will thus focus on the years from 1920 to 1947 in order to explain and contextualize the dual argument. Chapter 2 focuses on the context of interwar Vienna and the controversies known as the socialist calculation debates. I will argue that this attempt to intellectually disprove the possibility of socialism is a founding moment for neoliberalism, as it gave rise to a new conception of markets as mediators of modernity. Chapter 3 will focus on the 1938 Walter Lippmann Colloquium, and how ideas from the socialist calculation debates were used to argue also against social liberalism, as neoliberals realized they needed a theory of states as well as a theory of markets. Chapter 4 focuses on the war years, in which key neoliberal thinkers published versions of the dual argument and Hayek began preparations for putting together what he called "an army of freedom fighters" to renew liberalism after the war.

In Part II, we will see the dual argument "in action" at some of the most important sessions of the first meeting of what was to become the Mont Pelerin Society in 1947. Chapter 5 takes a closer look at the demographics and background of the attendees meeting, and Chap. 6 focuses on Hayek's key session on how to use states in order to make markets more competitive. Here the neoliberals went into largely unchartered territory in trying to square their idea that that economic planning leads to totalitarianism, with their claim that laissez-faire liberalism was an outdated creed, unfit for the modern world. The neoliberals agreed that state action was necessary to protect and spread the market order, but struggled to define its scope and nature when they were simultaneously arguing that state "interference" with the economy led to totalitarian dictatorship. Chapter 7 explores the context of post-war Europe

[5]My use of the concept of duality is thus different from how it is used in mathematics, where it refers to a form of mirrored symmetry. Instead, my use refers to its meaning within theology and philosophy, where a duality indicates two parts of a whole which are almost opposites, yet are equally important for the totality. It has also been used in history, for instance, in reference to the economic *dualism* between the north and south of Italy. See, for instance, Riall (2009, 100–104).

and the ways in which the neoliberals envisioned a new Europe where states were put in the service of the market mechanism. Chapter 8 summarizes the chaotic last week of the meeting and pays special attention to a decisive moment in which one of the conference attendees argued that the liberal interventions discussed by the neoliberals amounted to a form of economic planning in itself.

In the concluding chapter, I will summarize my findings and argue that my study indicates that neoliberalism has to be understood as something much broader than just a set of economic policies. Furthermore, I will argue against the notion, put forward in recent historiography, that the period in question was but a mildly interesting, European pre-history of neoliberalism, which only found its true form in a 1970s "Americanized" version, deemed by these historians to be more radical. (Burgin 2012; Jones 2012). Although the content of neoliberalism certainly changed over time, I will argue that this interpretation fails to take into account the novelty of the ideas put forward by early neoliberal thinkers in the interwar- and early post-war years. Their ideas about markets as mediators of modernity, and their opening towards using states in their service, represented an important innovation in liberal political thought, and this is the basis for later developments of neoliberalism, undertaken, for instance, by the second generation of Chicago School economists and the Virginia school of Public Choice theorists. I will argue that the best way to understand neoliberalism today is to study these original ideas carefully, something that can best be done by understanding the historical context out of which they grew.

Secondary Litterature

Audier, S. (2008). *Le Colloque Lippmann: Aux Origines du Néo-Libéralisme*. Paris: Le Bord de l'Eau.

Bell, D. (2014). What is liberalism? *Political Theory, 42*, 682–715.

Biebricher, T. (2018). *The political theory of neoliberalism*. Stanford, CA: Stanford University Press.

Boettke, P. (2019). *F. A. Hayek: Economics, political economy and social philosophy*. London: Palgrave Macmillan.

Bourke, R., & Skinner, Q. (2016). *Popular sovereignty in historical perspective*. Cambridge: Cambridge University Press.

Brown, W. (2015). *Undoing the demos—Neoliberalism's stealth revolution*. Cambridge MA: Zone Books.

Burgin, A. (2012). *The great persuasion: Reinventing free markets since the depression*. Cambridge, MA: Harvard University Press.

Butler, E. (2015). *Classical liberalism—A primer*. London: Institute of Economic Affairs.

Caldwell, B. (2004). *Hayek's challenge: Intellectual biography of F.A. Hayek*. Chicago: University of Chicago Press.

Constant, B. (1819). 1988. The liberty of the ancients compared with that of the moderns. *Political Writings*, 308–28. https://www.earlymoderntexts.com/assets/pdfs/constant1819.pdf.

Conway, D. (1998). *Classical liberalism—The unvanquished ideal*. New York: Palgrave.

Coogan, T. P. (2012). *The famine plot—England's role in Ireland's greatest tragedy*. London: Palgrave Macmillan.

Dardot, P., & Laval, C. (2013). *The new way of the world: On neoliberal society*. Brooklyn, NY: Verso.

Davies, W. (2009). The making of neo-liberalism. *Renewal—A Journal of Social Democracy, 17,* 88–92.

Djelic, M. (2014). Spreading ideas to change the world—Inventing and institutionalizing the neoliberal think tank. In *Political affair: Bridging markets and politics*. Edward Elgar.

Duménil, G., & Lévy, D. (2004). *Capital resurgent: Roots of the neoliberal revolution*. Cambridge, MA: Harvard University Press.

Ebenstein, A. O. (2003). *Friedrich Hayek: A biography*. Chicago: University of Chicago Press.

Edling, M., & Mörkenstam, U. (1995). Quentin skinner: From historian of ideas to political scientist. *Scandinavian Political Studies, 18,* 119–131.

Elliott, A. (2013). *Reinvention*. Shortcuts. New York: Routledge.

Fawcett, E. (2014). *Liberalism: The life of an idea*. Princeton: Princeton University Press.

Flew, T. (2014). Six theories of neoliberalism. *Thesis Eleven, 122,* 49–71.

Foucault, M. (2008). *The birth of biopolitics: Lectures at the Collège de France, 1978–79*. New York: Palgrave Macmillan.

Friedman, M. (1951). Neo-liberalism and its prospects. *Farmand,* 89–93.

Gamble, A. (1996). *Hayek: The iron cage of liberty*. Key Contemporary Thinkers. Cambridge: Polity Press.

Gleason, A. (1995). *Totalitarianism: The inner history of the cold war*. New York: Oxford University Press.

Hardhaug Olsen, A. (2015). *Keynes + Hayek*. Oslo: Civita.

Hartwell, R. M. (1995). *A history of the mont pelerin society*. Indianapolis: Liberty Fund.

Harvey, D. (2005). *A brief history of neoliberalism*. Oxford: Oxford University Press.

Innset, O. (2016). Nyliberalisme—filosofi eller politisk rasjonalitet? *Agora, 33,* 5–32.

Jainchill, A. (2008). *Reimagining politics after the terror—The republican origins of french liberalism*. Ithaca and London: Cornel University Press.

James, M. (2014). *Classical liberalism in the 21st century*. Buckingham: The University of Buckingham Press.

Jones, D. S. (2012). *Masters of the universe: Hayek, Friedman, and the birth of neoliberal politics*. Princeton: Princeton University Press.

Klein, D. B. (2004, February 13). The origin of "Liberalism." *The Atlantic*.

Levi, G. (1991). On Microhistory. In P. Burke (Ed.), *New perspectives on historical writing* (pp. 93–113). Oxford: Polity Press.

McMahon, D. M. (2014). Return of the history of ideas? In *Rethinking modern european intellectual history* (pp. 11–31). Oxford: Oxford University Press.

Mirowski, P. (2008). Review of David Harvey "A Brief History of Neoliberalism". *Philosophy and Economics, 24,* 111–118. https://doi.org/10.1017/S0266267108001715.

Mirowski, P. (2013). *Never let a serious crisis go to waste: How neoliberalism survived the financial meltdown*. London: Verso.

Mirowski, P., & Plehwe, D. (Eds.). (2009). *The road from Mont Pèlerin: The making of the neoliberal thought collective*. Cambridge, Mass: Harvard University Press.

Nordbakken, L. P. (2017). *Liberale tenkere for vår tid*. Oslo: Civita.

Riall, L. (2009). *Risorgimento: The history of Italy from Napoleon to Nation-State*. London: Palgrave Macmillan.

Richardson, J. L. (2001). *Contending liberalisms in world politics*. Boulder, CO: Lynne Rienner Publishers Inc.

Rodrigues, J. (2013). Between rules and incentives: Uncovering Hayek's moral economy. *American Journal of Economics and Sociology, 72,* 565–592.

Rorty, R., Scheewind, J. B., & Skinner, Q. (1984). *Philosophy in history: Essays in the historiography of philosophy*. Cambridge: Cambridge University Press.

Rosenblatt, H. (2018). *The lost history of liberalism*. Princeton, NJ: Princeton University Press.

Ross, D. (2002). *Ireland: History of a nation*. New Lanark: Geddes & Grosset.

Sabbadini, L. (2016). Popular sovereignty and representation in the English civil war. In *Popular sovereignty in historical perspective*. Cambridge: Cambridge University Press.

Skinner, Q. (2002). *Visions of politics, Volume 1, Regarding method*. Cambridge: Cambridge University Press.

Springer, S. (2012). Neoliberalism as discourse: between foucauldian political economy and marxian poststructuralism. *Critical Discourse Studies, 9*, 133–147.

Tribe, K. (1995). *Strategies of economic order—German economic discourse, 1750–1950*. Cambridge: Cambridge University Press.

Trivellato, F. (2011). Is there a future for Italian microhistory in the age of global history? *California Italian Studies 2*.

Tully, J. (1988). *Quentin skinner and his critics*. Princeton, NJ: Princeton University Press.

Venugopal, R. (2015). Neoliberalism as concept. *Economy and Society, 44*, 165–187.

Wacquant, L. (2011). Three steps to a historical anthropology of actually existing neoliberalism. *Social Anthropology, 20*, 66–79.

Zmirak, J. (2001). *Wilhelm Röpke—Swiss localist, global economist*. Wilmington, DE: ISI Books.

Part I
The Dual Argument (1920–1947)

Chapter 2
The Socialist Calculation Debates

> The World War of 1914–18 brought to a definite end the 'long' nineteenth century and inaugurated the age of modernity. Many who recognised this also assumed that nineteenth-century capitalism would be replaced by a new form of twentieth century, planned economy; that the correlate of the modern world was an organised economy in which rational deliberation would replace profit and the market as the mechanism for the allocation of resources. (Tribe 1995, 140)
>
> Keith Tribe, "The Logical Structure of the Economic World – the rationalist economics of Otto Neurath", in *Strategies of Economic Order*, 1995

In 1920, the Austrian economist and nobleman Ludwig von Mises (1881–1973) wrote an essay entitled "Wirtschaftsrechnung in sozialistische Gemeinwesen", later to be translated as "Economic Calculation in the Socialist Commonwealth". Only two years after events such as the Russian Revolution, the failed Spartacist revolution in Berlin, and the short-lived experiments of the Bavarian and Hungarian People's Republics, Mises claimed that collective ownership of the means of production meant "the abolition of a rational economy" (Mises 1990, 26). The ensuing debates between economists of liberal and socialist persuasions, known as "the socialist calculation debates", took many turns and lasted at least until the 1940s. In this chapter, I will argue that some of the ideas emerging from this controversy were foundational for the intellectual and political project of neoliberalism. First and foremost, this involved a novel conception of what markets really are. I will argue that Hayek and Mises essentially came to see markets as mediators of modernity: a mechanism whose very existence and operation was what made a modern world possible.

My analysis in this chapter is similar to that of Erwin Dekker in his recently published *The Viennese Students of Civilization—The Meaning and Context of Austrian Economics Reconsidered*. Like Dekker, I will argue that the context of Vienna in the interwar years contributed to a new view of markets as nothing less than the bedrock of civilization. "Civilization" was a concept used by the Austrian economists themselves, who would speak of developments in their time as "a revolt against civilization"; and of their fear of "the destruction of the Western civilization

O. Innset, *Reinventing Liberalism*, Springer Studies in the History of Economic Thought,
https://doi.org/10.1007/978-3-030-38885-0_2

altogether" (Dekker 2016, 9). Instead of "civilization", I have opted instead to impose the concept of "modernity" on my analysis of early neoliberalism. This is in order to shed light on how these thinkers felt that a *new* historical situation called for a *new* liberalism. Indeed, Dekker too writes that the Austrian economists´ analyses of civilization during the interwar years amounted to a confrontation "with the central problem of modernity" (Dekker 2016, 89). Throughout this chapter, we will get a closer idea of what this "problem of modernity" was conceptualized by the early neoliberals, and how they came to see markets as its solution.

In 1961, Carl E. Schorske claimed that "the word 'modern' has come to distinguish our perception of our lives and times from all that has gone before, from history as a whole, as such". Schorske saw the beginning of the modernist worldview in Mises' near past, *fin-de-siècle* Vienna, which "with its acutely felt tremors of social and political disintegration, proved one of the most fertile breeding grounds of our century's a-historical culture" (Schorske 1979, xvii). According to Schorske, "Modern architecture, modern music, modern philosophy, modern science – all these define themselves not *out* of the past, indeed scarcely *against* the past, but in independence of the past" (Schorske 1979, xviii). Marshall Berman has described modernity as a confusing *maelstrom* fed from many sources, such as:

> the industrialization of production, which transforms scientific knowledge into technology, creates new human environments and destroys old ones, speeds up the whole tempo of life, generates new forms of corporate power and class struggle; immense demographic upheavals severing millions of people from their ancestral habitats, hurtling them halfway across the world into new lives; rapid and often cataclysmic urban growth; systems of mass communication, dynamic in their development, enveloping and binding together the most diverse people and societies; increasingly powerful nation states, bureaucratically structured and operated, constantly striving to expand their powers; mass social movements of people, and peoples, challenging their political and economic rulers, striving to gain some control over their lives: finally, bearing and driving all these people and institutions along, an ever-expanding, drastically fluctuating capitalist world market. (Berman 2010, 16)

Berman wrote in the 1970s and 80s, and was engaged in debates regarding whether or not modernity had been replaced by something called post-modernity. Berman thought not, and although the socialist calculation debates are almost a century old, it is worth noting that the developments driving these debates bear semblance to the burning issues of our own times. A great number of the aspects of modernity highlighted by Berman were indeed addressed directly by early neoliberal thinkers. Their books, lectures, letters and closed debates centred on issues such as bureaucracy, capitalism, urbanization, social movements, democracy, science, corporations, diversity and class differences. In a time of economic crisis, revolutionary upheaval and total war, these colossal issues were at the forefront of contemporary debate, informing the development of neoliberal thought.

If the early neoliberals faced similar issues as we now do related to the problems of modernity, one major difference between their time and ours would still be how *new* many of these issues were to them. In *Consciousness and Society—The Reorientation of European Social Thought 1890–1930*, H. Stuart Hughes wrote of this period's "sense of the demise of an old society, coupled with an agonizing uncertainty as to what the forms of the new society might prove to be" (Hughes 1958, 14). The problem of traditional communities breaking up and being replaced by larger, more impersonal ones, was a central feature of these still rather early days of modernity. So too was the advent of various forms of movements for and ideas about *socialism*. Here I am not differentiating between various forms of socialism, like marxism, pre-Marxist socialism, market socialism or bolshevism, but referring to the broad, often contradictory movement for a non-capitalist society, which had existed for some time, but had arguably only become a significant force in European politics around the middle of the nineteenth century.[1] Socialism had arguably always been conceptualized as an answer to the problems of capitalism, but especially after Marx, and his Hegelian idea that socialism would be born out of capitalism, movements for socialism were almost exclusively modernist. I mean this in the sense that they pictured the socialist Utopia (or communist, in the case of Marx), not as a nostalgic return to a romanticized past, but a profoundly new type of society, born out of the modern present's radical independence of the past. A key point of my analysis is that early neoliberals, in their criticisms of socialism, ended up presenting *a competing solution* to how a modern world could function and bring prosperity to all. At its very basis, the solution they offered was markets (albeit deeply embedded in modern state structures), and as we will see it was a solution born out of a profound pessimism with regard to the potential for democratic deliberation. Modern states are not the anti-thesis to neoliberalism, popular democracy with its inbuilt threat of socialism is. Berman has remarked that twentieth-century critics of modernity, unlike more optimistic nineteenth-century writers on the topic like Marx and John Stuart Mill, "had little faith in the people":

> Many twentieth-century thinkers have seen things this way: The swarming masses who press upon us in the street and in the state have no sensitivity, spirituality or dignity like our own; isn't it absurd, then, that these 'mass men' (or 'hollow men') should have not only the right to govern themselves, but also, through their mass majorities, the power to govern us? (Berman 2010, 28)

The reason for beginning this history of early neoliberalism in 1920 with the socialist calculation debates is to show explicitly how the core ideas of neoliberalism were developed as a response to socialism. Scholars like Albert Hirschmann and Corey Robin have, in different ways, interpreted neoliberal thinkers like Friedrich Hayek as fundamentally *reactionary* (Hirschman 1991; Robin 2011). The point of this book is to go further and show that since socialism in many ways was what Schorske called a "modern philosophy", the neoliberalism developed to fight it had to be the same. Indeed, Jan-Werner Müller has described neoliberalism as an attempt to create a "counter-faith" to communism (Müller 2014, xxiv). As Keith Tribe points out in the epigraph to this chapter, many of those who recognized the years after World War I as inaugurating the age of modernity, thought that capitalism would be replaced by a new form of planned economy. Neoliberalism was a reaction to this

[1] As we will see, the early neoliberals themselves seldom differentiated between different forms of socialism, and even argued that social liberalism led to socialism, and furthermore that socialism, like fascism, was a form of *collectivism*.

trend, but it offered much more than a return to "laissez-faire" and past liberal wisdom. In attacking *both* planning and the doctrine of laissez-faire, neoliberalism became a competing theory of modernity, a theory of how the modern world, radically different from past worlds, could function. As we will see, this required serious intellectual innovation, and although the neoliberals built on previous creeds, I will show that they also added brand new ideas which can only properly be understood by studying the context out of which they rose.

Red Vienna

In 1920, Ludwig von Mises (1881–1973) was 39 years old and had worked as an economic policy advisor for the Vienna Chamber of Commerce for eleven years. Mises' was born in the outskirts of the Austro-Hungarian Empire, more precisely in what was then Lemberg, Galicia, now the Ukrainian city of Lviv. His father's family was of Jewish descent, and had been elevated into nobility in the nineteenth century, hence the "von" in his name. Mises arrived in Vienna at the turn of the century and had studied with the famous Austrian economist von Böhm-Bawerk (1851–1914). The end of the First World War, in which Mises served as an officer and economic advisor to the War ministry, led to the collapse of the Austro-Hungarian Empire and brought revolution to Vienna. The empire had been crumbling for some time before that, and since 1867 it had been divided into two parts, Austria and Hungary. Also in 1867, a liberal constitution from six years earlier was partly reversed, and, according to Dekker, these experiences severely disillusioned the Austrian economists who had trained and influenced Mises. Their liberalism was closely tied up with the idea of empire, but they eventually came to think that liberal ideas were too complicated for ordinary people to understand. Friedrich von Wieser (1851–1926), for instance, was amongst those "deeply disappointed about politics and their old ideals. They had truly believed that the masses could be elevated out of their poverty and mental backwardness, that they could learn to be responsible and autonomous individuals. This project failed" (Dekker 2016, 61). Dekker notes later that Mises (and Hayek) would not reject this elitist current of Austrian thought, but rather "build on it and develop it further" (Dekker 2016, 63), in a historical context in which the days of empire were conclusively over, but its memory still lingered.

The golden age of bourgeois culture and scientific discovery at the turn of the century, referred to as "The Age of Insight" by Eric Kandel (Kandel 2012) and "Wittgenstein's Vienna" by Allan Janik and Stephen Toulmin (Janik 2001), was increasingly a thing of the past in the Vienna inhabited by Mises. The workers' movement was growing, and socialists had won elections for municipal government. The historian Helmut Gruber writes: "There are few connections between the hermetically sealed world of bourgeois high culture Schorske has depicted and the "red Vienna" the socialists sought to create". This signalled a new engagement with politics also on the part of those who opposed socialism, and Gruber has written that "*Bildung* and culture as a substitute for politics among the bourgeoise came to an end in the republican Vienna emerging after 1918" (Gruber 1991, 12). The so-called Red Vienna of the Austrian Social Democratic Party (SDAP) was the most extensive experiment in municipal socialism the world had ever seen (Borkenau 1938, 160–175), including factory councils and wide-ranging cultural and educational programmes for workers (Gruber 1991, 21). These projects certainly built upon previous initiatives carried out by communists, socialists and social liberals, with the aim of empowering the urban proletariat and improve their living conditions, but the sheer scope and virtual takeover of what had up until recently been a city dominated by the bourgeoisie and aristocracy signalled the coming of a new age. The "Austro-Marxism" advocated by the SDAP included an attempt to bridge the widening chasm between revolutionary communists adhering to the Russian revolution and the Bolshevik-controlled Comintern, and the reformist Marxism of thinkers like Karl Kautsky and the German Social Democratic Party. In the tumultuous days of 1919, soldiers' and workers' councils, influenced by Soviet models in Bavaria and Hungary, threatened a revolution in Austria following the Bolshevik example, but the SDAP out-manoeuvred these elements within the councils themselves (Gruber 1991, 16). Austro-Marxists like Otto Bauer, Max Adler and Rudolf Hilferding preached a third way of socialism: between the orthodox, "quietist" parliamentarism of Kautsky, and the activist, revolutionary stance of Lenin. In theoretical terms, this was related to a Kantian quest to find a moral, a priori basis for socialism, transcending even the category of class. In more practical terms, their programme centred on Vienna as a socialist laboratory (Kolakowski 2005, 242). According to Gruber:

> Unlike other versions of Marxism, it [Austro-marxism] promised a foretaste of the socialist utopia of the future in the present by locating the beginning of the great transformation leading to a new socialist humanity within capitalist society itself, before the ultimate revolution. (Gruber 1991, 5)

This foretaste was the creation of a new, working class culture, taking place in one of the very centres of European bourgeois life. Karl Polanyi (1886–1964) called it "one of the most spectacular triumphs of Western history" (Polanyi 2001, 299). Mises' Chamber of Commerce and the intellectual circles he frequented were certainly influenced by what was going on around them. In a footnote to his magnum opus *The Great Transformation*, Polanyi remarked that he was "first drawn to the study of Speenhamland and its effects on the classical economists by the highly suggestive social and economic situation in Austria as it developed after the Great War". Polanyi further wrote:

> Here, in a purely capitalist surrounding, a socialist municipality established a regime which was bitterly attacked by economic liberals. No doubt some of the interventionist policies practiced by the municipality were incompatible with the mechanism of a market economy. But purely economic arguments did not exhaust an issue which was primarily social, not economic. (Polanyi 2001, 298)

As we will see, the issue was certainly more than economic also to the liberals, but they nonetheless did their best to frame the debate in economic terms. At one point during the time of Red Vienna, a Viennese mayor is to have proclaimed, in the presence of Mises that "The Viennese is born into Social Democracy. He lives in it and dies as he has lived". Mises is said to have responded with the Austrian proverb "Some say that even the owners of four-story houses are mortal", indicating that he did not think the experiment would last (Hülsmann 2007, 490). In these new, post-imperial times, the challenge of socialism meant that the debates within Viennese intellectual circles were about nothing less than the possibility of a functioning social system and world order. Outside of the salons, but not entirely disconnected to the most radical members of the bourgeoisie, such as Polanyi, the labour movement was in power; carrying out reforms and demanding political representation, justice and freedom from abject poverty. It was into this context that Mises, the nobleman advisor of business leaders, struck his blow against the very idea of socialism.

Mises' Argument

It should be mentioned that Mises was not the first Austrian economist to criticize socialism. In 1866 Max Menger (1838–1911), the older brother of the more famous Carl Menger (1840–1921) and more of a politician than a theoretical economist, had gone directly to workers and independent shop-owner to try to convince them that socialism was not the answer to their problems. In a lecture to the society of printers, he argued that socialism was a denial of the basic laws of the economy (Dekker 2016, 52). This is the line that Mises developed further, in a context where the issue was arguably an even more pressing concern than it had been in the days of Marx and Ferdinand Lasalle. Mises' 1920 essay on socialist calculation was based on a lecture he had delivered in 1919, and was presented as a response to the socialist economist Otto Neurath (1882–1945). Neurath had presented a proposal for a centrally planned, socialized economy without the use of money (Dale 2010, 20), which built on one of his own works on economic planning from 1917 (Becchio 2007, 134). Dekker notes that "the Viennese society, especially during the Habsburg period, was extremely unequal. The cultural (and political) elite was formed by a couple of hundred families". Thus, everyone knew (or were related to) everyone else who mattered in Viennese cultural and intellectual life (Dekker 2016, 29). There was some room for left-leaning thinkers in parts of this milieu, at least in the left-wing of the Wiener Kreis (Vienna Circle) of logical positivists, of which Neurath was a member. Due to his working class background, insistence on wearing a working man's cap and refusal to adjust his accent however, Neurath was denied entry into the house of Moritz Schlick (1882–1936), the Kreis' most prominent member (Dekker 2016, 37).

Neurath had for many years been trying to understand the workings of a war economy and was attempting to transplant those ideas into a blueprint for a socialist economy in peacetime (Tribe 1995, 153). Keith Tribe has noted that Max Weber also criticized Neurath's ideas strongly, but that his assessment was less overtly anti-socialist, and consequently had little influence over the ensuing calculation debates (Tribe 1995, 160). In *Economic Calculation in the Socialist Commonwealth*, Mises made certain references to Neurath directly and also to other prominent Marxists of the time, such as Otto Bauer and Karl Kautsky, but he mainly directed his arguments to Marxists and socialists in general. Mises claimed that even though socialist parties had obtained power in Russia, Hungary, Germany and Austria, "they still cautiously avoid the crucial question, leaving it to be tackled by the despised 'Utopians.' (...) The only possible conclusions from all these writings is that they are not even conscious of the larger problem of economic calculation in a socialist society" (Mises 1990, 40). Neurath had indicated that socialization would lead to a "natural economy" without the use of money, and in a footnote, Mises let this stand as the ultimate folly of the project of socialization: "Neurath merely overlooks the insuperable difficulties that would have to develop with economic calculation in the socialist commonwealth" (Mises 1990, 24).

In what was also a scathing critique of the labour theory of value, Mises noted that without money there would be no *commensurability* (the possibility of weighing different means up against each other), and hence no possibility for rational calculation. Using the hypothetical example of whether or not to build a new railroad line, he wrote "It is not possible to attain the desired end merely by counterbalancing the various physical expenses and physical savings. Where one cannot express hours of labor, iron, coal, all kinds of building material and other things necessary for the construction and upkeep of the railroad in a common unit, it is not possible to make calculations at all" (Mises 1990, 24–25). In a later article on the importance of capital goods, Mises would write: "All material civilization is based upon this "capitalistic" approach to the problems of production" (Mises 2007, 31). Capitalism was thus the basis of civilization, and on the question of "rational calculation", Mises truly hammered home his anti-socialist message:

> Without economic calculation there can be no economy. Hence, in a socialist state wherein the pursuit of economic calculation is impossible, there can be – in our sense of the term – no economy whatsoever. (...) Would there, in fact, be any such thing as rational conduct at all, or, indeed, such a thing as rationality and logic in thought itself? Historically, human rationality is a development of economic life. Could it then obtain when divorced therefrom? (Mises 1990, 21)

Capitalism was to be understood as human rationality itself,[2] and socialism as an attack on this. Indeed, Dekker finds that "the defence of markets is the defence of civilization itself" for both Mises and later Hayek (Dekker 2016, 89). The degree to which this very political undertaking is based on economic reasoning and arguments about supply and demand and the appropriate methods of production is worthy of note. Mises was keen to base his critique of socialism on what he claimed were rational, objective facts; hence turning a political, civilizational debate concerning, amongst other things, power and representation, into an intellectual, or even technical debate. This Austrian position is not to be confused with the *positivism* of the Wiener Kreis or the idea that the economy is a domain better left to the experts. In a way,

[2]It is still debated what Mises really meant by "rational" and also the word "impossible", which appears at other points in his texts. Günther Chaloupek notes that "The impossibility of a socialist economy does not imply the impossibility of goods production as such under socialism; but it does imply the impossibility of economically rational production..." (Chaloupek 1990, 661).

Mises was arguing against precisely the notion that the economy could be tinkered with by technocrats in order to create a better society. Yet Mises presented his view as that of an expert, an expert who knows how markets work and therefore understands that they are the bedrock of civilization, and not to be dispensed or tinkered with.

In the following year of 1921, Mises published a tome called *Sozialismus*, in which he claimed, among many other things, that "it is characteristic of Socialism to discover in social institutions the origins of unalterable facts of nature, and to endeavour, by reforming these institutions, to reform nature" (Mises 1932, 102). In *Sozialismus* he would use a variety of arguments against socialism, and the contempt with which he held the very ideal is clear. Methodologically, Mises was not known for making naturalistic arguments, and the rhetorical excess cited above is not generally seen to be symptomatic of his writing (Gane 2014). However, the suggestion that human rationality would wither away in a socialist society and the claim that socialism was an attempt to reform nature, suggests that at base this was far from a technical policy issue as far as Mises was concerned. Instead, it was a highly charged question concerning nothing less than the modern social order and the progress of humankind.

The Emergence of Hayek

Friedrich von Hayek was 18 years younger than Mises, born in Vienna in 1899 to a medical doctor and the heiress of a wealthy, land-owning family. His connections to the lost world of *Fin-de-siècle* Vienna were thus strong; indeed Hayek was the second cousin of none other than Ludwig Wittgenstein. Upon returning from service in the First World War, Hayek studied law and political science at the University of Vienna. There he had originally been drawn to the politics of his first mentor, von Wieser (Caldwell 2004, 142), who according to a later biographer of Hayek was "slightly tainted by Fabian Socialist sympathies" (Ebenstein 2003, 26). These stains of socialism disappeared quickly when Hayek started working for Mises at the Chamber of Commerce in 1920. He later said of Mises' 1921 book *Sozialismus* that it "fundamentally altered the outlook of many of the young idealists returning to their university studies after World War I", adding: "I know, for I was one of them" (Caldwell 2004, 144).

Intellectuals in Vienna would hold private seminars in these days, centred around the different *Kreise* (circles). The Mises Kreis met every Friday evening in Mises' home. They had several rituals, including specially written songs, which Dekker calls "alternative strategies to establish legitimacy (Dekker 2016, 30). The existence of circles and private seminars was due in part to the fact that the University of Vienna had few chairs, not to mention a culture of anti-semitism; therefore they did not employ most of the leading lights of Viennese intellectual life (Janik 2001, 248). The subject of socialist accounting became a hot topic in the *Kreise*, and also in the many Viennese journals and publications relating to economics, politics and philosophy. Karl Polanyi was editor of the economics journal *Volkswirt*, and he was amongst those who dedicated his own *Privatseminar* to the issue of socialist accounting

(Peck 2008, 79). Hayek was one of the participants in Mises' seminar, along with later Mont Pelerin Society members like Fritz Machlup (1902–1983) and Gottfried von Haberler (1900–1995) (Butler 2012, 12). Hayek also organized his own circle, known as the *Geistkreis* (Dekker 2016, 33). Also in attendance in Mises' seminar at one point was the young British economist Lionel Robbins (1898–1984), who was much taken with Mises and the staunch anti-socialism of Austrian economics. Robbins, who had become professor at the early age of 29, was a student of the liberal economist Edwin Cannan (1861–1935), and in 1933 he persuaded his new acquaintance Hayek to take up a position at the London School of Economics. This was a conscious effort on Robbins' part of bringing Austrian economic ideas to Great Britain, and as we shall see, the changed context contributed to an important development of Hayek's ideas.

From Socialism to Business Cycles

Even though the guild socialism of G.D.H. Cole (1889–1959) had been inspirational to some Viennese socialists, in particular the before-mentioned Karl Polanyi (Levitt and McRobbie 2006, 317), the economic debates in Great Britain were quite different from those on the continent. Although certainly not radical, there was a different approach in the UK to what Mark Blaug called "interventionism":

> It was the Austrian School that was markedly conservative and given over to attacks on socialism and the espousal of laissez-faire. The aversion to radical politics was a characteristic note in Vienna seminars, just as interventionism and a bored attitude to Marxism was characteristic of the Cambridge economist. (Blaug 1962, 283)

In Great Britain, Robbins was thus not debating with socialists, but rather with the teachings of Alfred Marshall (1842–1942), the grand old man of Victorian economics (Heilbroner 2011, 172), and in particular the interventionist economics of Marshall's very popular new protégé: John Maynard Keynes (1883–1946). In his 1926 lecture "The End of Laissez-Faire", Keynes had heralded a new era in economic policy-making, one in which increased government spending was to be put to use to create demand and ameliorate slumps in the business cycle. Robbins hoped that Austrian capital theory, as expounded by Mises and Hayek, would be a powerful antidote to Keynes' claims in *Treatise on Money* from 1930, where he had argued specifically for higher government spending. What has later been called the Austrian Business Cycle Theory is a somewhat more technical issue than the attack on socialism, but it amounted to a claim that economic slumps resulted from artificially low interest rates. The Austrian school thus prescribed policies of governmental passivity in order to let the downturn run its course, instead of making things even worse by injecting capital and "artificially" inflating the economy (Burgin 2012, 21–22). Dekker has drawn lineages between this line of reasoning in Austrian economics with what was known as the "therapeutical nihilism" of Viennese medicine. In this tradition, the limited capacity of the scientist or doctor to fully understand nature was highlighted, and so "the role of the doctor is not to be a healing artist, but he should be a student of nature". The physician Joseph Dietl (1804–1878) wrote "Whether a treated illness finally cures is not dependent on the treatment of the doctor, rather it is dependent on the relevant forces of nature that determine the outcome of the illness" (Dekker 2016, 113). Similarly, the Austrian argument against counter-cyclical spending was that the economy had to run its course, since government interventions based on a lacking appreciation of how the economy works, would only lead to more interventions, and eventually to full socialism. "Either capitalism or socialism; there is no middle of the road", wrote Mises in 1926 (Mises 1926). Fritz Machlup wrote in 1930: "The drowning man clings to all those who still have their head above water and pulls them with him. But if we want to save the other, we should suppress our pity, and let the drowning man drown" (Dekker 2016, 113).

As is suggested by his above quoted statements regarding the book *Sozialismus*, Hayek adopted Mises' project of fighting socialism. Furthermore, he took it in directions the more traditional Mises did not agree with. The fact that the British debate related more to technical issues of how to deal or not to deal with periods of boom and bust than with the possibility of socialism, did not stop Hayek from bringing the ideas of the socialist calculation debate to an English language context. At his 1933 inaugural lecture at LSE, entitled "The Trend of Economic Thinking", Hayek said that in his new country, there were "very few people left today who are not socialists" (Caldwell 1997, 14). As we will see, this was something he sought to rectify this by doing more than just giving obscure lectures on business cycle theory.[3]

Collectivist Economic Planning

In a critique of Bruce Caldwell's intellectual biography of Hayek, Philip Mirowski has argued that "the key to understanding the turns and reversals in his [Hayek's] thought lay in his politics, and not as Caldwell has it, in some abstract philosophical doctrines" (Mirowski 2015, 351). I think this is a fair assessment, and would agree that the fight against socialism was the main motivating force behind the development of Hayek's thought. An important part of this project was his 1935, edited volume entitled *Collectivist Economic Planning*. It included the first English translation of Mises' original article, translations of early contributions by N.G. Pierson, Georg Enrico Barone and Georg Halm, plus a preface and an epilogue by Hayek himself (Hayek 1935). Hayek's own texts were entitled "The Nature and History of the Problem" and "The Present State of the Debate". The volume was published in conjuncture with a book called *Economic Planning in Soviet Russia* by Boris Brutzkus (1874–1938). In his preface, Hayek wrote:

[3]Hayek's lecturing style in these days was famously rather difficult, with a heavy use of mathematical equations and a thick Austrian accent that did little to further his communication. See, for instance, Wapshott (2011, 65–81).

> It is the purpose of this volume therefore to present within two covers the main results of the critical analysis of socialist planning attempted by Continental scholars. Together with the translation of Professor Mises‘ major work and the companion volume containing Professor Brutzkus' studies on Russia it should give a fairly comprehensive survey of the problems raised by any kind of planning. (Hayek 1935, 39)

Hayek was indicating that the arguments against socialism would cause problems for *any kind of planning*, echoing Mises' remarks that there was no middle road between capitalism and socialism, and foreshadowing his own later arguments in *The Road to Serfdom*. In his concluding essay, Hayek probed deeply into the problems posed by a theoretical socialist society, focusing especially on problems of competition and the function of the entrepreneur. He suggested that the criterion of marginal costs would cause problems for socialism, and that the analysis of Austrian economics had "enabled us not only to examine some of the supposed advantages which are commonly associated with any form of planning but also to indicate certain problems which will necessarily accompany planning under socialism" (Hayek 1935, 226). Yet again, the argument against socialism was thought to have implications for "any form of planning". Hayek argued that a socialist society might possibly be more equal and "improve the relative position of the working class", but that the gains of that would depend "entirely on the extent to which productivity is reduced" (Hayek 1935, 240). He admitted to having no definite conclusion as to whether or not this would happen, but of course suggested as much with his whole intervention, and especially in this final paragraph:

> … at least the decision cannot be made before the alternatives are known, before it is at least approximately realized what the price is that has to be paid. That there is still so little clarity on this point, that it is still possible to deny that it is impossible to have the best of both worlds, is mainly due to the fact that most socialists have little idea of what the system they advocate is really to be like, whether it is to be a planned or a competitive system. (…) But nobody has yet demonstrated how planning and competition can be rationally combined; and so long as this is not done one is certainly entitled to insist that these two alternatives are kept clearly separate, and that anybody who advocates socialism must decide for one or the other and then demonstrate how he proposes to overcome the difficulties inherent in the system he has chosen. (Hayek 1935, 241)

The duality between "planning" and "competition" had thus been established. As we will see however, it was to become a somewhat ambiguous duality, when the neoliberals themselves decided that states were important to achieve competition.

The Challenge of Market Socialism

Thus far, I have referred to the socialist calculation debates in the plural, following for instance the philosopher John O'Neill who holds that "There was not one debate, but many" (O'Neill 1998, 112). It has now become common to divide the controversy into a German language debate and an English language debate (Chaloupek 1990). The German language debate was initiated by Mises and took place mainly in Vienna. The English language debate was instigated by Hayek's publication of *Collectivist Economic Planning*, some 15 years after Mises' original intervention. It seems reasonable to see this publication as a follow-up to Hayek's comment two years earlier that in Britain, very few people were not socialists (Caldwell 1997, 14). It also seems reasonable to assume that within the context of that remark, Hayek thought of Keynes as a type of socialist, due to the latter's wish that governments "interfere" in markets to counter slumps in the business cycle. This seemed to constitute a form of planning. However, it was not Keynes who responded to Hayek, but socialist economists such as Oskar Lange (1904–1965) and Abba Lerner (1903–1982), later to be known as *market socialists.* In the German language debate, Mises engaged with Marxists of various stripes, guild socialists and others. What he never encountered were socialist, neoclassical economists like Lange and Lerner. Marxists and guild socialists did not adhere to the principles of the marginal revolution that had been put forward more or less simultaneously by Stanley Jevons (1835–1882), Léon Walras (1834–1910) and Carl Menger (Mirowski 1989, 254). The marginal revolution entailed a move within economics towards formalized equilibrium-based models of the economy, away from the labour theory of value of classical political economists like Smith, Ricardo and Marx. Menger is known as the founding father of Austrian economics, and we have seen that Mises' critique of socialism was partly based on a critique of the labour theory of value. The ideas of market socialists thus represented a new challenge to Austrian economists, since they too based their thinking on the neoclassical framework.

The Polish economist Oskar Lange's article "On the Economic Theory of Socialism" was published in two parts in the *Review of Economic Studies* in 1936 and 1937. In 1938 he co-authored a book with the much older American economist Fred Taylor (1855–1932), who had written on the issue earlier, under the same title (Rothbard 1991). Since Lange was to become the most famous, socialist participant in the socialist calculation debate, some scholars have wrongly referred to the whole controversy as "The Mises-Lange Debate" (Heilbroner 1980, 1100). Unlike those who had argued with Mises in the German language debates, Lange made his arguments on the basis of neoclassical economics. He thus conceded several of Mises' arguments out of hand, since Mises too was operating largely within the same framework, namely neoclassical economics, which accepted both the marginal theory of value and the need for monetary units. In his intervention, Lange conceded to Mises' argument about the use of money, and more importantly, to the argument that the price mechanism was vital for a modern, social order. Still, he claimed that a society with socialized production could have mechanisms similar to markets, and that this would enable a planning agency to carry out the calculation necessary in order for a socialist economy to be "rational" by Mises' standards. Referring to earlier work done by Vilfredo Pareto (1848–1923) and Enrico Barone (1859–1924), Lange could state that economic calculation was mathematically possible, and also claim that these markets would be more efficient than the markets of a capitalist economy. *Market socialism* thus became the name for a current of thought, very different from Marxism, which argued that a socialist society was the best way to achieve the ideals of efficiency posited by neoclassical economics (Roosevelt and Belkin 1994).

The idea of incorporating the mechanisms of prices and markets into a socialist system was a tremendous challenge to Hayek. These were the very mechanisms he and Mises had claimed that the modern social order rested on, and that would be lost in a socialist society. Market socialism was a brand new idea, itself inspired by the contributions of Mises,[4] and it avoided most of the attacks made by Mises in the German language debates. According to Peter J. Boettke, economist and former president of the Mont Pelerin Society, "Lange's response on neoclassical grounds took the Austrians by surprise (…) In response, both Mises and Hayek started to articulate more clearly and precisely what differentiated Austrian economics from the neoclassical orthodoxy" (Boettke 1997, 16–17). The economist Giandomenica Becchio confirms: "In the debate on socialism, the strongest arguments against the Austrians were raised by neoclassical economists" (Becchio 2007, 133). Because of this, Murray N. Rothbard claims that Hayek later had to abandon Mises' "extreme position". According to him, Hayek and Lionel Robbins "fell back on a second line of defence" (Rothbard 1991, 54). In this, Hayek would turn the debate away from questions of commensurability, efficiency and rationality, towards the questions of epistemology, that is, theories of knowledge and how it is arrived at. The challenge put forth by market socialists was to occupy Hayek's attention for many years. As late as 1946 or 1947, he would devote a whole seminar at LSE to dissect the arguments of Abba Lerner's 1944 book *The Economics of Control*.[5]

The Knowledge Argument

In Mises' original article, the market was indispensable mainly because it allowed human beings to calculate different ends up against each other through the use of monetary units (O'Neill 1998, 117). But after Lange and others had demonstrated the theoretical possibility of market-like calculation carried out by a central planning unit, Hayek's case gradually became transformed into a claim that rational calculation itself was actually impossible, since the grand total of the different ends to which individuals aspire was never known in advance, but only found through participation in the market order. "Competition" was the key term as Hayek began arguing that the knowledge of what a society ought to produce and how was only truly arrived at through the competitive process; something which made a mockery of the idea that this could somehow be planned in advance:

[4]In his 1936 article, Lange famously wrote:" Socialists have certainly good reason to be grateful to Professor Mises, the great *advocatus diaboli* of their cause. For it was his powerful challenge that forced the socialists to recognize the importance of an adequate system of economic accounting (…) the merit of having caused the socialists to approach this problem systematically belongs entirely to Professor Mises. Both as an expression of recognition for the great service rendered by him and as a memento of the prime importance of sound economic accounting, a statue of Professor Mises ought to occupy an honourable place in the great hall of the Ministry of Socialization or of the Central Planning Board of the socialist state".

[5]Interview with Mrs. Dorothy Hahn, 22.12.2015.

> … the method which under given conditions is the cheapest is a thing which has to be discovered, and to be discovered anew, sometimes almost from day to day by the entrepreneur… (…) it is the main merit of real competition that through it use is made of knowledge divided among many persons which, if it were to be used in a centrally directed economy, would all have to enter the single plan. To assume that all this knowledge would be automatically in the possession of the planning authority seems to me to miss the main point. (Caldwell 1997, 133–134)

Hayek would develop what is sometimes referred to as the "Knowledge Argument" (Birner and van Zip 1994) in a series of articles written through the 1930s and 40 s, including the classic "The Use of Knowledge in Society", published in 1945. His argument against socialism and in favour of capitalism was that only a capitalist society with private ownership can have markets in any meaningful sense of the term. The main functioning of markets was now thought to be epistemological: Markets gather knowledge about what to produce and how to do so in the most efficient way. Thus, markets effectively transpose the diverse wishes and preferences of the millions of people which are bound together in modern societies into a functioning social order, in a way that planning could never achieve nor mimic. Hayek thus conceived the notion of markets as mediators of modernity. It could be argued that Mises had already hinted at this appreciation of the epistemological workings of the market mechanism, but it was only in Hayek's work that it came to full fruition.

Differing Accounts

Accounts and interpretations of the socialist calculation debates are many and differing, and so it is worth commenting briefly on other accounts to understand what the contribution of this chapter has been. John O'Neill holds that "the story told of it [the socialist calculation debate] are myths" (O'Neill 1998, 112), whereas Peter J. Boettke has compiled a nine-volume work entitled *Socialism and the Market*, including both original contributions and commentary. Work on this controversy is abundant. Yet it is my contention that much of it suffers from combining the approach of intellectual history with the desire to take sides along political lines and thereby continuing the debate. As mentioned in the introduction, I find this type of rational reconstruction wholly legitimate, but it is a different endeavour to my own, which comes closer to what Richard Rorty called historical reconstruction and intellectual history (Rorty et al. 1984). In this respect, Boettke, who was recently the president of the Mont Pelerin Society, sits rather firmly on the Austrian side and O'Neill occupies a position trying to rescue some of the ideas of socialism, although he favours a non-market version. The sociologist Johanna Bockmann could be considered something of a modern market socialist, whereas the before-mentioned Murray N. Rothbard was a form of Austrian libertarian, somewhat like Boettke, but of the so-called anarcho-capitalist type, and therefore almost as critical of Hayek as he was sympathetic to Mises.

This tension between the two main protagonists on the neoliberal side is worth exploring. According to O'Neill, the extent to which Hayek built on Mises' argument has been severely overestimated. O'Neill argues that Hayek departed from both Mises and from neoclassical economics. He claims that knowledge was not essential to Mises' arguments,[6] and writes that in focusing on epistemic issues, "it is not Lange that departs from Mises here, but Hayek" (O'Neill 1998, 120). Additionally, O'Neill brings attention to Otto Neurath's original positions on problems of rationality and commensurability. Part of the reason why Neurath argued for a natural economy was because he criticized the notion that monetary calculations of value could ever be rational in any meaningful sense of the word. As noted, Mises had argued against these positions, claiming that rational decision-making required money so that comparisons could be made when choosing to prioritize one possible end over another. Lange then conceded to this argument, but went on to show the mathematical possibility of economic calculation with central planning. O'Neill argues persuasively that Hayek, in his subsequent criticism of Lange, turned the debate on his head, actually making use of Neurath's original arguments. Mises had argued that socialism would abolish rationality, whereas Hayek would go on to claim that *rationalism* was one of the main intellectual errors behind socialism. The rationality Mises wanted to save from socialism was not the same as the rationalism of which Hayek accused socialists of all kinds, but the terminology does say something about the varying strategies employed to argue against socialism in the work of Mises and Hayek, respectively.

It is possible to find commonalities between Hayek and Mises too of course, and Becchio has noted that Mises did have an emphasis *both* on prices and the role of knowledge. According to her, this "was the starting point for Hayek when, in the mid-1930s, he reconstructed the debate and wrote his English language articles on the role of knowledge and on the meaning of competition in order to explain the mechanisms of a free market" (Becchio 2007, 142). The key role of Hayek in framing the debate for the second, English language round is emphasized also by Johanna Bockmann. She claims that Hayek, when arriving in London, "created the Socialist Calculation Debate from the scattered writings of Mises, Lange and earlier authors, and thus provided a strategy for right-wing and libertarian groups for decades to come" (Bockman 2011, 31). This seems a stretch, since there certainly was a German language socialist calculation debate before Hayek's edited volume in 1935, but Hayek's very active role in the transmission of ideas when framing the German debate to an English speaking audience is worthy of close scrutiny.

In 1940, Hayek wrote the article "Socialist Calculation III: The Competitive 'Solution'", in which he admitted that there were indeed two very different arguments against socialism in play:

> Two chapters in the discussion of the economics of socialism may now be regarded as closed. The first deals with the belief that socialism will dispense entirely with calculation in terms

[6] Although perhaps not *essential*, it should be noted that the focus on knowledge was at least *present* also in Mises:" The naive assumption that the behaviour of the Absolute Good is quite arbitrary. We have no standard on which to base a valid decision between what is good and what is evil in this context" (Mises 1932, 351).

> of value and will replace it with some sort of calculation in natura based on units of energy or of some other physical magnitude. Although this view is not yet extinct and is still held by some scientists and engineers, it has been definitely abandoned by economists. The second closed chapter deals with the proposal that values, instead of being left to be determined by competition, should be found by a process of calculations carried out by the planning authority, which would use the technique of mathematical economics. (Hayek 1948, 181)

In this paragraph, Bockmann's contention that Hayek, through his framing of the debate, "dehistoricized socialism and narrowed its definition to mean only state ownership and central planning" (Bockman 2011, 33), starts to seem more plausible. By presenting the socialist calculation debates in a certain way, Hayek made it seem as if Hayek and Mises had effectively proved socialism an impossibility. Later neoliberals would certainly take their cue from Hayek's interpretation, claiming that Hayek and Mises had "prove(d) with almost mathematical precision... that socialism was an unrealisable and unworkable concept" (Shtromas 2003, 101). From Mises in 1919 to Hayek in the 1940s, the claim that socialism would both be practically impossible and, importantly, lead to a complete *perversion* of the socialist's original aims for a better society, remained the same.[7]

A New Vision of Markets

Regardless of how much Hayek departed from Mises, it is clear that there was serious intellectual work taking place in Hayek's attempts to fight socialism by arguing intellectually against its very plausibility. The argument I wish to make is that the socialist calculation debates is where we find the first seeds of the very important neoliberal conception of what the market really is and does. Philip Mirowski has described this as a change from a standard neoclassical view of markets as static devices for the allocation of resources, to something much bigger and more metaphysical. Mirowski argues that neoliberals' unconsciously borrowed a metaphor from the developing field of computing sciences and started seeing The Market as an "information processor", "more powerful and encompassing than any human being or organization of humans" (Mirowski 2013, 98). Especially Hayek's interventions made the alleged impossibility of socialism into a question of epistemology, one of how knowledge is arrived at in a modern, intertwined world, and this amounted to a whole new way of seeing markets. No longer merely imagined sites of commerce and exchange, markets were seen as mediators of modernity.

In some ways, this was a continuation of previous naturalizations and metaphysical conceptions of the market order, but in the context of the 1930 s' debates on the modern social order, this was to take on a whole new meaning. Dekker has argued that Austrian economics did not conceptualize markets as natural, but as *cultural*, in that they were allowed to function and flourish precisely by human culture (Dekker 2016,

[7]For a more thorough analysis of the "perversity-thesis" in reactionary rhetoric, see Hirschman (1991).

89). "Cultural" sounds like the opposite of "natural", and the Austrian understanding of markets did consider them to be fragile systems of human interaction embedded in morals and values (Rodrigues 2013a, b). In more practical purposes, however, this conceptualization of markets as cultural devices did place them similarly out of reach for politics and "interventions" as a naturalization would, since it was argued that markets were simply too complex for humans to understand. The opposite concepts of nature and culture thus take on similar properties in Austrian thought, in that markets are deemed so complicated that politicians or economists would do best not to "interfere" with them or try to improve economic outcomes in any way.

Both Mises and Hayek wrote about the functioning of markets and the price mechanism as if they were merely describing something that was already there, something actually existing in the real world that they, unlike their counterparts, were able to comprehend. This was an important part of Hayek's self-understanding, as noted by his biographer Bruce Caldwell: "The question he set out to answer was: Why did contemporary public opinion on economic issues differ so dramatically from that held by professional economists like himself?" (Caldwell 1997, 13). Of course, there were plenty of economists whose views were different to those of Hayek, that was why he was summoned to Great Britain in the first place. But as we will see repeatedly, a general idea underpinning both Hayek's work and indeed the whole neoliberal argument against not only socialism, but certainly also Keynesianism, was a notion that the whole world had gone mad and forgotten some essential economic "truths". Without acknowledging it, both Mises and especially Hayek described markets in a new way, and as we shall see, this was to lead Hayek to brand new conclusions about the role of modern states. In what I will call the dual argument, the neoliberals also attacked the old liberalist notion of laissez-faire. After all, when the market order was seen to have such amazing properties, it made perfect sense to use states to defend them against mounting opposition.

I have argued briefly that Hayek's more technical work on Austrian Business Cycle Theory should not be seen as completely unrelated to his very active participation in the socialist calculation debates. Both activities relate to a desire, similar to that of Mises, to use the academic field of economics to argue politically against various progressive elements wanting to change economic outcomes either through government spending or whole-scale socialization. Keynes and those who followed his lead fall into the former category, and Viennese Austro-Marxists fall in the latter, but as suggested in his LSE inaugural lecture, Hayek considered them all to be socialists of some form. We will see in the next chapter how Hayek would gather a group of thinkers inspired by the Austrian positions in the socialist calculation debates to start using these arguments against Keynes and other social liberals. As we get closer to the second half of the 1930s, the issues of business cycles and socialist calculation blended with a third concern in Hayek's work: the relation between liberty and scientific economic planning. The historian Ben Jackson has written that "Neo-liberals had initially objected, in the early 1930s, to the impossibility of rational economic calculation... the later 1930s and 1940s saw this replaced as the dominant line of neoliberal argument by an emphasis on the destructive consequences of central planning for individual liberty" (Jackson 2010, 140). Jackson thus sees a replacement of one type of enquiry and arguments with another. Similarly, Bruce Caldwell's concept of "Hayek's transformation" suggests that the philosophical issues to which Hayek would increasingly devote his attention had little to do with the socialist calculation debates, which in turn is believed to have had little to do with Austrian Business Cycle Theory (Caldwell 1988). I suggest instead that the difference between the three have been exaggerated, and that they all come together in the so-called Knowledge Argument: targeting the many different economic and political positions Hayek bundled together under the rubric of "planning".

Primary Sources

Interview with Mrs. Dorothy Hahn, Cambridge, 22.12.2015.

Secondary Literature

Becchio, G. (2007). The early debate on economic calculation in Vienna (1919–1925). *Storia del Pensiero Economico*, 133–144.
Berman, M. (2010). *All that is solid melts into thin air*. London: Verso.
Birner, J., & van Zip, R. (1994). *Hayek, co-ordination and evolution: His legacy in philosophy, politics, economics and the history of ideas*. London & New York: Routledge.
Blaug, M. (1962). *Economic theory in retrospect*. Cambridge: Cambridge University Press.
Bockman, J. (2011). *Markets in the name of socialism: The left-wing origins of neoliberalism*. Stanford: Stanford University Press.
Boettke, P. J. (1997). Where did economics go wrong? modern economics as a flight from reality. *Critical Review, 11,* 11–64.
Borkenau, F. (1938). *Austria and after*. London: Faber and Faber.
Burgin, A. (2012). *The great persuasion: Reinventing free markets since the depression*. Cambridge, Mass: Harvard University Press.
Butler, E. (2012). *Friedrich Hayek: The ideas and influence of the libertarian economist*. Harriman Economic Essentials. Petersfield, Hampshire: Harriman House.
Caldwell, B. (1988). Hayek's transformation. *History of Political Economy, 20,* 513–541.
Caldwell, B. (1997). *Socialism and war. The collected works of F.A. Hayek*. Chicago: Chicago University Press.
Caldwell, B. (2004). *Hayek's challenge: Intellectual biography of F.A. Hayek*. Chicago: University of Chicago Press.
Chaloupek, G. K. (1990). The Austrian debate on economic calculation in a socialist economy. *History of Political Economy, 22,* 659–675.
Dale, G. (2010). *Karl polanyi: The limits of the market. Key contemporary thinkers*. Cambridge: Polity.
Dekker, E. (2016). *The viennese students of civilization–The meaning and context of Austrian economics reconsidered*. Cambridge: Cambridge University Press.
Ebenstein, A. O. (2003). *Friedrich Hayek: A biography*. Chicago: University of Chicago Press.
Gane, N. (2014). Sociology and neoliberalism: A missing history. *Sociology, 48,* 1092–1106.
Gruber, H. (1991). *Red Vienna: Experiment in working-class culture, 1919–1934*. New York: Oxford University Press.

Hayek, F. (1935). *Collectivist economic planning*. London: Routledge & Kegan Paul Ltd.
Hayek, F. (1948). *Individualism and economic order*. Chicago: The University of Chicago Press.
Heilbroner, R. L. (1980). Analysis and vision in the history of modern economic thought. *Journal of Economic Litterature, 28,* 1097–1114.
Heilbroner, R. L. (2011). *The worldly philosophers: The lives, times and ideas of the great economic thinkers*. Simon and Schuster.
Hirschman, A. O. (1991). *The rhetoric of reaction: Perversity, futility, jeopardy*. Cambridge, Mass: Belknap Press of Harvard University Press.
Hughes, H. S. (1958). *Consciousness and society–The reorientation of European social thought 1890–1930*. New York: Alfred A. Knopf.
Hülsmann, J. G. (2007). *Mises: The last knight of liberalism*. Auburn, Alabama: Ludwig von Mises Institute.
Jackson, B. (2010). At the origins of neo-liberalism: The free economy and the strong state, 1930–1947. *The Historical Journal, 53,* 129–151.
Janik, A. (2001). *Wittgenstein's Vienna revisited*. New Brunswick, USA: Transaction.
Kandel, E. (2012). *The age of insight: The quest to understand the unconscious in art, mind, and brain, from Vienna 1900 to the present*. New York: Random House.
Kolakowski, L. (2005). *Main currents of marxism: The founders, the golden age, the breakdown*. New York: W.W. Norton & Company.
Levitt, K., & McRobbie, K. (2006). *Karl Polanyi in Vienna: The contemporary significance of the great transformation*. Black Rose Books Limited.
Mirowski, P. (1989). *More heat than light*. Cambridge: Cambridge University Press.
Mirowski, P. (2013). *Never let a serious crisis go to waste: How neoliberalism survived the financial meltdown*. London: Verso.
Mirowski, P. (2015). Naturalizing the market on the road to revisionism: Bruce Caldwell's Hayek's challenge and the challenge of hayek interpretation. *Journal of Institutional Economics, 3,* 351–372.
Mises, L. (1926). *A critique of interventionism*. New York: Arlington House.
Mises, L. (1932). *Socialism*. Indianapolis: Liberty Fund.
Mises, L. (1990). *Economic calculation in the socialist commonwealth*. Auburn, Alabama: Ludwig von Mises Institute.
Mises, L. (2007). *Economic freedom and interventionism*. Indianapolis: Liberty Fund.
Müller, J. W. (2014). The place of liberal thought and practice in post-war European politics. In *Re-Inventing Western Civilization: Transnational Reconstructions of Liberalism in Europe in the Twentieth Century*, xiii–xxiv. Newcastle upon Tyne: Cambridge Scholars Publishing.
O'Neill, J. (1998). *The market: ethics, knowledge and politics*. London–New York: Routledge.
Peck, J. (2008). Remaking laissez-faire. *Progress in Human Geography, 32,* 3–43.
Polanyi, K. (2001). *The great transformation: The Political and economic origins of our time. 2nd beacon* (Paperback ed.). Boston, Mass: Beacon Press.
Robin, C. (2011). *The reactionary mind: Conservatism from edmund burke to sarah palin*. New York: Oxford University Press.
Rodrigues, J. (2013a). The political and moral economies of neoliberalism: Mises and hayek. *Cambridge Journal of Economics, 37,* 1001–1017.
Rodrigues, J. (2013b). Between rules and incentives: Uncovering Hayek's moral economy. *American Journal of Economics and Sociology, 72,* 565–592.
Roosevelt, F., & Belkin, D. (1994). *Why market socialism?*. Armonk, NY: M.E. Sharpe Inc.
Rorty, R., Scheewind, J. B., & Skinner, Q. (1984). *Philosophy in history: Essays in the historiography of philosophy*. Cambridge: Cambridge University Press.
Rothbard, M. N. (1991). The end of socialism and the calculation debate revisited. *The Review of Austrian Economics, 5,* 51–76.
Schorske, C. E. (1979). *Fin-de-siècle Vienna: Politics and culture* (1st ed.). New York, Knopf : Distributed by Random House.

Shtromas, A. (2003). *Totalitarianism and the prospects for world order: Closing the door on the twentieth century*. Lexington Books.

Tribe, K. (1995). *Strategies of economic order-German economic discourse, 1750–1950*. Cambridge: Cambridge University Press.

Wapshott, N. (2011). *Keynes hayek: The clash that defined modern economics* (1st ed.). New York: W.W. Norton & Co.

Chapter 3
The Lippmann Colloquium

> The real world of liberalism is shot through with tensions. Its unity has always been problematic. Natural law, free trade, private property, the virtues of market equilibrium – these were so many dogmas in the liberal thought dominant in the mid-nineteenth century. [...] A wide variety of political critiques flowered... (Dardot and Laval 2013, 21).
>
> Pierre Dardot & Christian Laval, *The New Way of the World*, 2013.

The event known as *le colloque Walter Lippmann* was held in Paris over five days in 26–30 August 1938, and a number of historians agree on its importance as a precursor for the meeting at Mont Pèlerin in 1947 (Hartwell 1995, 20; Walpen 2004; Audier 2008; Burgin 2012, 65–67; Jones 2012, 31; Dardot and Laval 2013, 49–75). Towards the end of the previous chapter, I noted that Hayek's and Mises' arguments against socialism could be used to criticize just about any form of "planning". Whereas the chapter on the socialist calculation debates showed that neoliberalism was a response to socialism, this chapter on the 1938 Lippmann Colloquium will show how the neoliberal critique also targeted other currents within liberalism, notably social liberalism. In addition to understanding neoliberalism as a response to socialism, it also has to be situated within the diverse currents of liberal thought at the time. As we will see, this is where the term *neoliberalism*, which in 1938 was the preferred label also of many of the actors themselves, becomes especially instructive. Social liberals and neoliberals alike wanted to reform liberalism and update the creed to a modern world, but they chose to do so in very different ways. The neoliberals' theory of markets as mediators of modernity meant that their philosophy and policy conclusions developed as an all-out attack not only on socialism but also on other forms of liberalism.

O. Innset, *Reinventing Liberalism*, Springer Studies in the History of Economic Thought,
https://doi.org/10.1007/978-3-030-38885-0_3

The Rise of Fascism

By the time of the colloquium in 1938, the threat of communist revolution in Western Europe seemed to have diminished, and instead, fascism was on the rise. The pressure for international revolution had been coordinated from Moscow since the Russian Revolution of 1917, but it faded in the second half of the 1930s. The Soviet Union's rigid foreign policy, which had instructed Europe's Communist Parties not to cooperate with social democrats and instead label them "Social Fascists", changed after 1934 (Borkenau 1981, 3). Alarmed at the prospect of German invasion, Stalin opted instead to form a "Popular Front" with the liberal democracies against fascism (Hobsbawm 2000, 148). This was the geopolitical backdrop of the Soviet Union's controversial involvement in the Spanish Civil War from November 1936 (Borkenau 1937, 281), where NKVD agents[1] went in behind republican lines and actively purged the coalition of revolutionary elements. The motivation behind this was seemingly to prove to potential Popular Front countries like France and Great Britain that they could be a moderate, non-revolutionary ally in a future war against Germany (Borkenau 1938, 407); Adolf Hitler and the National Socialist Party had taken power in 1933 after the German Weimar Republic had been "one large weak spot" since 1930 (Neumann 1966, 33). Fascism first came to power in Italy in 1922, and by the 1930s various forms of right-wing autocracies had been established in countries such as Spain, Portugal, Hungary, Romania and Austria. Causes commonly cited for this in the historical literature are dysfunctional parliamentary democracies and the effect of economic depression (Mazower 1999; Hobsbawm 2000; Kershaw 2016). According to Mark Mazower "Opinion in Europe at the end of the 1930s was by no means opposed to the idea of an authoritarian reconstruction of Europe under German leadership" (Mazower 1999, 143). In 1938, the battle lines were still very much unclear, with liberal democracies, fascist dictatorships and the Soviet Union all displaying both similarities and differences, animosities and allegiances.[2] As we now know, the forthcoming wartime alliances would also be anything but clear-cut.

It is common knowledge that fascism, like neoliberalism, was a response to socialism, so it is not surprising to find certain affinities between the political movements. In Vienna, Ludwig von Mises had acted as a close advisor to two Engelbert Dollfuss, who assumed dictatorial powers and suppressed the socialist movement in the short Austrian civil war of 1934, in which the Austro-Marxists were defeated and the experiment of *Red Vienna* was definitely abandoned (Hoppe 1997, 11–26). In his 1927 book *Liberalismus*, Mises was highly critical of the economics of fascism as he observed it in Italy and Germany, calling it "altogether antiliberal" and "completely interventionist". Even so, Mises referred to fascism as "the lesser evil", expressing much sympathy for the fascist fight against communism, and even excusing the violence of fascist groups as "emotional reflex actions evoked by indignation at the

[1] A precursor to the Cold War era's KGB and present-day FSB.

[2] Duncan Bell argues that the concept of "liberal democracy" also appeared at precisely this moment in time. "Barely visible before 1930, in the ensuing decades it began to supplant existing appellations for Euro-Atlantic states" (Bell 2014, 703).

deeds of Bolsheviks and Communists". According to Mises, "As soon as the first flush of anger had passed, their policy took a more moderate course and will probably become even more so with the passage of time", something he claimed was due to "the fact that traditional liberal views still continue to have an unconscious influence on fascists" (Mises 2005, 28). In conclusion, Mises wrote:

> It cannot be denied that Fascism and similar movements aiming at the establishment of dictatorships are full of the best intentions and that their intervention has, for the moment, saved European civilization. The merit that Fascism has thereby won for itself will live on eternally in history. (Mises 2005, 30)

The Popularity of Economic Planning

As we will see, in spite of Mises' praise and the rather close ties to fascism exhibited by other members of the movement, neoliberal thinkers managed in the immediate post-war years to establish their creed as more or less the opposite of fascism. This was because the ideas developed in the socialist calculation debates about markets as mediators of modernity served as an effective critique also of the economics of fascism. At the time, the gyrations of the world economy led practically all political movements to follow Keynes and move to replace the old-fashioned policies of laissez-faire with a more active government policy to improve economic conditions. Economic historians call this period "The Great Slump" (Eichengreen 1992, 213–239), and according to Eric Hobsbawm it led to nothing less than "the fall of liberalism" (Hobsbawm 2000, 109). The volumes of *American Political Science Review* (a main international outlet then as now) reveal that "economic planning" was indeed a hot topic at the time. Some of the articles on the subject matter published at the time include "Social Planning Under the Constitution" (Feb, 1932); "Does City Planning Assist Economic Planning?" (Jul, 1932); "Some Political Aspects of Economic Planning" (Aug, 1932); "Scientific Management and Economic Planning" (Mar, 1933); "Reserve Bank Policy and Economic Planning" (Mar, 1933); "Economic Planning and Foreign Trade" (Jul, 1935); "Transportation and Economic Planning" Sep (1936), and "Economic Regulation and Economic Planning" (Dec, 1939).

This list is indicative of how, during The Great Depression, governments were forced to take a more active part in managing economic life. The problems and opportunities involved with this was the subject of heated debate, not only among political scientists and economists, but also in public life as such. Many argued that centralized coordination of the economy was the only way to avoid a complete civilizational collapse. The German sociologist Karl Mannheim, for instance, wrote in his 1935 book *Mensch und Gesselschaft in Zeitalter Umbaus*, translated in English to *Man and Society in an Age of Reconstruction*, that a new world order of "planned freedom" had to be installed, in order to safeguard human dignity under what he saw as the inevitable rise of a totalitarian state (Jászi 1941). Similarly, the German historian and ex-communist Franz Borkenau wrote in *The Totalitarian Enemy* from 1940 that the economic aspects of totalitarianism had to be incorporated into a free, democratic society, in order to combat what he called totalitarianism's pseudo-religious aspects (Borkenau 1940, 244).

The desire to use government power to improve economic conditions was certainly one of several affinities between the supposed arch-enemies of fascism and communism, but it was also a similarity between fascism and the economic policies pursued in liberal democracies. In 1930, Keynes was invited by Williamstown University in Massachusetts to participate in the project "World Economic Planning". The programme would be a three-year study from 1931 to 1933 on "economic organization under (a) the individualist capitalist system, (b) the Fascist system, (c) the Communist system", and would include lectures from Anglo-Saxon, Italian and Russian representatives. The chairman of the Institute of Politics wrote to Keynes that he had secured "the hearty cooperation of Premier Mussolini", and also that of President Herbert Hoover and Secretary of State Henry L. Stimson.[3] Another striking example of the similarity of economic policy between various types of regimes at this time is the answer given by Nazi propaganda minister Joseph Göbbels when asked by an American television journalist how he viewed the "New Deal" economic policies of Franklin D. Roosevelt: "Wir betrachten die wirtschaftliche Entwicklung in Amerika mit den aller größten positiven Interesse" (We look upon the economic development of America with the greatest, positive interest) (Propaganda Minister Joseph Goebbels 2013). There was indeed a certain congruence of economic policy between politicians leaning towards fascism, communism *and* liberalism. This fact lends credence to the standard neoliberal claim that they were the only ones working against the tide of economic planning and strong state involvement in the economy. At the same time, it somewhat weakens their claim that communism and socialism were essentially the same as fascism and Nazism, since what supposedly linked them was the penchant for economic planning (Schivelbusch 2006). If economic planning made socialists into Nazis, then Keynes, Hoover and Roosevelt should also be considered Nazis. That was hardly the claim of neoliberals, although the connection is certainly made from time to time in the world of US libertarian think tanks (Gordon 2006; Boaz 2007; Hornberger 2009), and there are of course *degrees* of economic planning and state control of industry. As we will see however, the notion of a *slippery slope* towards totalitarianism certainly suggested the connection between social liberalism and totalitarian rule.

The Totalitarian Enemy

What the Italian political scientist Marco D'Eramo has called "the discourse of the twin-totalitarianisms" (D'Eramo 2013, 21) was largely in place by 1938. It is relatively unknown that the first people to use the term as a comparative tool for the

[3]Kings College Cambridge, Modern Archives, John Maynard Keynes Papers, AV1, Box 38.

study of both fascism and Bolshevik communism were German socialists critical of the Soviet Union and the German communist party (KPD). Their use of the term, and the comparative approach itself, first began as a continuation of their Marxist analyses of fascism. As shown in the book *The Lost Debate* by William David Jones, the concept of totalitarianism was developed in *milieus* like the German underground resistance group *Neu Beginnen*, with the support of left-wing thinkers like Franz Borkenau, Franz Neumann and Richard Löwenthal (Jones 1999). All of these thinkers had a somewhat unresolved relationship to both Communism and Marxism at the time, but nevertheless built on Vladimir Lenin (1870–1924) and Rosa Luxemburg's (1870–1919) theories of imperialism as the last stage of capitalism. Thinkers like the Austro-Marxist Rudolf Hilferding (1877–1941), who incidentally had wanted to join the discussion at the Walter Lippmann Colloquium in Paris but was excluded (Mirowski and Plehwe 2009, 47), denounced Stalin and interpreted the Soviet Union as a parallel phenomenon to the German Third Reich. Thus, in 1936, Leon Trotsky could write in *The Revolution Betrayed*: "Stalinism and fascism, in spite of a deep difference in social foundations, are symmetrical phenomena" (Trotsky 1972, 271–272).

It was this tradition Lippmann, Hayek and the other neoliberals were building on when they used the concept of totalitarianism to describe the consequences of economic planning. Unlike the original left-wing tradition of totalitarianism studies however, they also built on the liberal tradition of criticizing, and wanting to limit, popular democracy. As mentioned in Chap. 1, French liberals like Tocqueville had argued in the nineteenth century that democracy could lead to a whole new form of tyranny (Tocqueville 2007, 319). Tocqueville conceptualized this as the possible "tyranny of the majority". The British historian Lord Acton (1834–1902) also arrived at the conclusion that "the sphere of enforced command ought to be restricted within fixed limits" (Hayek 1948, 29), and these ideas also owe something to Benjamin Constant's before-mentioned conceptualization of modern liberal liberty as a freedom *from* society. Albert Hirschmann has noted that "From the last third of the nineteenth century to the First World War and beyond, a vast and diffuse literature—embracing philosophy, psychology, politics and belles letters—amassed every conceivable argument for disparaging the "masses", the majority, parliamentary rule, and democratic government" (Hirschman 1991, 5). Hirschmann referred to Vilfredo Pareto (1848–1923) and Gustave Le Bon (1841–1931), both of whom were thinkers who, like Mises, flirted with fascism. The neoliberal theory that economic planning is what leads to totalitarianism thus had less in common with the theories of, for instance, Leon Trotsky, and was instead a branch of this "elitist liberalism", described in the introduction. To the neoliberals, the concept of totalitarianism was a way of proving that past liberals they admired had been right about the dangers of democracy. They did this by inserting elitist liberalism and ideas from the socialist calculation debates into the concept of totalitarianism, thus claiming that dictatorship was a result of economic planning.

The Good Society

An Enquiry Into the Principles of The Good Society was published by the American journalist Walter Lippmann (1889–1974) in 1937. Lippmann was a wealthy Harvard graduate, whose German-American family is said to have taken annual holidays to Europe. His 1922 book *Public Opinion* and his 1925 *The Phantom Public* had earned him a reputation as a sharp critic of democracy, who was nonetheless very committed to its ideals. Lippmann identified the main problem of democratic rule as the ease with which public opinion could be manipulated and voters could be misinformed. This critique of democracy would be popular amongst neoliberals, but Lippmann dedicated his life to journalism in order to ameliorate the problem he had identified (Lippmann 1997, 10–20). His own politics varied over the years. He was rumoured to have been a member of a socialist party in his youth, and Crauford D. Goodwin describes him as a "lifelong Keynesian" (Goodwin 2014, 51). After the Second World War, he would abandon the neoliberal course and become highly critical of the work of Friedrich Hayek. In between, however, he wrote one of the classic texts of neoliberalism and inspired the first organized meeting of neoliberal intellectuals.

In *The Good Society*, Lippmann sought to criticize the growth of state power and what he saw as the hollowing-out of the rule of law under the policies of the New Deal (Burns 2009, 49). In doing so, he looked to Europe and argued that attempts to subordinate the market economy to centralist planning had been the defining feature of Italy and Germany's descent into dictatorship. He likened these fascist dictatorships to their supposed arch-enemy the Soviet Union, and labelled them all "Totalitarian regimes" (Lippmann 2004, 54–91). Writing of the "necessary absolutism" of totalitarian regimes, Lippmann claimed that:

> They [collectivists] speak of the chaos and the confusion of free regimes and feel inspired to eliminate the interaction of all the numerous private interests of individuals, groups and classes, of local and regional communities. Collectivists are profoundly monistic in their conception of life because they regard variety and competition as evil. (Lippmann 2004, 56)

According to Lippmann, this "monism" was due to the impossibility of economic planning in peacetime: "Planning is theoretically possible only if consumption is rationed", he wrote. "For a plan of production *is* a plan of consumption. If the authority is to decide what shall be produced, it has already decided what shall be consumed. In military planning this is precisely what takes place: (…) A planned production to meet a free demand is a contradiction in terms and as meaningless as a square circle" (Lippmann 2004, 101–102). It was this intellectual error and contradiction in terms which was bound to set collectivism and economic planning onto a slippery slope towards totalitarianism. Lippmann wrote: "There is nothing in the collectivist principle which marks any stopping place short of the totalitarian state" (Lippmann 2004, 52). His controversial claim was that the USA and other liberal democracies were headed in that very direction, due to the "collectivism" of social programmes like the New Deal.

However, Lippmann's claim that government interference led to totalitarian dictatorship did *not* lead him to advocate policies of laissez-faire. On the contrary, he also attacked laissez-faire liberals, calling them "latter day liberals" who had "lost the intellectual leadership of the progressive nations" (Lippmann 2004, 192). In passages almost similar to some of today's *critiques* of neoliberalism (when wrongly perceived as a laissez-faire programme), Lippmann attempted to break down the very idea that the economy was a separate sphere with which politics could not tinker:

> The title to property is a construction of the law. Contracts are legal instruments. Corporations are legal creatures… It is, therefore, misleading to think of them as existing somehow outside the law and then to ask whether it is permissible to 'interfere' with them… (Lippmann 2004, 269)

One could imagine that such a strong attack on state "interference" in the economy as presented by Lippmann in *The Good Society,* would lead to a laissez-faire position: an argument that the state would stay out of the economic sphere all together. This was not the case, because the notion that economic planning lay behind totalitarianism did not lead Lippmann to criticize state involvement in the economy as such. Instead, he argued that laissez-faire liberalism had proven futile in the face of the totalitarian danger, and that modern states had to be put to use to protect and foster the price mechanism. Markets as *mediators of modernity* were too important to allow liberals to advocate just "letting go", in the vane hope that the mechanisms would sort themselves out. This was the dual argument. Lippmann was inspired by Mises and Hayek's ideas from the socialist calculation debates, but to a certain extent, this strand of thought was developing independently in the United States among what would be called the first generation of Chicago School economists, see especially Henry Simons' 1934 pamphlet *A Positive Programme for Laissez-Faire* (Simons 1934) and the work of Frank Knight. Lippmann's keen intellect brought US criticisms of the New Deal together with the neoliberal theory of totalitarianism as developed in Europe on the basis of ideas from the socialist calculation debates. It is a fascinating irony of history that one of the main building blocks of neoliberalism would be put in place by someone who later disavowed this group and would prefer a much less conservative form of liberalism (Goodwin 2014, 250–251). One of the reasons for this may be the approach to popular democracy. In spite of seeing clearer than many others the problems involved in a rule of the people, Lippmann nonetheless remained committed to the ideal.

The Importance of Hayek

Friedrich Hayek and Lionel Robbins at the LSE in Great Britain had read Walter Lippmann attentively for some time, through articles in the *Atlantic Monthly* in 1936 and 1937 which were in fact chapters from the upcoming book (Jackson 2012, 55–56). The two had entered into eager correspondence with Lippmann and, among other things, Hayek had sent Lippmann, on 11 June 1937, a list of "the few real liberals known to me",[4] to whom Lippmann later sent copies of his book. Robbins and Hayek were no strangers to the claim that economic planning leads to totalitarian dictatorship; for instance, in all likelihood, they had both been in attendance at the Swedish economist Gustav Cassel's lecture "From Protectionism Through Planned Economy to Totalitarian Dictatorship" at the LSE in 1934. Cassel was familiar with the work of Mises, and in his lecture, he claimed that "The arbitrariness, the mistakes and the inevitable contradictions of such policy [economic planning] will, as daily experience shows, only strengthen the demand for a more rational coordination of the different measures and, therefore, for unified leadership. For this reason, Planned Economy will always tend to develop into Dictatorship" (Cassel 1934). Hayek and Robbins had been moving towards this idea also in their own writings, and Lippmann had in fact been inspired by the Europeans to make his own argument. On 12 March 1937, he wrote the following in a letter to Hayek:

> I am profoundly grateful to you for sending me your book and your papers, but I should want you to know at once that I already possess the book and your papers and have studied it very carefully, and have been very influenced by it… In a crude way I had discerned the inherent difficulty of the planned economy, but without the help I have received from you and Professor von Mises, I could never have developed the argument.[5]

The book Hayek had sent to Lippmann, which the latter had already read and taken great inspiration from, was *Collectivist Economic Planning*. Lippmann's reference to "Professor Mises" makes it abundantly clear that his arguments about markets as the only devices that could make a modern society function, were taken from the Austrian interventions in the socialist calculation debates. In the context of the 1930s and the rise of fascism, the Austrian argument against socialism had become one saying that fascism too was a type of socialism, and that liberal democracies were headed in the same direction if they did not stop tampering with the markets that made the modern social order possible.

In his letter to Lippmann, Hayek divided the true liberals known to him into subsections, starting with "The Cannan-group", in which he included himself and other UK based economists like Lionel Robbins and William Harold Hutt (1899–1988). The next section were "people who owe their conversion mainly to Mises", a group in which he included his close Austrian friend Fritz Machlup and the German economist Wilhelm Röpke (1899–1966). Finally, there was "the interesting little group in Freiburg in Germany", led by Walter Eucken (1891–1950), and the Italian group led by Luigi Einaudi (1874–1961).[6] A month later, on July 10th, Hayek wrote to Lippmann with the news that a man named Louis Rougier was about to contact him concerning the French rights to *The Good Society*. Rougier (1899–1992) had not been on the exclusive list enclosed with the June letter, but Hayek nonetheless

---

[4]Yale University Library, Walter Lippmann Papers, Selected correspondence 1931–1974, Box 10, Folder 11: Hayek.

[5]Yale University Library, Walter Lippmann papers, Selected correspondence 1931–1974, Box 10, Folder 11: Hayek.

[6]Yale University Library, Walter Lippmann papers, Selected correspondence 1931–1974, Box 10, Folder 11: Hayek.

characterized him as "a distinguished French philosopher who is highly respected for his work on epistemology". It appears from the letter that Rougier was at that point also planning French translations of Mises, Robbins, Hayek and the before-mentioned Russian economist Boris Brutzkus,[7] to be published by the newly founded publishing house Librairie de Médicis (Mirowski and Plehwe 2009, 46). By spring 1938, Rougier had organized for *The Good Society* to be translated and published in French as *La Cité Libre*, and on the basis of Hayek's list of "true liberals", he arranged for a five-day colloquium to take place in Paris. Here, French and European thinkers would discuss Lippmann's book, and the greater question it posed regarding the future of economic and political liberalism.

The Colloquium

French scholars, like François Denord, Serge Audier and Dardot and Laval, tend to see the Lippmann Colloquium as "the founding moment of neo-liberalism"; the latter two claiming that "the Mont Pelerin Society emerges as an extension of the 1938 initiative"(Dardot and Laval 2013, 49). Their 2009 book *La nouvelle raison du monde: Essai sur la société néolibérale* was published in English in 2013 as *The New Way of the World*, and much of the factual information upon which their reading of the Walter Lippmann Colloquium is based is taken from Denord's 2007 publication *Néo-liberalisme—version française*. Audier has also written extensively on the colloquium, and his 2008 publication *Le colloque Walter Lippmann—aux origines du néo-liberalisme* also include a reprint of the proceedings from the 1938 meeting (Audier 2008, 299–355). Recently the minutes were translated to English together with an introduction by Audier and Jurgen Reinhoudt (Audier and Reinhoudt 2019).

The twenty-eight men gathered in Rue Montpensier looked at the Popular Front government in France and the general political climate in favour of centralized economic planning with great disdain. Amongst them were international guests like Mises, Hayek, Röpke and Karl Polanyi's brother Michael (1891–1976); but a good half of them were French, including intellectuals like Raymond Aron (1905–1983), Jaques Rueff (1896–1978), and Etienne Mantoux (1913–1945). In his opening address, Louis Rougier said:

> Le drame moral de notre époque, cést dès lors, l´aveuglement des hommes de gauche qui rêvent d´une démocratie poltique et d´un planisme économique, sans compredre que le planisme économique implique l´État totalitaire et qu´un socialisme liberal est une contradiction dans les termes. (Hartwell 1995, 21)

> (The moral drama of our time concerns the (willing) blindness of the men of the left, who dream of a democratic politics and economic planning, without understanding that economic planning implies a totalitarian state and that a liberal socialism is a contradiction in terms.)

[7]Yale University Library, Walter Lippmann papers, Selected correspondence 1931–1974, Box 10, Folder 11: Hayek.

Throughout this book we will become well acquainted with this tone of despair and expression of outsider status which characterized Rougier's comments. Both were in many ways the *elocutio* of neoliberalism. I believe that the people in question did see themselves as confronting a deep crisis of civilizational proportions, but the idea that they were complete outsiders has to be nuanced: Neoliberal intellectuals would often complain at great length that no one ever listened to them, and that everything was moving in the wrong direction. There was *some* truth in this of course, but Rougier, who held a doctorate from Sorbonne and a chair at the University of Besançon, also had close ties with many resourceful French industrialists interested in funding right-wing intellectuals. One of these was M. Bourgeois, who was present at the colloquium, and Denord has noted that Rougier's initiative 'attracted members of the ruling elite seeking an answer to "the crisis of capitalism"' (Mirowski and Plehwe 2009, 45). Another point which ties the Lippmann Colloquium closer to the political and economic establishment of the time is The Institute for Intellectual Cooperation, in whose headquarters the meeting was held. The institute had been established in Paris in 1924 and was a precursor to the post-war United Nations organization UNESCO. The historian Hagen Schulz-Forberg has shown how the Institute for Intellectual Cooperation in Paris, its local branches in other European countries, and indeed the Geneva-based League of Nations itself, served as an important node for early neoliberal thought. The League of Nations has been the subject of renewed scholarly interest in recent years (Pedersen 2016), and the historian Quinn Slobodian has conceptualized "Geneva school" neoliberalism as fundamentally a response to the fall of empire (Slobodian 2018). Through various American philanthropic foundations like the Carnegie Trust and the Rockefeller Foundations, international institutions connected to the League of Nations commissioned reports from several of the intellectuals involved with neoliberalism (like Mises), and forged contacts across national borders within the framework of transnational cooperation between politics, diplomacy and the social sciences (Schulz-Forberg 2014, 13–41). The French attendees of the colloquium included men like Jaques Rueff, who would become important post-war policymakers (Chivvis 2010), and Schulz-Forberg argues that the burgeoning transnational elite of the interwar years is an important *milieu* for the development of neoliberalism.

The sessions of the meetings were certainly inspired by Lippmann's book, but they were organized under a broader theme: that of liberalism and how to save it. The five sessions of the conference were entitled: "The reasons for the decline and retreat of liberalism"; "Is the decline of liberalism due to endogenous causes?"; "Is liberalism capable of fulfilling its social tasks?"; "If the decline of liberalism is not inevitable, what are its real causes (exogenous causes)?"; and "If the decline of liberalism is not inevitable, what remedies can we take to analyse it's causes?" (Session titles translated from the French original) (Audier 2008, 249–250). The titles indicate a clear idea among the participants that liberalism was in "retreat" and had to be rescued, but also pointed to problems with liberalism itself. On the one hand, the colloquium participants sought to change and update liberalism; on the other, they sought to return to past, liberal wisdom.

The Price Mechanism

I noted in Chap. 1 that laissez-faire liberalism developed in the late eighteenth and early nineteenth century as a new form of what James L. Richardson calls "elitist liberalism". As political questions were increasingly framed as economic ones, the doctrine of non-interference with trade and business built on previous arguments against popular democracy and in favour of a negative view on liberty (Richardson 2001, 32). New currents of liberalism then developed in opposition to laissez-faire, and social liberals like Thomas Hill Green and Leonard Hobhouse argued that active policies had to be pursued in order to secure liberty for all (Frieden 2005, 4). By the time of the Lippmann colloquium, this social liberalism, at times labelled "new liberalism", was a dominant force in politics: exemplified by the New Deal policies pursued by Franklin D. Roosevelt in the USA (Rodgers 1998). The intellectual doctrine of laissez-faire as such seemed to have been given its final blow by Keynes in his 1924 essay *The End of Laissez-Faire* (Keynes 2004). The neoliberals gathered in Paris, however, worried that what *they* perceived as liberal values were being thrown out with the bathwater. Yet as Lippmann's book showed, they did not want an easy return to laissez-faire either. At the end of their conference, they founded the Centre International d'Études pour la Rénovation du Libéralisme (CIRL), an international centre for studying the *renewal* of liberalism. The collective decision to call themselves *neoliberals* (Jones 2012, 35) indicates that their approach to the problem went beyond a simple restatement of laissez-faire. In fact, the neoliberals wanted to move beyond that and make active use of the state; but due to their view of markets as the bedrock of civilization and mediators of modernity, their preferred use of the state would have to be very different than that of social liberals like Keynes. They agreed with the principle of active state policies, but they did not agree with the idea that there was something wrong with markets (in their idealized form). In the Lippmann colloquium, the notion used to get out of this conundrum was *the price mechanism*. The participants agreed that state policies, however active, still had to respect the workings of the price mechanism. An active policy had to be pursued which did not suspend or replace said mechanism, but instead facilitated its proper functioning (Centre International d'Études pour la Renovation du Libéralisme 1938).

I believe that this distinction between *different uses* of the state better captures the neoliberal position in these years than the more typically drawn divisions concerning whether or not to use the state at all. Several scholars have opted for this latter, standard narrative when discussing the divisions within the Lippmann Colloquium. Mises did distinguish himself at the colloquium, as he would at the first meeting of the Mont Pelerin Society nine years later, by representing laissez-faire views that were believed to be outdated by many of the colloquium's attendees. This caused, for instance, Alexander Rüstow to confess in private to Wilhelm Röpke that he thought both Mises' *and* Hayek's place "was in the museum, in formalin. People like them were responsible for the great crisis of the twentieth century" (Dardot and Laval 2013, 56). This comment later led political scientist C.J. Friedrich to claim, in a review article about neoliberalism written in 1955, that Hayek and Mises "take a more traditional view, and are therefore referred to by the neo-liberals as *paleo-liberals*" (Friedrich 1955, 512). As late as in 2014, Edmund Fawcett referred to tensions within the Walter Lippmann Colloquium by describing Hayek and Mises as "free-market purists" (Fawcett 2014, 277). While this may be a reasonable representation of Mises' position, it does not do justice to Hayek's thinking at the time. In the published minutes of the meeting, Hayek first appears to have kept quiet during the whole colloquium, but in a footnote to the introduction, Rougier explains that the interventions in French and German were better captured in the minutes than the ones made in English: "En particulier, les trés intéressantes interventions du professeur F.A. von Hayek ne purent être reconstituées par lui de mémoire"(Centre International d'Études pour la Renovation du Libéralisme 1938, 8) (In particular, he [the secretary] was not able to reconstruct from memory the very interesting interventions of Professor F.A. von Hayek). Hayek did speak, "interestingly" even, if we are to believe Rougier, but his interventions were not captured in the minutes since he appears to have made them in English.

As we have seen, Hayek was more than a little involved behind the scenes of the colloquium both in the intellectual sense and in the organizational sense, by compiling lists of "real liberals" and pushing for international cooperation between them. However, it was Rougier who was given the organizational credit for the meeting, and Lippmann was given the intellectual credit. If we read Hayek's own writings from this time, it seems odd that Rüstow would conflate his position with that of Mises, but perhaps Hayek was afraid to upset his mentor. Along with Röpke,[8] Walter Eucken and Franz Böhm (1895–1977), Rüstow belonged to the Freiburg based school of economists and lawyers who would later be called "ordoliberals", named after their jointly edited publication series *Ordnung der Wirtschaft*, later to become the journal *ORDO*. The ordoliberals were well aware of the socialist calculation debates, and Röpke's biographer John Zmirak writes: "Working alongside other economists of the German neoliberal movement such as Walter Eucken and Alexander Rüstow, Röpke built on the insights of the Austrian school" (Zmirak 2001, 54). Röpke, who was not based in Freiburg and thus something of an outsider in these early days of ordoliberalism, claimed that reading Mises saved him from the dangers of idealistic interwar-years socialism. Very much like Hayek, he wrote:

> [I]t was his book *Nation, Staat und Wirtschaft* (1919) which set me on his track really and which was in many ways the redeeming answer to the questions tormenting a young man who had just come back from the trenches. (Zmirak 2001, 59)

Even so, the ordoliberals departed significantly from Mises because they had come to think that the best way to create a society based on the market mechanism was through constitutional foundations put in place by a strong state (Vanberg 1998, 17). They thus wholeheartedly agreed with Lippmann's attack on laissez-faire and claimed that a competitive, market society needed state intervention. Paired with a

[8]In Hayek's list of "true liberals", sent to Lippmann in 1937, Röpke was categorized not as part of the Freiburg group, but among "those who owed their conversion mainly to Mises". Yale University Archives, Walter Lippman Papers, Selected Correspondence 1931–1974–77, Box 10, Folder 11: Hayek.

claim that state intervention lay behind the rise of totalitarian dictatorship, this was the dual argument in full.

We don't know what Hayek said during the colloquium, but already at this point, he was in more or less full agreement with the ordoliberals. In another letter from 1937, Hayek wrote to Lippmann:

> I have always regarded it as the fatal error of classical liberalism that it interpreted the rule that the state should only provide a semi-permanent framework most conducive to the efficient working of private initiative as meaning that the existing legal framework must be considered unalterable.[9]

This is key to understanding the neoliberals' reconfiguration of liberalism. The proper functioning of the state and how to further theorize it within the realm of liberalism had already been Hayek's concern before the colloquium in 1938. Thus Rüstow and later commentators who have quoted him were wrong to conflate Hayek's position with Mises'. The explicit desire to make use of the state meant that the neoliberals had something in common with social liberals like Keynes, who wanted to reform liberalism both by abandoning the policies of laissez-faire, and by challenging the dogma of the self-regulating market. The neoliberals were on board with the first step of this programme, but not so much the second. Dardot & Laval observe: "... while neo-liberals accept the need for state intervention and reject pure governmental passivity, they are opposed to any action that might frustrate the operation of competition between private interests" (Dardot and Laval 2013, 47).

According to Schulz-Forberg, neoliberalism can best be understood as an attempt by liberal establishment figures to take into account "the social", but without jeopardizing what they referred to as the price mechanism (Schulz-Forberg 2016, 2). It is true that the attendees of the Lippmann Colloquium did focus some attention on social questions and how to ameliorate social ills while still preserving what they thought of as a liberal society. What set the Lippmann Colloquium apart from social liberalism and the "New Deal liberalism" that Lippmann sought to criticize was precisely the focus on the price mechanism as something which could not be tampered with. This is what made neoliberalism a reaction against not only Keynes' project of saving capitalism from itself, but also against social liberalism as such. Keynes acknowledged that there were some problems internal both to capitalism and the mechanisms of markets, which had to be solved through government action. The neoliberals at the Lippmann Colloquium, inspired by Mises and Hayek's contributions to the socialist calculation debates, instead insisted that the mechanism itself was key, and that government action had to spread and foster this mechanism, not replace it. I would therefore insist that we do not conflate neoliberalism with social liberalism. The Lippmann colloquium is perhaps the most "social" moment of the history of neoliberalism, yet even at this time, the front against social liberalism was quite clear. John Dewey wrote in the mid-1930s that "liberalism has meant in practice things so different as to be opposed to each other" (Dewey 1935, 3). According to Duncan Bell, "there was little sophisticated or thorough discussion of liberalism as

---

[9]Yale University Archives, Walter Lippman Papers, Selected Correspondence 1931–1974–77, Box 10, Folder 11: Hayek.

an intellectual tradition until the early twentieth century" (Bell 2014, 693). The rise and legitimacy of social liberalism was the main bone of contention at this time, and a sympathetic observer like Michael Frieden sees the work of Green and Hobhouse as "teasing out of liberalism implicit and underplayed features that created an ideological turn" (Frieden 2005, 4–5). I argue that neoliberalism was not part of this turn within liberalism, but rather a response to it.

Ordoliberalism

Austrian economics arguably laid the foundations of the neoliberal view of markets as mediators of modernity, and Chicago School economics would become the most influential strand of neoliberal thought from the 1970s, at least outside Europe. In the period from the 1930s to the post-war years however, ordoliberalism was arguably the most important of the three main currents of neoliberal thought. This was precisely due to their important admission that states had to be put to use to organize competitive markets. Despite the caricature of Hayek as a "free-market purist", his ideas at this time regarding the use of modern states to secure a competitive market society, had much in common with those of the ordoliberals. Hayek was in contact with Röpke, and the latter's wife prepared the German translation of his 1944 book *The Road to Serfdom* (Tribe 1995, 215n). Hayek is also said to have met Eucken as early as 1928, and remained in close contact with him until Eucken's death in 1950. He would later takeover Eucken's chair at the University of Freiburg in 1961, and when doing so he stated that he wanted to carry on Eucken's work, and that their "friendship of many years standing" had been "based on the closest agreement on scientific as well as on political questions" (Streit and Wolgemuth 2000, 227). According to the historian of economics Stefan Kolev, Hayek's work is best categorized into three phases in which: first Hayek is a cycle theorist; he then becomes an ordoliberal social philosopher; only to become an evolutionary social philosopher in his third phase (Kolev 2010, 2). This partition implies that the only early neoliberals who wanted to use the state actively were the ordoliberals, and so the attack on laissez-faire implicit in the dual argumen*t* could be understood as an ordoliberal influence on early neoliberalism. It is true that Mises more or less remained a champion of laissez-faire as far as his policy advice was concerned. There were disagreements between the different wings of early neoliberalism concerning the use of the state, but as opposed to the idea that the ordoliberals were the odd ones out, I would argue that here Mises was the outsider. As we will see in Part II, practically all the other neoliberals apart from Mises were seeking ways to actively use the state, and their attempts at theorizing how the state may be put to use *in the service* of the market mechanism was indeed one of their main innovations.

Keith Tribe claims in a footnote to his treatment of ordoliberalism in German economic thought that "It would be incorrect to refer to these writers as neo-liberals, since the characteristic feature of the writings discussed here is that they envisage a wide-ranging programme of social policy reform, whereas the attention of neo-liberals is focused on competition policy" (Tribe 1995, 207n). Tribe then goes on to contradict this, when writing that ordoliberals gave "extremely limited attention" to the linkage between economic and social policy (Tribe 1995, 238). Tribe's dismissal of the label of neoliberalism might have something to do with the state of research on neoliberalism at the time of writing (1995). Tribe's reading of Hayek's critique of planning as fundamentally different to that of the ordoliberals is interesting, but does not contradict my claim that the ordoliberals were neoliberals too.[10] The mere participation in both the Lippmann Colloquium and the Mont Pelerin Society of virtually all thinkers central to ordoliberalism speaks for itself. Part II of this book will show that the ordoliberal view of the state as a guarantor and enforcer of a modern market society was central to early neoliberalism, and was accepted both by Austrians like Hayek, and Chicago economists like Aaron Director alike.

But what was this ordoliberal view of the state which was shared by Hayek and many other neoliberals? One way to contextualize their ideas is to look at their contemporaries. Looking to their left, Michel Foucault claimed that the *Freiburger Schule* essentially took up the same problem as the Marxists of the *Frankfurter Schule*: that is, a displacement of Marx's problem of analysing the logic of capital by Max Weber's problem of the "irrational rationality of capitalist society". Various Marxist thinkers like Luxemburg, Hilferding and Lenin considered the economic downturns of the early twentieth century and the rise of finance capital, and what they called "monopoly capitalism", to show capitalism's inner contradictions coming to final fulfilment. It was clear to the ordoliberals too that capitalism was not working especially well, and, unlike laissez-faire liberals, they came to think that market society rested on conditions which could be said to lie outside of the economy itself. The philosopher Oscar Dybedahl has conceptualized the problem facing liberalism as a sort of prisoner's dilemma, in which a competitive system would be beneficial for all economic actors, but where it is also in the interest of all participants to try and avoid the imperatives of competition whenever possible (Dybedahl 2016). According to Foucault, Frankfurt philosophers like Marx Horkheimer tried to define new forms of social rationality "so as to nullify economic irrationality". The ordoliberals, by contrast, went about "redefining, or rediscovering, the economic rationality that will make it possible to nullify the social irrationality of capitalism" (Foucault 2008, 106). This is where these economists and lawyers turned to "Ordnung der Wirtschaft": expert-constructed rules and regulations which would make markets operate rationally, that is in the most competitive way possible. Foucault wrote: "for the neo-liberals, the most important thing about the market is not exchange", and described "a shift from exchange to competition in the principles of the market" (Foucault 2008, 118). We are reminded of Mirowski's thesis that neoliberalism entailed a new conceptualization of markets as information processors; very different from the standard neoclassical view that they are simple devices for the efficient allocation of

[10](Tribe 1995, 208) Tribe also claims that Hayek re-introduced "the purity of an order governed by *laissez-faire* principles", whereas he sees Röpke as opposed to this in suggesting "an alternative to both *laissez-faire* and planning" (Tribe 1995, 214).

resources. A shift to competition as the main principle of markets also fits with my own contention that neoliberals understood markets in a new way, as mediators of a modern society, and we may add: based on the principles of competition. In later writing, especially the 1983 book *Knowledge, Evolution and Society*, Hayek would emphasize the idea that *altruism* was a relic of tribal societies, and an ethical principle upon which a modern social system could not be built. According to him, modern, intertwined societies could only work if organized as markets in which people act self-interestedly in competition with others (Gamble 1996, 26–49).

Looking to the ordoliberals' right, many scholars have in recent years focused attention on the similarities between ordoliberal conceptions of the state and those of another contemporary: Carl Schmitt (1888–1985), crown jurist of the Third Reich. Schmitt made a separation between a qualitative total state and a quantitative total state. A quantitatively total state is a weak state, intervening in all possible areas due to all kinds of societal pressures. According to Schmitt, the liberal state of the Weimar republic had been overwhelmed by the demands of mass democracy and the state was thus unable to keep a distance from society as such, becoming "total in its weakness and defencelessness". Schmitt's solution lay in a qualitatively total state, elevated above conflicts of economic interest and protected from the masses. Hayek would make several references to Schmitt in later works on the constitutional structure of market society, and Dybedahl suggests that Schmitt's view on the relationship between state and society is the same as that of German neoliberalism. Hayek accepted Schmitt's distinction between liberalism and democracy, and according to Dybedahl, the constant tension between the two is addressed by neoliberalism in a doctrine about a strong state meant to protect market society from mass democracy (Dybedahl 2016, 14). As Röpke wrote in *Die Gesellshaftskrisis der Gegenwart*: "The free market requires an active and extremely vigilant policy" (Röpke 1950, 228).

The Myth of Laissez-Faire

The second aspect of the dual argument thus involved an attack on the quietist programme of laissez-faire. Keynes had ridiculed this doctrine as somewhat absurd, writing that: "The beauty and the simplicity of such a theory are so great that it is easy to forget that it follows not from the actual facts, but from an incomplete hypothesis introduced for the sake of simplicity" (Keynes 2004, 31). Lippmann argued along similar lines, when he claimed that laissez-faire and non-intervention made little sense, and that it was "misleading" to think of corporations "as existing somehow outside the law and then to ask whether it is permissible to 'interfere' with them…"(Lippmann 2004, 269). Lippmann clearly considered the very constructed nature of the complicated legal arrangements making a capitalist economy possible, for instance, the inventions of modern firms (Micklethwait and Wooldridge 2005), and limited liability regulations (Djelic 2013). We remember also Hayek's letter to Lippmann in 1937, in which he considered it "the fatal error of classical liberalism" to consider the existing legal framework unalterable.

It is worth turning again to Michael Polanyi's brother Karl, who in *The Great Transformation* studied the transition from feudalism to capitalism in England, and claimed that the idea of laissez-faire had always been rhetoric and a utopia. Karl Polanyi was an active socialist, and in spite of his family relations, he appears to not have been very aware of the development of neoliberal ideas about using the state in the service of markets. He therefore focused his energy on the perceived enemy of laissez-faire liberalism. As we have seen, the neoliberals theorized totalitarianism as a result of economic planning and abandonment of liberal principles, while Karl Polanyi instead blamed liberalism for what he called "the cataclysm"; claiming that it was a result of "the Utopian endeavour of economic liberalism to set up a self-regulating market system" (Polanyi 1985, 29). "Utopian" is a key term in his thesis, since Polanyi saw the full separation of the economy from society as impossible. Throughout his life, Polanyi argued that "the pursuit of material self-gain as the *institutionally enforced* incentive to participate in economic life eroded social and community life…" (Polanyi 1971, xii) He used England in the early stages of the industrial revolution as the example of how laissez-faire capitalism was in fact a constructed order, one which he argued was fundamentally at odds with the reality of human nature.

A key insight of what I have referred to as a "Foucauldian" approach to neoliberalism is the claim that active use of a strong state to impose market structures in all of society is the very essence of neoliberal doctrine. This insight in fact owes something to *The Great Transformation*, and the notions have been further developed by the institutionalist tradition of political economy which followed in Polanyi's wake (Dale 2010; Block and Somers 2014). Karl Polanyi in many ways deconstructed the main contradiction of neoliberalism as present already in laissez-faire liberalism. Foucault noted how neoliberalism was not so much an attack on the state, as it was an attempt to redefine it. It was Polanyi, however, who first showed how even the old liberal order was constructed and far from a natural state of affairs. "Laissez-faire was planned" was his controversial claim (Polanyi 2001, 151). The economist João Rodrigues contends that the members of the Mont Pelerin Society had "recognized early on that the creation of new markets is a political process, requiring the intervention of an organized power" (Rodrigues 2012, 1008), thus in fact agreeing with Michael Polanyi's socialist brother (Mirowski 2014). We may find that the true importance of the neoliberals was not so much that they were the first to open up the Pandora's box of using state power to uphold a liberal order, but that they were to first liberals to thoroughly theorize it.

Primary Sources

Yale University Library, New Haven, Connecticut, USA:
Walter Lippmann Collection

Kings College Archive Centre, Cambridge, UK:
John Maynard Keynes Collection.

Secondary Literature

Audier, S. (2008). *Le Colloque Lippmann: Aux Origines du Néo-Libéralisme*. Paris: Le Bord de l'Eau.

Audier, S., & Reinhoudt, J. (2019). *The Walter Lippmann Colloquium—the Birth of Neo-Liberalism*. London: Palgrave Macmillan.

Bell, D. (2014). What is liberalism? *Political Theory, 42,* 682–715.

Block, F., & Somers, M. R. (2014). *The power of market fundamentalism—Karl Polanyi's critique*. Cambridge, Mass: Harvard University Press.

Boaz, D. (2007). *Hitler, Mussolini*. Cato Institute: Roosevelt.

Borkenau, F. (1937). *The spanish cockpit*. London: Faber and Faber.

Borkenau, F. (1938). *The communist international*. London: Faber and Faber.

Borkenau, F. (1940). *The totalitarian enemy*. London: Faber and Faber.

Borkenau, F. (1981). *End and beginning*. New York: Columbia University Press.

Burgin, A. (2012). *The great persuasion: Reinventing free markets since the depression*. Cambridge, Mass: Harvard University Press.

Burns, J. (2009). *Goddess of the market: Ayn Rand and the American Right*. Oxford: Oxford University Press.

Cassel, G. (1934). From protectionism through planned economy to dictatorship. *International Conciliation*, 307–325.

Centre International d´Études pour la Renovation du Libéralisme. (1938). *Compte-rendu des séances du Colloque Walter Lippman*. Paris: Libraire de Médicis.

Chivvis, C. S. (2010). *The Monetary Conservative—Jacques Rueff and Twentieth-Century Free Market Thought*. De Kalb, Illinois: Northern Illinois University Press.

Dale, G. (2010). *Karl Polanyi: The limits of the market*. Key Contemporary Thinkers. Cambridge: Polity.

Dardot, P., & Laval, C. (2013). *the new way of the world: On neoliberal society*. Brooklyn, NY: Verso.

D'Eramo, M. (2013). Populism and the new oligarchy. *New Left Review, II,* 5–28.

Dewey, J. (1935). *Liberalism and political action*. New York: Prometheus Books.

Djelic, M.-L. (2013). When limited liability was (Still) an issue: Mobilization and politics of signification in 19th-Century England. *Organization Studies, 34,* 595–621.

Dybedahl, O. (2016). Nyliberalismens sterke stat. *Vardøger, 16,* 7–22.

Eichengreen, B. (1992). The origins and nature of the Great Slump revisited. *The Economic History Review, 45,* 213–239.

Fawcett, E. (2014). *Liberalism: The life of an idea*. Princeton: Princeton University Press.

Foucault, M. (2008). *The Birth of Biopolitics: Lectures at the Collège de France, 1978–79*. New York: Palgrave Macmillan.

Frieden, M. (2005). *Liberal languages*. Princeton and Oxford: Princeton University Press.

Friedrich, C. J. (1955). The political thought of Neo-Liberalism. *American Political Science Review, 49,* 509–525.

Gamble, A. (1996). *Hayek: The iron cage of liberty*. Key Contemporary Thinkers. Cambridge: Polity Press.

Goodwin, C. D. (2014). *Walter lippman: Public economist*. Cambridge Massachusetts: Harvard University Press.

Gordon, D. (2006). Three new deals: Why the nazis and fascists loved FDR. *Mises Daily Articles*, September 22.

Hartwell, R. M. (1995). *A history of the mont Pelerin society*. Indianapolis: Liberty Fund.

Hayek, F. (1940). *Individualism and economic order*. Chicago: The University of Chicago Press.

Hirschman, A. O. (1991). *The rhetoric of reaction: Perversity, futility, Jeopardy*. Cambridge, Mass: Belknap Press of Harvard University Press.

Hobsbawm, E. J. (2000). *The age of extremes: A history of the world, 1914–1991*. Incorporated: Peter Smith Publisher.

Hoppe, H.-H. (1997). The meaning of the Mises papers. *The Free Market* 15.

Hornberger, J. G. (2009). The socialism and fascism of the new deal. *The Future of Freedom Foundation*.

Jackson, B. (2012). Freedom, the common good, and the rule of law: Lippmann and Hayek on economic planning. *Journal of the History of Ideas* 73.

Jászi, O. (1941). Reviewed works: Man and society in an age of reconstruction by Karl Mannheim; The contempt of freedom; The Russian experiment and After by M. Polanyi. *The American Political Science Review*, *35*, 550–553.

Jones, D. S. (2012). *Masters of the Universe: Hayek, Friedman, and the Birth of Neoliberal Politics*. Princeton: Princeton University Press.

Jones, W. D. (1999). *The Lost Debate: German Socialist Intellectuals and Totalitarianism*. Champaign: University of Illinois Press.

Kershaw, I. (2016). *To hell and back—Europe 1914–1949*. New York: Viking.

Keynes, J. M. (2004). *The End of Laissez-Faire & The Economic Consequences of the Peace*. Amherst, New York: Prometheus Books.

Kolev, S. (2010). F.A. Hayek as an Ordo-liberal. *HWWI Research Paper* 5.

Lippmann, W. (1997). *Public opinion*. New York: Simon & Schuster.

Lippmann, W. (2004). *The good society*. New York: Little Brown.

Mazower, M. (1999). *Dark continent: Europe's Twentieth Century*. London: Penguin.

Micklethwait, J., & Wooldridge, A. (2005). *The company—A short history of a revolutionary idea*. New York: Modern Library Chronicles.

Mirowski, P. (2014). *Polanyi vs.* Hayek. In: University of Sydney.

Mirowski, P., & Plehwe, D. (Eds.). (2009). *The road from Mont Pèlerin: The making of the neoliberal thought collective*. Cambridge, Mass: Harvard University Press.

Mises, L. (2005). *Liberalism—The classical tradition*. Auburn, Alabama: Liberty Fund.

Neumann, F. L. (1966). *Behemoth: The structure and practice of national socialism, 1933–1944*. New York: Harper Torchbooks.

Pedersen, S. (2016). *The guardians: The league of nations and the crisis of empire*. Oxford: Oxford University Press.

Polanyi, K. (1971). *Primitive, archaic, and modern economies: Essays of Karl Polanyi* (1st ed.). Garden City, N.Y.: Beacon Press.

Polanyi, K. (1985). *The great transformation*. Boston: Beacon Press.

Polanyi, K. (2001). *The great transformation: The political and economic origins of our time. 2nd Beacon* (Paperback ed.). Boston, Mass: Beacon Press.

Propaganda Minister Joseph Goebbels. (2013).

Richardson, J. L. (2001). *Contending liberalisms in world politics*. Boulder, Colorado: Lynne Rienner Publishers Inc.

Rodgers, D. T. (1998). *Atlantic crossings: Social politics in a progressive age*. Cambridge, Mass: Belknap Press of Harvard University Press.

Rodrigues, J. (2012). Where to draw the line between state and markets? *Journal of Economic Issues*, *46*, 1007–1033. https://doi.org/10.2753/JEI0021-3624460409.

Röpke, W. (1950). *The social crisis of our time*. Chicago: The University of Chicago Press.

Schivelbusch, W. (2006). *Three New Deals: Reflections on Roosevelt's America, Mussolini's Italy and Hitler's Germany, 1933-1939*. New York: Metropolitan Books.

Schulz-Forberg, H. (2014). Laying the groundwork: The semantics of neoliberalism in the 1930s. In *Re-Inventing Western Civilisation: Transnational Reconstructions of Liberalism in Europe in the Twentieth Century*. Newcastle upon Tyne: Cambridge Scholars Publishing.

Schulz-Forberg, H. (2016). The intellectual and institutional roots of early neoliberalism. In *WZB*, Berlin.

Simons, H. C. (1934). *A positive program for laissez faire*. public policy pamphlet 15. Chicago: The University of Chicago Press.

Streit, M. E., & Wolgemuth. (2000). The market economy and the state—Hayekian and Ordoliberal conceptions. In *The Theory of Capitalism in the German Economic Tradition*. Hanover: Springer.

Slobodian, Q. (2018). *Globalists: The end of empire and the birth of neoliberalism*. Cambridge Mass.: Harvard University Press.

de Tocqueville, A. (2007). *Democracy in America* (1st ed.). New York: W.W. Norton & Company.

Tribe, K. (1995). *Strategies of economic order—german economic discourse, 1750–1950*. Cambridge: Cambridge University Press.

Trotsky, L. (1972). *The revolution betrayed*. New York: Pathfinder Press.

Vanberg, V. J. (1998). The Freiburg School—Walter Eucken and Ordoliberalism. *Freiburger Diskussionspapiere zur Ordnungsökonomik* 4.

Walpen, B. (2004). *Der Plan, das Planen zu beenden*. Amsterdam: University of Amsterdam.

Zmirak, J. (2001). *Wilhelm Röpke—Swiss Localist, Global Economist*. Wilmington, Delaware: ISI Books.

Chapter 4
The Economic Consequences of the War

> …before the Great Depression, the gamblers ran capitalism and brought the economies down. And what happened? The war followed the Great Depression. In wars you mobilize everything. Governments tore down the railings in Britain and America to make bullets. They rationed food, they conscripted people, and they sent them to die. The state took over. And after the war people said, 'If you can plan for war, why can't you plan for peace?' When I was 17, I had a letter from the government saying, 'Dear Mr. Benn, will you turn up when you're 17 ½? We'll give you free food, free clothes, free training, free accommodation, and two shillings, ten pence a day to just kill Germans'. People said, 'well, if you can have full employment to kill people, why in God's name couldn't you have full employment and good schools, hospitals, good houses?'
>
> British Labour politician Tony Benn in the 2000 PBS documentary *Commanding Heights*.[1]

The outbreak of World War II leads to the abandonment of the Centre International d'Études pour la Rénovation de Libéralisme (CIRL). The neoliberal intellectuals who had gathered in Paris to discuss the writings of Walter Lippmann, at the invitation of Louis Rougier but thanks to the initiatives of Friedrich Hayek, went into a period of isolation from each other, as opposed to the period of transnational collaboration they had been envisioning. The institute met a second time in January 1939, but Germany occupied parts of Czechoslovakia in violation of the Munich Treaty in March that same year, and then went on to invade Poland on September 1st. Another meeting of the organization had been planned to take place in Geneva that very month, but as Great Britain and France declared war on Germany, the plans had to be abandoned. By June 1940, the French army had collapsed and France was under German control. This chapter focuses on the activities of neoliberal intellectuals in the years between 1938 and 1947, but also on the significance of World War II for their ideas and their political project. Volume 10 of Friedrich Hayek's collected works has been entitled

[1]Full transcript of the interview is available at http://www.pbs.org/wgbh/commandingheights/shared/minitext/int_tonybenn.html (last accessed 03.03.2017).

O. Innset, *Reinventing Liberalism*, Springer Studies in the History of Economic Thought,
https://doi.org/10.1007/978-3-030-38885-0_4

"Socialism and War" by its editor, Bruce Caldwell, and war plays an ambiguous role in early neoliberal thought. On the one hand, neoliberal intellectuals worked hard to link the horrors of war and dictatorship to economic ideas of the wrong kind. Michel Foucault claims that through "a series of theoretical and analytical *coups de force*", the German ordoliberals were able to establish their project as the opposite of Nazism. The centrally planned economy of the Nazi administration was held as proof that "the defects and destructive effects traditionally attributed to the market economy should instead be attributed to the state" (Foucault 2008, 116). As we will see, this was fraught with contradictions, both because many ordoliberals had not opposed Nazism as strongly as they would later claim, but also because an important role was reserved for the state also within their own doctrine. Even so, the link established by the early neoliberals between economic planning and the dictatorships who had thrown the world into total war helped the neoliberals in branding their doctrine as the anti-totalitarian alternative to both fascism and socialism.

On the other hand, the experiences with economic planning in wartime were seen by many as positive, something which signalled a new era of more rational economic management. As in the interwar years, this was not a position held only by socialists, rather it transcended most political boundaries. In the post-war years, Keynesian economists would see to it that active government policies of demand management and redistribution became the order of the day across the Western world (Hall 1989). This was the tide that the neoliberals set out to combat, and this fight included turning away from the principles of laissez-faire, in an attempt to create a new liberalism capable of fighting the influence of both social liberalism and social democracy. Where Chap. 2 discussed the socialist calculation debates and suggested that the core idea of neoliberalism was a notion of markets as mediators of modernity, Chap. 3 showed how the rise of fascism arguably became a more pressing concern than the possibility of socialist revolution as the 1930s wore on. In spite of belonging squarely on the political right and even expressing some sympathy for the goals of fascism, neoliberal intellectuals like Ludwig von Mises criticized the economics of fascism with tools developed in the socialist calculation debates. Replacing the mechanisms of markets and using the power of the state to control the economy seemed a common feature of the socialist Soviet Union and the fascist regimes of Italy and Germany. It was, however, a feature these regimes also shared with liberal democracies like Great Britain and the USA. Inspired by the writings of Walter Lippmann, neoliberal intellectuals thus developed an argument saying that socialism and fascism were expressions of the same essential programme of subverting markets, and that liberal democracies were headed in the same direction, due to the "collectivism" which was to be found in social liberalism as well as in socialism and fascism. As shown towards the end of the previous chapter, this strong stance did not lead the neoliberals to argue in favour of the old policies of laissez-faire. Instead, neoliberals brought forward a dual argument which included a powerful charge against laissez-faire, and began the process of thinking actively about how to use modern states without subverting the mechanisms of markets.

Hayek in the Blitz

My research shows that although many other men contributed and were important to the neoliberal project, Hayek was the central figure both intellectually and organizationally. In 1938, Hayek gave a lecture in Zürich entitled "Die politischen Folgen der Planwirtschaft" ("The Political Consequences of Economic Planning"), in which he asserted that the most important thing for "Freiheit und Demokratie" (Freedom and democracy) was "dass der Staat nicht allzu weit in das Wirtschaftsleben eindringt" ("that the state does not penetrate too far into economic life").[2] To him, the role of the state in economic affairs was not a question of dull economic policy and mathematical theorems explaining booms and bust, but one regarding freedom and democracy. The concern that civilization itself was falling apart was typical for neoliberal intellectuals in general, and the Austrians in particular. Dekker has written that "A wider circle of Viennese scholars had the feeling of witnessing the same development as they had seen in Austria and previously in the Habsburg empire" (Dekker 2016, 132). This sense of impending doom and of seeing the same thing happen twice, led Austrian scholars like Hayek and Karl Popper to describe their work in this period as their "war effort" (Dekker 2016, 133). Recently, Quinn Slobodian has conceptualized early neoliberalism as a way of coming to terms with the end of empire and envisioning a market-based world order in the age of universal suffrage and independent nation states (Slobodian 2018).

Throughout the war, Hayek was able to keep in contact with at least some of the "real liberals" he had assembled in Paris in 1938. Other issues were more pressing in a time of war, however, and one of the very few correspondences that Hayek kept in his personal archive is a peculiar one between himself and Frederic Ogilvie, general director of the BBC. On 9 September 1939, Hayek sent him a nine-page document entitled "Some notes on propaganda to Germany",[3] together with a kind of job application in which he wrote: "I am free and anxious to put my capacities to the best use which, after careful consideration, I believe to be in propaganda-work". Three days later he sent the same memo and a similar letter to the newly appointed Minister of Information, Lord Macmillan. Ogilvie responded briefly to Hayek, saying he "was very much interested to know that you had applied for a post at the Ministry of Information", but there was never any real response. In the following month, Hayek sent increasingly more agitated letters to Ogilvie in which he criticized various aspects of the BBC's propaganda broadcasts to Germany. Hayek appears to have sent at least ten of these letters, sometimes several per day. On October 15th, for instance, he noted that one of the speakers had a voice which made him sound Jewish, writing: "he will inevitably be taken by most German listeners to be a jew and in concequence [sic] deprive the broadcast, and even what preceded it, of most of its effect".

---

[2]Hoover Institution Library and Archives, Friedrich Hayek Collection, Box 105, Folder 24: "Die politischen folgen der Planwirtschaft".

[3]Hoover Institution Library and Archives, Friedrich Hayek Collection, Box 105, Folder 26.

Few copies of Hayek's own letters have been kept for the archives, but the short responses these provoked give us some insight into how they may have been phrased, and the way in which members of the British establishment dealt with an eccentric Austrian émigré professor, whose help they clearly felt they could do without. One example from October 3: "Thank you very much for your letter of 30th. I was very glad to have your valuable comment but hope very much that "verächtlich" for "verachtungsvoll" is not to be regarded as so appalling a blunder as you suggest..." Hayek received several notes from various officials at the Ministry of Information thanking him for his feedback, but altogether avoiding the issue of employment.[4] Hayek later wrote to Fritz Machlup, who had migrated to the US, that he was "getting really annoyed by the refusal to use a person like myself on any useful work" (Hayek 2007, 10).

Hence, Hayek ended up having time on his hands to organize the liberal insurrection that he hoped would follow the war. His close colleague Lionel Robbins, who had brought him to London in the first place, was, unlike Hayek, highly trusted by the British government. After the outbreak of war, he became director of the economics section at the Offices of the War Cabinet (Pinder 1998, 45). Therefore, Robbins was busy working for the government when Hayek, along with the rest of the LSE faculty, moved to Peterhouse at Cambridge to escape the German bombings. There Hayek started writing the book that would become *The Road to Serfdom* (Wapshott 2011, 192).

The Road to Serfdom

In the book, Hayek claimed not only that markets were indispensable for economic calculation, hence the impossibility of centrally planned socialism; but also that even if calculation was possible, it would be impossible to know what to calculate for without the help of markets. Hayek's insistence on the price mechanism and the market process as the only possible mediator between the many individuals that comprise a modern society was taken more or less directly from Mises, who had written: "(...) no single man can ever master all the possibilities of production, innumerable as they are, as to be in a position to make straightway evident judgments of value without the aid of some system of computation" (Mises 1990, 16). This was Mises' original argument against socialism, as Hayek had presented it to an English language audience in his influential 1935 volume. At that time, Hayek had yet to use the term "totalitarianism" as a description of the unwelcome results of economic planning, but his theory of the importance and functioning of the market order was already largely in place. So too was his comparison between fascism and communism. In a memo to Sir William Beveridge, already written in 1932, Hayek wrote, under the title "Nazi-Socialism" that:

[4]Hoover Institution Library and Archives, Friedrich Hayek Collection, Box 61, Folder 5.

> The persecution of the Marxists, and of democrats in general, tend to obscure the fundamental fact that National Socialism is a genuine Socialist movement, whose leading ideas are the final fruits of the anti-liberal tendencies which have been steadily gaining ground in Germany since the later part of the Bismarckian era (…) What must be realised is that this is only the ultimate and necessary outcome of a process of development in which the other nations have been for a long time steadily following Germany, albeit at a considerable distance. The gradual extension of the field of state activity… sympathy with central economic planning and the widespread playing with dictatorship ideas, all tend in this direction (Hayek 2007, 245–248).

What Abbot Gleason and many others have referred to as the "slippery slope"—argument concerning the connection between economic planning and totalitarianism (Gleason 1995, 64) may have first been put forward by Lippmann in *The Good Society* in 1937; but as we have seen, he was far from the first to compare fascism with communism, and the specific economic argument Lippmann proposed had clear antecedents in Hayek's elaboration on Mises' arguments against the possibility of economic rationality in socialism. This argument was developed over more than a decade, but arguably only came to full fruition in Hayek's own words in 1944. The overarching claim of *The Road to Serfdom* was precisely that "the rise of fascism and naziism (sic) was not a reaction against the socialist trends of the preceding period but a necessary outcome of those tendencies" (Hayek 2007, 59). Furthermore, Hayek's claim was not only that fascism was a version of, more than a reaction against socialism; but also that democratic countries were becoming more socialist by the hour, and thus also coming closer to totalitarianism. "For at least twenty-five years before the spectre of totalitarianism became a real threat, we had progressively been moving away from the basic ideas on which Western civilization has been built", he wrote. The key point in this was an abandonment of "that freedom in economic affairs without which personal and political freedom has never existed in the past". Writing from a Britain under siege by the German bomber planes, Hayek claimed that contrary to popular opinion it was "the prevalence of socialist views and not Prussianism" (Hayek 2007, 63) that had led to totalitarianism in Germany, and that it would do so also in Britain if his warnings were not heard in due time.

Hayek then cited several developments in Germany in the years of the Weimar Republic and as far back as to the rule of Otto von Bismarck as proof of how what he called "social constructivism", in the form of economic planning, had led to totalitarianism. These developments were all political attempts by socialists, fascists and social liberals to subvert the workings of the price mechanism and the "free" market. Hayek repeatedly stated that "… the very complexity of the division of labour under modern conditions (…) makes competition the only method by which such coordination can be adequately brought about" (Hayek 2007, 95). This was an echo of Mises, but Hayek further contended that economic planning presupposed "the existence of a complete ethical code in which all the different human values are allotted their due place" (Hayek 2007, 101). He then went on to state that there is no "complete ethical code" available for human beings to grasp, so choices in a planned society would be have to be made by someone, between the diverse preferences of different groups. Since this someone can never have all the knowledge automatically embedded in the market through the price mechanism, these choices would be bad ones. More importantly for the question of how economic planning leads to totalitarianism: "People who are not satisfied with the priorities made by planners will feel unjustly treated. There will always exist inequalities…" Hayek wrote, "But when these things occur in a society which is consciously directed, the way in which people will react will be very different from what it is when they are nobody's conscious choice" (Hayek 2007, 137). This is a key element in the road to totalitarianism described by Hayek: The impossibility of planning, be it by a democratically elected entity or not, leads to inefficiency and social unrest, thus "The cry for an economic dictator is a characteristic stage in the movement toward planning" (Hayek 2007, 108). According to Hayek, this stage would be followed by massive propaganda to secure full support for the economic policies that could be neither fair nor effective (Hayek 2007, 171). Finally, it would become obvious that the leading group within a totalitarian state, "is not likely to be formed by the best but rather by the worst element of any society" (Hayek 2007, 160). And it all starts with economic planning.

The Contested Definition of Economic Planning

The question of what Hayek really meant by "economic planning" is highly contested to this day, and I argue that the notion of a dual argument shows us that neoliberalism can best be understood as an attempt to reconcile the attack on planning with an attack on laissez-faire. In the book, Hayek attempted to separate between "planning for competition" and "planning *against* competition" (Hayek 2007, 90). To some of Hayek's critics in our time, the existence of successful post-war welfare states in Europe seem to disprove Hayek's theory of totalitarianism as a result of economic planning and government intervention in the economy (Farrant and McPhail 2010). In the second part of the twentieth century, many countries engaged actively in a variety of policies that might fall under most definitions of economic planning; including state ownership of industries, counter-cyclical spending, widespread redistribution through high rates of taxation and extensive welfare systems. But if these countries are to be labelled totalitarian, then the concept loses much of its power and relevance, especially in relation to the atrocities committed by the European dictatorships that the concept was intended to describe. Bruce Caldwell claims that Hayek was merely "arguing against the dangers of socialist central planning, not the welfare state", and that "it was only in later books, after the demise in the west of 'hot socialism', that he took up the question of the dangers of the welfare state, and when he did so it was in more measured and gradualist terms" (Caldwell 2011, 2).

Thus, we arrive at the very crux of the question of the role assigned to the state by early neoliberals. As I suggested in the previous chapter, it is entirely plausible that Hayek never meant to argue against government *involvement* in the form of "a legal system designed both to preserve competition and to make it operate as beneficially as possible", or even "an extensive system of social services" (Hayek 2007, 87). As we can see, this is pointed out in the text itself, and Hayek was reported to have been disheartened by the popularity of his book amongst American business conservatives, who mainly sought new arguments for lower taxes and less government involvement in what they perceived as their affairs. Much later, in *Law, Legislation and Liberty* (1973), Hayek also wrote, "What I meant to argue … was certainly not that whenever we depart, however slightly, from what I regard as the principles of a free society, we shall ineluctably be driven to go the whole way to a totalitarian system" (Hayek 1998, 58). Hayek here shows a more moderate side than the caricature of a free market fundamentalist we find in some of the critical literature. Yet, as should be clear from the previous chapter and from Hayek's critique of the welfare states later in life, his disagreements with laissez-faire liberals and business conservatives in the US was not mainly related to welfare programmes. American business leaders took Hayek's book to be a spirited attack on government involvement in economic affairs; it was, but they missed the other aspect of the dual argument, the more subtle critique of laissez-faire and Hayek's novel approach to the role of modern states in both guarding and constituting liberal market order.

We thus return to the common misunderstandings which are apparent when scholars, politicians and journalists refer to neoliberalism and the doctrine of writers like Hayek as somehow "anti-state". Johanna Bockmann has observed that the state/market dichotomy is arguably useless for real social analysis, and that it "easily blurs into other dichotomies: between socialism and capitalism, between central planning and the market, between Keynesianism and monetarism…" (Bockman 2011, 5). According to João Rodrigues, one of Hayek's main contributions was the idea that "the development of markets demands an expanding state with the power to impose the rules that markets require" (Rodrigues 2013, 1007). This is the point where Hayek, along with several of the other early neoliberals, departed from laissez-faire liberalism; and Hayek postulated that "the question whether the state should or should not 'act' or 'interfere' poses an altogether false alternative, and the term laissez-faire is a highly ambiguous and misleading description of the principles on which a liberal policy is based" (Hayek 2007, 84). This expresses the fundamental tension in Hayek's work between attacking economic planning on one side and attacking laissez-faire liberalism on the other. As Bruce Caldwell writes about Hayek: "Within the covers of the same book he will both argue that policies that aim at income redistribution violate the rule of law, and endorse the provision of a 'safety net' that is itself an instrument of redistribution" (Caldwell 2004, 5). Caldwell indicates that Hayek contradicted himself, but the two aspects of the dual argument can also be understood as creating a tension, which pushed both Hayek and other neoliberal thinkers forward to try and reconcile the attack on planning with their admission that laissez-faire was an outdated programme.[5]

[5] Erwin Dekker sees a similar type of tension in the work of Austrian thinkers like Hayek and Popper, namely "the tension between on the one hand, the strong conviction of the futility of science or art in the face of tyranny, and on the other hand, the feeling that one has the moral duty to do something" (Dekker 2016, 136).

Other Versions of the Dual Argument

The dual argument, stating both that economic planning led to totalitarianism *and* that liberals would have to do better than laissez-faire to stop it, was expressed by all the European protagonists of the neoliberal movement in the war years separating The Walter Lippmann Colloquium in 1938 and the founding meeting of the Mont Pelerin Society in 1947. In *Les mystiques économiques*, published in 1938, Louis Rougier claimed that liberal democracy "finds itself transformed into a totalitarian state", and argued that "la mystique libérale" of laissez-faire was not enough to counter the trend towards economic planning (Burgin 2012, 69). As mentioned, Wilhelm Röpke never worked at the University of Freiburg, but was instead based in Jena and Marburg before fleeing Germany; first for Turkey and then to Switzerland, where he remained for the rest of his life. *Die Gesselschaftscrisis der Gegenwarts* (translated in 1950 as *The Social Crisis of Our Time*) was thus "written in the latter part of 1941, at a time when Hitler was at the very height of his triumph, and in the solitude of the Swiss alps which was then a small island in a continent swamped by tyranny" (Röpke 1950, preface). But what was the cause of this tyranny? "What uncanny disease has invaded our world and what exactly has been happening in those countries which have already succumbed to it?" (Röpke 1950, introduction) Röpke saw a "spiritual crisis", and waxed lyrically about the "process of social decomposition and agglomeration for which the term 'collectivization' has been coined", lamenting the "healthy society, firmly resting on its own foundations, [which] possesses a genuine structure with many intermediate stages; it exhibits a necessarily hierarchical composition (…) where each individual has the good fortune of knowing his position" (Röpke 1950, 10).

These lamentations of a lost world with traditional hierarchies were arguably present also in Hayek's thought, but Röpke put his notion of a spiritual crisis at the centre both of *The Social Crisis of Our Time* and *Civitas Humana* from 1944, two books which are indeed very similar to each other. At times Röpke appeared more balanced than Hayek, at one point even decrying "the vague and thoughtless use of terms such as 'planned economy' and 'socialism'". Röpke, somewhat similar to Karl Polanyi, insisted that collectivism was a response to something else, but the driving force was not, like in *The Great Transformation* a double movement protecting society from the attempt at giving market efficiency primacy over social relations, but instead the "spiritual crisis". Yet this crisis remained a rather unclear entity, simultaneously the cause and the effect of social unrest. Röpke did claim that "This juxtaposition of totalitarianism and socialism is more than a mere comparison; the two tendencies are, on the contrary, so closely interrelated that as can be proved in detail, they are, in the last analysis, one" (Röpke 1950, 19). When it came down to this last analysis, Röpke rested on precisely the same argument as Hayek: "Since decisions regarding the use of the economy's productive forces are no longer made through the market but in the office of a government agency, they become politicalized [sic]", (Röpke 1950, 88) he wrote. But "an ideal democracy presupposes … that people are in almost complete agreement on questions of government… How would it be possible to effect even a tolerable agreement on all those questions of detail which are the essence of economic process and which affect individual interests most directly and acutely?" (Röpke 1950, 89). This was a reprise of Hayek's intervention in the socialist calculation debates, and Röpke was in some respects probably closer to the Austrian school than other ordoliberals. Although he quoted Mises, he was not engaging with questions of commensurability, rather with questions of epistemology and knowledge. In *Civitas Humana* called "the Market" "the unsurpassed Master of Calculation" (White 1950, 576), similar to how another ordoliberal, von Stackelberg, wrote that the market order operated as if it was an automatic calculating machine (Tribe 1995, 136). Röpke too saw the market as the only possible mediator of modern social life, the process through which the diverging ends of different individuals and groups were aligned. Although he used a more "spiritual" approach than Hayek, the actual arguments of both *The Social Crisis of Our* Time and *Civitas Humana* were very similar to those of Hayek's in *The Road to Serfdom.*

It could be argued that Röpke was in fact the neoliberal thinker who most closely resembled Hayek before 1947. He also did so at such an early stage that it is difficult to contend that the influence went only one way; Röpke too must have influenced Hayek. Already in *The Economics of the Free Society*, which Röpke published in 1937, he put forward that: "The processes peculiar to economic life in a free society make evident the fundamental superiority of the *spontaneous order* over the *commanded order*". Bruce Caldwell has argued that Hayek went through a "transformation" from simply arguing for a spontaneous order, to actually trying to explain it around the time of his essay "Economics and Knowledge" from 1936, just one year earlier (Caldwell 2004, 205). Furthermore, when it came to embracing the concept of *totalitarianism* as an apt description of modern European dictatorships, Röpke claimed as early as 1935 that Fascism was "distinctly illiberal [and] decidedly totalitarian" in an article published in LSE's journal *Economica* (Röpke 1935, 85). Thus the dual argument owes much not only to Hayek and Mises, but also to Röpke.

Against "Scientism"

In a letter to Walter Lippmann on 28 May 1940, before the Blitz and the relocation to Cambridge, but after the declaration of war, Hayek wrote:

> While I by no means despair about the situation and while I do not dream of running away while the crisis lasts, there is one thing where I want to make preparations in time for all eventualities. If the worst were to come, it might be too late to write about it.
>
> I have for some time been engaged in preparatory work on a book, which I believe, if I ever come to do it, might be of real importance, but which in certain eventualities I should not be able to continue here. I enclose a synopsis of the first part of the planned book – the second part would be essentially an elaboration of the argument of my pamphlet on Freedom and the Economic System.

Hayek then went on to ask Lippmann to keep the synopsis "in case I should at some later date have to ask you to use it on my behalf in some connection".[6] The synopsis referred to has not been kept in the archives, but it seems reasonable to assume that it was not a synopsis for *The Road to Serfdom*, but instead for a never-completed project entitled *The Abuse of Reason*. In a letter to Fritz Machlup sent just a few weeks later, on June 21st, Hayek wrote "... I am already at work on my new book, a history of the influence of scientific and technological development on social thought and policy (to be called The Abuse and Decline of Reason)".[7] The mentioned text, "Freedom and the Economic System", was of a policy pamphlet Hayek had published on Chicago University Press in 1939. According to Caldwell, "pieces of *the Abuse of Reason* project ... were published separately: A part of the first section appeared as an article entitled "Individualism: True and False" ... The second section was published as "Scientism and the Study of Society", ... and parts of the historical account appeared as the essays "The Counter-Revolution of Science" ... and "Comte and Hegel" (...) The final section became *The Road to Serfdom*" (Caldwell 2004, 241).

In using the word "scientism", Hayek was criticizing contemporary thinkers like Karl Mannheim, who, like many others at the time, advocated a planned society. Other European neoliberals, notably Michael Polanyi and Karl Popper, also combined a theory of science with the trademark neoliberal theory of totalitarianism and the dual argument (Bedeleem 2017). Michael Polanyi was present both at the Walter Lippmann Colloquium and the first Mont Pelerin Society meeting in 1947, whereas Popper only took part in the latter event. In 1938 Popper was teaching in New Zealand and would have been unable to attend the meeting in Paris. Popper was in close contact with his Austrian compatriot Hayek however, and the latter admitted to having been influenced by Popper's 1934 work *Logik der Forschung* (Burgin 2012, 50). Popper sent Hayek the manuscript for his later very famous work *The Open Society and its Enemies*, and Hayek acted as a sort of agent for him in Great Britain, eventually securing Popper a publication deal and a chair at the LSE. *The Open Society and its Enemies* was published in 1945 and has become one of the most famous philosophical theories of totalitarianism. In it Popper offered "an attractive, high-end analogy between experimental science and open-minded liberal politics" (Fawcett 2014, 279) to show how the world had descended into anti-liberal totalitarian politics. Popper made liberalism the political equivalent of scientific discovery, and "divided the world into open, liberal-minded spirits who accepted change, uncertainty, and the provisional character of life and knowledge, and closed-up, illiberal spirits who craved sameness, fixity and security. Good societies came from the first, bad from the second", writes Edmund Fawcett (Fawcett 2014, 280). In Popper's grand narrative, Plato, Hegel and Marx were the villains of history who had imposed "closed" orders

[6]Yale University Library, Walter Lippmann papers, Selected correspondence 1931–1974, Box 10, Folder 11: Hayek.

[7]Hoover Institution Library and Archives, Fritz Machlup Collection, Box 43, Folder 15: "Hayek, Friedrich—1933–1944".

and ways of thinking, fundamentally opposed to the openness of liberalism (Popper 2003).

Michael Polanyi, who was Karl Polanyi's brother but shared none of his socialist views, (Congdon 1997) had already struck a similar chord in his 1935 essay "Soviet Economics—Fact and Theory". There he claimed that there were only two imaginable ways of organizing an economy: centralized planning or a market system (Mitchell 2006, 21). Polanyi had had great success as a chemist before migrating to philosophy and social theory during these years. Like Hayek, his quarrel was with the communists' claim to "scientific planning", which was given intellectual credence by engineers and sociologists like Mannheim, who advocated the complete rationalization and planning of society in order to avoid civilizational collapse. Like Hayek, Polanyi argued that a central authority could not possibly gather and assimilate information about all possible aspects of the economic system: "the central authority, however properly constituted it may be as a government, is in fact ignorant of the desires of its constituents as far as their day-to-day-wants are concerned" (Mitchell 2006, 22). Polanyi argued that as with scientific discovery, society as a whole with all its social and economic factors was too complicated to make economic planning possible. He continued along these lines in articles called "Collectivist Planning" in 1940 and the book *USSR Economics* in 1936. As early as 1919, in the essay "New Scepticism", Polanyi observed that "society is so complicated that even science cannot calculate the future effect either of any institution or of any measure and people involved with politics, with their rough minds and passionate fancies, are a thousand times less able to foresee whether the institutions they demand will meet their interests in the last analysis" (Polanyi 1997, 30). Michael Polanyi actually coined the phrase "spontaneous order", and his ideas about "tacit knowledge" were to become very important for Hayek, (Mitchell 2006, 22) with whom he was in correspondence (Dekker 2016, 142).

In an essay entitled "Collectivist Economic Planning", Michael Polanyi also went on to express the full dual argument, arguing that liberals should not be so opposed to government intervention. There was nothing wrong with the right *kind* of intervention, he claimed, and this would be absolutely necessary to protect the market economy:

> The orthodox Liberals maintain that, if the market is limited by the fixation of some of its elements, then it must cease to function, the implication being that there exists a logical system of complete *laissez-faire*, the only rational alternative to which is collectivism. That is precisely the position which collectivists want us to take up when asserting that none of the evils of the market can be alleviated except by destroying the whole institution root and branch. (Polanyi 1997, 140)

Thus Polanyi too found himself arguing both that economic planning was an epistemic impossibility, *and* that there was absolutely nothing wrong with government intervention. Once again, we are starting to glimpse the crucial importance for the early neoliberals of defining *which kinds* of interventions were possible and not harmful to the market order.

War and Planning

Like Lippmann had done in *The Good Society,* Hayek and Röpke went to great lengths in their 1944 publications to show how the wartime command economy was *not* an example to be followed after the war was over.[8] Their reasoning behind this should be clear by now. In the article "Austria: Advance Post in Europe" from 1946, Hayek stressed the importance of quickly abandoning price controls and rationing, noting that "The needs of reconstruction will force the Austrian government to make decisions that will be highly unpopular with their own citizens".[9] Lionel Robbins was a leading member of the neoliberal group who, unlike Hayek and Röpke, was directly involved in organizing the economic war effort through his position as the director of the economic section of the Offices of the War Cabinet (Pinder 1998, 45). This must have had a profound impact on Robbins, making him somewhat less prone to abstract generalizations about the alleged impossibility and totalitarian effects of planning and coordination outside of the market order. Robbins certainly remained a strong defender of liberalism and "free" trade, but as time went on, he focused his energy on more concrete questions of international cooperation. In 1937, Robbins was invited to speak at Institut Universitaire des Hautes Études Internationales in Geneva. This Institute was founded by William Rappard (1883–1958) in 1927, and it hosted several other neoliberals throughout the years, including Mises, Frank D. Graham and the Chicago economist Jacob Viner (1892–1970) (Mirowski and Plehwe 2009, 12). Robbins delivered a lecture that would later be published under the title *Economic Planning and International Order*. In the lecture he performed a very vocal critique of laissez-faire liberalism, stating bluntly that: "If planning is an attempt to create institutions conducive to the satisfaction of the citizens, then international liberalism is a plan", (Pinder 1998, 45) and "The characteristic institutions of a liberal society are inconceivable without government" (Pinder 1998, 50). As we have seen, this attack on laissez-faire was an integral part of the dual argument and the emerging neoliberal programme. Robbins was also focused on disproving left-wing theories of totalitarianism and the causes behind the Great Depression and rise of dictatorships in Europe. In *The Economic Causes of War* from 1939, he engaged actively with theories of imperialism by thinkers like Lenin, Luxembourg, Hilferding and also John Hobson (1858–1940), trying to disprove the contention that there were structural problems in capitalism that lay behind society's present ills (Robbins 1968, 19–57). Robbins work in the years between 1938 and 1947 thus attacked socialism and economic planning, but also often took the form of defending capitalism. Much like the other neoliberals (and Carl Schmitt), Robbins saw democracy and the economy torn up by

[8]In a lecture to the infamous Conservative Monday Club in London, in 1980, Hayek would also claim that rationing and economic planning would be less efficient even during wartime. Hoover Institution Library and Archives, Friedrich Hayek Collection, Box 104, Folder 4: "Problems of War Economy".

[9]Hoover Institution Library and Archives, Friedrich Hayek Collection, Box 107, Folder 6: "Austria: Advance Post in Europe".

what he called "group interests". In a preface to a collection of essays published in 1939, he claimed that:

> The modern world, deluged by the *clichés* of propaganda and second-rate thinking, believes that it is becoming collectivist. But this is self-deception. The apologia for many recent tendencies, from the 'co-ordination' of British transport to the corporative chambers of the fascist state, is collectivist. But the substance is essentially something different. It is the consolidation of group interest. (Robbins 1939, vii)

Like the other neoliberals, Robbins claimed that group interests were "incompatible with general interest", which according to him was best served not by "unified collectivism… [but] by that system of decentralized initiative which, within a suitable framework of law, is provided by private property and free markets" (Robbins 1939, vii). In his 1947 publication *The Economic Problem in Peace and War*, however, he seemed to perform something of a U-turn on questions of Keynesian economic planning. He stated that within his own tradition there had been "a tendency to ignore certain deep-seated possibilities of disharmony, in a way which, I now think, led sometimes to superficiality and sometimes to positive error. I owe much to Cambridge economists, particularly to Lord Keynes and Professor Robertson, for having awakened me from dogmatic slumbers in this very important respect" (Robbins 2007, 68).

More than seeing this shift as a radical conversion of beliefs, we should take it as an argument for not conceding too easily that "Keynes vs. Hayek" was the ultimate political battle of the twentieth century. Keynes famously wrote to Hayek, after reading *The Road to Serfdom* while on his way to the Bretton Woods conference in 1944, that he found himself "in deeply moved agreement" with the bulk of the text. In some ways, Keynes' attack on laissez-faire from 1924 had been motivated by the same urge to "save capitalism" from the threat of Marxism as had Hayek's version 20 years later. Both Hayek and Keynes sought to establish a form of state intervention that could ameliorate some suffering, while at the same time leaving property relations intact and nurture "market forces", instead of stifling them. Keynes' appraisal of *The Road to Serfdom* has made some commentators believe that Hayek was more moderate than the free market fundamentalist he is often portrayed as. I argue instead that Keynes' letter, rather than showing us that Hayek was somewhat Keynesian, instead suggests that Keynes was somewhat sympathetic to neoliberalism. Although he did not share all of Hayek's views on the origins of totalitarian dictatorship, Keynes certainly also wanted to salvage capitalism from the possibility of socialism. The economic teachings of Keynes and the philosophies of social liberalism were indeed targets for neoliberals from the very beginning. However, the difference between the two has been somewhat misunderstood and exaggerated, as both strands criticized laissez-faire and wanted to use the state actively. The main difference was the type of state intervention advocated and the neoliberal idealization of the *market mechanism*. Neoliberal forms of state intervention were meant to safeguard and spread this mechanism and make it the *mediator of modernity*, not to stabilize it or improve upon its workings. The distinction is surely slippery, but it is fundamentally what differentiated neoliberalism from social liberalism and Keynes from Hayek—not whether one should use the state *at all*. Even this division is not clear-cut, as Hayek, at least at times, seemed to accept the ordoliberal position that market mechanisms themselves did have in them a tendency to create monopolies and concentrations of power. Furthermore, Keynes is reported to have undergone something of a swing to the right towards the end of his life, stating, for instance, "I find myself more and more relying for a solution of our problems on the invisible hand which I tried to eject from economic thinking twenty years ago" (Skidelsky 2000, 470).

Neoliberals in Wartime

Of the German economists present at the Lippmann Colloquium in 1938, Alexander Rüstow and Wilhelm Röpke had already left Hitler's Germany a few years previously. Their first port of call was Istanbul, where Mustafa Kemal, president of the new Turkish republic since 1923, took advantage of the situation in Germany to recruit European émigré academics like Röpke, Rüstow and Erich Auerbach (1892–1957) to a new university on the Bosporus. Röpke founded the Institute for Social Sciences there in 1933, but moved on to Geneva four years later to teach at Rappard's Institute for Graduate Studies. Rüstow remained in Istanbul until after the war, working on his three-volume treatise on the demise of liberal politics, *Ortsbestimmung der Gegenwart*, English title: *Freedom and Domination*. The original edition of Röpke's *Die Gesselschaftskrisis der Gegenwart* actually included an appendix essay written by Rüstow, a sort of "thumbnail sketch" of Rüstow's own work that showed the extent to which these two thinkers considered themselves engaged in the same project (Zmirak 2001, 101).

In celebratory accounts of ordoliberals and early neoliberalism, much is made of the fact that Walter Eucken was twice questioned by the Gestapo (Gerken 2000, 97) and that other ordoliberals were both questioned and at times even imprisoned (White 2012, 241). Quoting a letter from Röpke to Hayek, Ronald Hartwell claims it was "a miracle" that Eucken survived the war (Hartwell 1995, 20). Less attention is paid to the fact that the whole Freiburg school, including Franz Böhm and Ludwig Erhard (1897–1977), actively tried to influence the Nazi administration with policy proposals (Mirowski and Plehwe 2009, 119). John Zmirak claims that unlike Röpke and Rüstow, Eucken and Böhm made "their criticism of Nazi economics implicit in their technical work", (Zmirak 2001, 35) but Ralf Ptak points to how this sort of "revisionist history of the wartime ordoliberals is not supported by facts". By reading papers published by the Freiburg-circle between the mid-1930s and early 1940s, Ptak concludes that "ordoliberal concepts were designed to be implemented under the auspices of a Nazi government" (Mirowski and Plehwe 2009, 117). This interpretation is supported also by the work of Bernhard Walpen in his Gramscian study of the Mont Pèlerin Society (Walpen 2004, 93–97). The more celebratory historiography on ordoliberalism is very much based on the notion that these ideas arose in opposition to Nazism. In a 1979 lecture, Foucault said that "Nazism was, in a way, the epistemological and political 'road to Damascus' for the Freiburg

School", which is not quite the same as the rather banal hagiographic accounts that see ordoliberalism as a brave and ingenious response to the horrors of Nazism. Foucault continues: "That is to say, Nazism enabled them to define what I would call the field of adversity that they had to define and cross in order to reach their objective" (Foucault 2008, 106). This is another way of describing totalitarianism as neoliberalism's Other, as Fawcett has noted (Fawcett 2014, 275). The contributions of Walpen and Ptak represent a serious challenge to the hagiographic accounts of the history of ordoliberalism and the Freiburg School, yet their work has so far been largely ignored. The ordoliberals were to greatly influence post-war economic policy in West Germany, and historian of economics Keith Tribe has insisted that rather than treating this period "as an awakening from the nightmare of National Socialist Germany", continuities should be emphasized (Tribe 1995, 6).

Louis Rougier, the man behind the Walter Lippmann Colloquium in 1938, was to disappear from the subsequent history of neoliberalism. The reasons are said to lie in his dealings with the Vichy regime. In October 1940, he acted as an envoy to Winston Churchill in London on behalf of Philippe Pétain, the leader of the collaborationist Vichy government. Rougier is to have made a "gentleman's agreement" with Churchill that France would resume the war on Britain's side once the British could provide more assistance. For this he was branded as a collaborator by many of his peers (Burgin 2012, 77). "Perhaps it has been unavoidable that you should have been entangled in all the misunderstanding and confusions of French opinion in this country...", Walter Lippmann wrote to Rougier in a letter dated 3 February 1941. Rougier had arrived in New York and wanted to write an article explaining his dealings with the Vichy regime. Lippmann, however, advised against this, writing that "publication of this article would be a disastrous mistake. It will be entirely misunderstood. It will make you, in this country, the propagandist of Petain".[10]

Lippmann and Rougier had had a disagreement after the Colloquium in 1938. Rougier had organized a dinner in Lippmann's honour, which included several backers of fascist movements and where the word "propaganda" had been used without negative connotations. Lippmann felt that the dinner had not been an effort to discuss ideas, but a tactical meeting in a group with clear political aims. He wrote to Rougier on 1 July 1938: "I feel I must tell you, that as a matter of principle to which I have adhered for more than fifteen years, I never participate in propaganda or political movements of any kind whatsoever".[11] But when Rougier ended up in trouble because of his dealings with the Vichy regime, Lippmann stood by him and helped him when he arrived in the US. Other neoliberals like Röpke and Hayek, by contrast, grew wary of Rougier's "pro-Vichy tendencies" and, according to Angus Burgin, they were "hesitant to maintain relations". Rougier then refused to recognize the legitimacy of De Gaulle and France Libre, and found himself marginalized at the New School for Social Research where he had been given a position (Mirowski

[10] Yale University Library, Walter Lippmann papers, Selected correspondence 1931–1974, Folder 1848: Louis Rougier.

[11] Yale University Library, Walter Lippmann papers, Selected correspondence 1931–1974, Folder 1848: Louis Rougier.

and Plehwe 2009, 51). After the war, the British' would deny Rougier's account of the events surrounding his agreement with Churchill, throwing him into further disrepute (Burgin 2012, 77). Thus Rougier would not present at the Mont Pelerin Society meeting in 1947 and was only admitted to the organization in 1960.

Individualism True and False

Not long after the end of the war, on 17 December 1945, Hayek gave a lecture entitled "Individualism True and False" at University College Dublin. There he turned against liberals of his own time, making crystal clear his attacks on social liberalism and his aim to carve out a new liberalism not tainted by this history. The lecture opened with a quote from Tocqueville on how there had been two currents of thought since the eighteenth century: one towards free institutions and one towards absolute power (Hayek 1948, 2). Here we see Hayek attempting to continue Tocqueville's project of criticizing democracy in the same way as earlier liberals had criticized absolutism. Hayek stated: "Terms like 'liberalism' or 'democracy', 'capitalism' or 'socialism', today no longer stand for coherent systems of ideas. (…) No political term has suffered worse in this respect than 'individualism'" (Hayek 1948, 2–3). He then took it upon himself to clear up this confusion and at the same time purge liberalism of those he labelled "false individualists". This was a tradition that Hayek, with his deep appreciation of British liberalism, found mainly in "French and other continental writers", blaming "the Encyclopedists, Rousseau and the Physiocrats", and later deriding such thinkers as Goethe, Humboldt and also John Stuart Mill. In a typical case of what Thomas Gieryn has called "boundary work" in order to police demarcations of political creeds, (Gieryn 1983) Hayek argued that "it was only liberalism in the English sense that was generally opposed to centralization, to nationalism and to socialism, while the liberalism prevalent on the Continent favoured all three". Hayek also engaged in what Duncan Bell has called "canonical protocol" (Bell 2014, 687) by positing as opposed to this "rationalist individualism [which] always tends to develop into the opposite of individualism, namely socialism or collectivism", thinkers like John Locke, Bernard Mandeville and Edmund Burke (1729–1797). He added: "In the nineteenth century I find it represented most perfectly in the work of two of its greatest historians and political philosophers: Alexis de Tocqueville and Lord Acton" (Hayek 1948, 3).

Hayek then defended what he called the "anti-rationalism" of these thinkers, with special reference also to Adam Smith, because they had realized how "many of the institutions on which human achievements rest have arisen and are functioning without a designing and directing mind" (Hayek 1948, 7). According to Hayek, "design theories necessarily lead to the conclusion that social processes can be made to serve human ends only if they are subjected to the control of individual human reason, and thus lead directly to socialism", whereas "true individualism believes on the contrary that, if left free, men will often achieve more than individual human reason could design or foresee" (Hayek 1948, 12). Hence the case was clear for limiting state power, also if it happened to be exercised by a legitimate democracy: "From the awareness of the limitations of individual knowledge and from the fact that no person or small group of persons can know all that is known to somebody, individualism also derives its main practical conclusion: its demand for a strict limitation of all coercive or exclusive power". Hayek followed Tocqueville and Acton to the letter in arguing that the most important thing about democracy was to limit its reach:

> While democracy is founded on the convention that the majority view decides on common action, it does not mean that what is today the majority view ought to become the generally accepted view-even if that were necessary to achieve the aims of the majority. On the contrary, the whole justification of democracy rests on the fact that in course of time what is today the view of a small minority may become the majority view.

According to Hayek, "the merit of competition is precisely that it gives the minority a chance to prevail" (Hayek 1948, 29–30). He also contended that: "it should be said at once that true individualism is not equalitarian [sic] in the modern sense of the word. (…) it also denies government the right to limit what the able or fortunate may achieve" (Hayek 1948, 30). Hayek then turned on the "much abused and misunderstood phrase of 'laissez-fare'" and claimed that along with the "still older formula of 'the protection of life, liberty and property' it is not much help: In fact, in so far as both tend to suggest that we can just leave things as they are, they may be worse than no answer; they certainly do not tell us what are and what are not desirable or necessary fields of government activity" (Hayek 1948, 17). Readers will recognize this as the fundamental theme of neoliberal thought, and Hayek then went on to try and distinguish between rule-based exercise of power based on abstract principles, and the more direct and arbitrary kind, which he opposed.

In a sense Hayek attacked the "false individualists" amongst the liberals for wanting to take individualism, and thus liberalism, too far. Due to the advances of social liberalism in the second half of the nineteenth century, liberalism had come to be a rather progressive and democratic creed (Bell 2014, 694). In 1904, for instance, the American political theorist William Dunning argued that as opposed to conservatism, "fundamentally, nineteenth century liberalism meant democracy" (Dunning 1904, 803). We can see in "Individualism True and False" how Hayek was doing his upmost to see that the twentieth century meaning of the term would be something different: He attacked laissez-faire, but also evoked the epistemology of "spontaneous order", to argue that human beings cannot change the social order consciously. This realization, he claimed, was the basis of the liberal tradition of limiting democracy. It is hard not to see Hayek's arguments as part of what Domenic Losurdo has called liberalism's "de-politicization and naturalization of economic and social relations" (Losurdo 2011, 193). In an essay much later in life, Hayek would once again comment on his fight to separate liberalism from democracy and socialism, writing: "It [liberalism] later became allied with socialism because agreement as to some of the ultimate ends for a time obscured the utter incompatibility of the methods by which the two movements tried to reach their goal" (Hayek 1948, 270).

The Acton-Tocqueville Army

When *The Road to Serfdom* was published in 1944, it brought Hayek a great degree of fame and success. This was especially so in the US, where the book was turned into, amongst other things: a condensed *Reader's Digest*-version distributed to millions; a radio programme aired on NBC[12]; and a cartoon, first published in *Look Magazine* and later distributed to all General Motors' employees in Detroit (see Fig. 4.1).

The cartoon clearly shows only one aspect of the dual argument: the theory that economic planning leads to totalitarian dictatorship. Panels 4 and 5 explain the theories from the socialist calculation debates, whereas the rest of the panels picture Hayek's theory of the detailed steps from war-induced interference with markets to totalitarian tyranny.

Hayek also travelled to the US and undertook an extensive lecture tour there in 1945 and 1946. On tour, Hayek spread the dual argument to a larger audience, and began recruitment to a closed society based on this insight. The roots of the dual argument in the history of liberal thought were perfectly clear to Hayek, and he proposed to call the society "The Acton-Tocqueville society".[13] At a speech at "The Economic Club" in Detroit in April 1945, Hayek argued that:" My attempt has been not merely to restate an old argument, but to reformulate it and adapt it to our time and to take account of what we have learned since the philosophy of free enterprise was first formulated a long time ago", insisting that what was needed was guidelines for good government intervention, not futile arguments about whether to have intervention or not.[14] At Stanford University in Palo Alto, California, Hayek stated ominously: "... if we are not careful we may find ourselves saddled with an omnipotent state whose machinery so thoroughly controls the people and their opinions that even the retention of the forms of democracy would not alter its totalitarian character".

There was, however, some cause for optimism too; and although Hayek claimed that it was the abandonment of liberalism that lay behind the threat of totalitarianism, he could also look to the history of liberal thought for answers to how to combat this trend. In the Stanford lecture he claimed that through Edmund Burke, American political ideas "became the foundation of English whiggism and later liberalism", but also noted that "the problems of these writers are not yet the problems of to-day; while they created much of the traditions and institutions, they did not yet know the particular dangers to which they would be exposed or which they would themselves produce". He then moved on to what we may recognize as the second step of liberal thought in which limitation on liberal institutions became a refrain, and he introduced

[12]Hoover Institution Library and Archives, Fritz Machlup Collection, Box 43, Folder 16: "Radio Script".

[13]Hoover Institution Library and Archives, Friedrich Hayek Collection, Box 61, Folder 8: "Memorandum on the Proposed Foundation for an Academy of Political Philosophy, Tentatively Called 'The Acton-Tocqueville Society'—Typescript 1945".

[14]Hoover Institution Library and Archives, Friedrich Hayek Collection, Box 106, Folder 8:"The Road to Serfdom Speech—The Economic Club of Detroit, Michigan—April 24, 1945".

Fig. 4.1 The illustrated road to serfdom

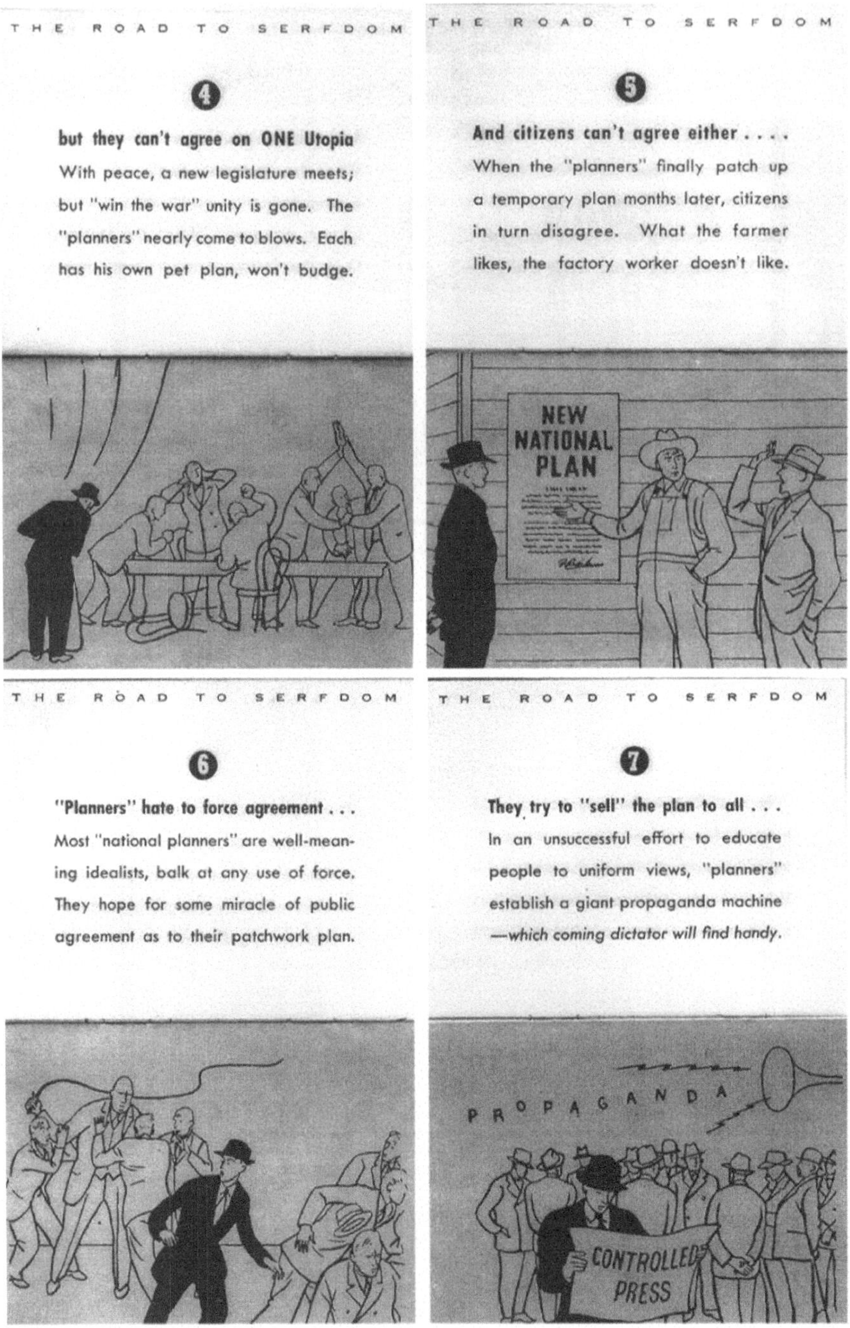

Fig. 4.1 (continued)

Fig. 4.1 (continued)

Fig. 4.1 (continued)

THE ROAD TO SERFDOM

16

Your thinking is "planned" . . . .

In the dictatorship, unintentionally created by the planners, there is no room for difference of opinion. Posters, radio, press—*all tell you the same lies!*

THE ROAD TO SERFDOM

17

Your recreation is "planned" . . . .

It is no coincidence that sports and amusements have been carefully "planned" in all regimented nations. Once started, "planners" can't stop.

THE ROAD TO SERFDOM

18

Your disciplining is "planned" . . . .

If you're fired from your job, it's apt to be by a firing squad. What used to be an *error* has now become a *crime* against the state. ***Thus ends the road to serfdom!***

Fig. 4.1 (continued)

Tocqueville and Acton as the saviours of the twentieth century. Here Hayek is worth quoting at length:

> My search for a satisfactory statement of the basic liberal philosophy led me in the end to two great historians who seem to me to have achieved the most complete synthesis of the basic principles of a free society and in particular to have developed the Burkean philosophy to the highest point it has yet reached. It was in the fragments of Lord Actons inachieved [sic] great history of freedom and in de Tocqueville's study of American democracy where I found the ripest fruits of the age-long speculation on the reconciliation of liberty and government which is again troubling us to-day

According to Hayek, this phase of liberal thought had "immediate relevance to the problems of to-day…[and]… show the amazing foresight of these men which still makes them the best guides to our task". He then quoted various passages from the two writers with comments such as: "What could be more penetrating [than] the following discussion by Lord Acton of what to-day we call totalitarianism", or "the amazingly prophetic words, concluding de Tocqueville's Democracy in America", adding that "these men were much more aware of the problems we face to-day than even we are, and … they provide a basic philosophy which might well provide the foundation from which our further work can start".

Hayek then continued to outline the organization that could carry out a new programme of reinventing liberalism to counter the totalitarian threat. This lecture also seems to be one of the first instances in which Hayek elaborated on a theme that was to consume much of his political energy: the power of ideas. As in later books, he quoted the then very recently deceased Keynes, who famously claimed that little else than the ideas of economists and political philosophers ruled the world. He then noted that the extent to which socialists had "succeeded in permeating all our thinking is not least due to their courage to be 'utopian'", another theme he would return to in a later call to arms for liberal intellectuals in his oft-quoted 1949 article "The Intellectuals and Socialism". He concluded: "we must raise and train an army of fighters for freedom".[15]

This "army" was to be the Mont Pèlerin Society: a new version of the Centre International d´Études pour la Rénovation du Libéralisme (CIRL) from 1938, formed nine years later and still active today. The first mention of the idea had come at a seminar at Cambridge in 1944, lead by economic historian John Clapham. Hayek had read a paper on the need for a post-war society dedicated to "opposition to all forms of totalitarianism, whether it be from the Right or from the Left". This is also where Hayek first came up with the idea of naming it after "some great figure who embodies in an especially high degree the virtues and ideals which such an organization would have to serve and whose name could serve as a flag under which men who agree could unite" (Hartwell 1995, 27–29).

The proposed naming of the society after two past liberal thinkers is of great interest. Was neoliberalism mainly a restatement of the ideas of Tocqueville and Acton? In a six-page memorandum written in August 1945, Hayek referred to the

[15] Hoover Institution Library and Archives, Friedrich Hayek Collection, Box 107, Folder 7: "The Prospects for Freedom, 1946".

ideas of Tocqueville and Acton as a "foundation from which to start", and referred to the work of the society as a process of "putting our own house in order". It was the house of liberalism that needed to be put in order; but it was not merely a question of a rediscovery of lost ideals, but also of how these ideals would lead to new ideas for a new time. The discovery process itself was not straightforward, either. It involved finding the right parts of the work of each thinker in Hayek's liberal pantheon, a process we can glimpse in the memorandum when he writes of Acton and Tocqueville that their thought

> is largely a development of ideas of Edmund Burke, but does not include the whole of Burke's philosophy but only that part of which Acton could say that 'Burke at his best is England at its best'. It is Burkes's wisdom purged of its excrescences and developed in the light of the experience of the last century, as to develop it further will be the task of our own.)

According to Hayek, Acton and Tocqueville had picked up the best parts of Burke, and now it was up to the neoliberals to pick up the best parts of Acton and Tocqueville, and develop that further. Yet at the same time, Hayek insisted that what the neoliberals were looking for were "the timeless truths, rather than the application to the problems of our time which we have yet to find".[16] Perhaps this is the true meaning of the phrase "classical liberalism", so often invoked by neoliberal thinkers to this day? Perhaps it is meant not as one philosophy found within the work of a particular thinker or set of thinkers, but rather a scattered whole of timeless truth, appearing in the work of different thinkers at different times.

The more practical problem was how to raise money for such a society, but a fortunate set of events would make Hayek's dream a reality. Wilhelm Röpke harboured plans of his own to unite "true liberals" in the wake of the Second World War and the collapse of the Institute pour le Rénovation de Libéralisme. In August 1945, Röpke had circulated a letter with plans for an international periodical, and Hartwell has commented that Röpke's motivations were "remarkably like that of Hayek". They were indeed: Röpke was concerned about totalitarianism and collectivism and wanted his international periodical to be used as a "clearly visible and effective platform for discussion with the double purpose of clarifying and working out ideas and making known the results" (Hartwell 1995, 29). In a circular filled to the brim with rhetorical despair, Röpke announced to his fellow liberals that "It will be difficult enough to eradicate the evils which Fascism and National Socialism have left in their wake; already another danger has become manifest, namely that the hatred sown by them will be misused to set up in their stead other forms of *Collectivism* (Röpkes emphasis)".[17] Röpke was helped in his efforts by the Swiss businessman Albert Hunold (who held a doctorate but was mainly engaged in the Swiss watch-making business), who set about using his contacts to raise money for the journal. Hunold was able to acquire a considerable amount from sources like the Swiss Chamber of

[16]Hoover Institution Library and Archives, Friedrich Hayek Collection, Box 61, Folder 8, "Memorandum on the proposed foundation of an international academy of political philosophy tentatively called 'The Acton-Tocqueville Society'".

[17]Hoover Institution Library and Archives, Mont Pelerin Society, Box 5, Folder 10, "Plan for an international periodical".

Commerce (Wirtschaftsförderung) and Credit Suisse/Schweizerische Kreditanstalt. (The money from Credit Suisse is not mentioned in Hunold's report to the society, but can be traced instead through some of his correspondence.)[18] According to Hartwell, the journal plans were abandoned because not enough money was raised; however in Hunold's own report, he stated that the reason for the abandonment of the journal plans were disagreements with the publisher A. Francke & Co. in Bern. They had wanted to also publish a journal on economic theory, and that project included a Professor Sahlin, who had recently suggested raising wages in Switzerland. Hunold apparently thought this proposal, and consequently Sahlin himself, so unacceptable that he refused to publish with A. Francke & Co. Although they supposedly had offers also from Amstutz and Herdeg, a publisher in Zürich, there were now complications with some of the funders and also with Röpke, so that the plans for a journal had to be completely abandoned.[19]

Nevertheless, both Hayek's proposal for a society and Röpke and Hunold's proposal for a journal were now circulating amongst the network of neoliberal intellectuals in Europe, and regardless of the reason for the abandonment of the journal project, this lead Hunold to suggest that the funds he had already raised for it could be used for Hayek's project instead (Hartwell 1995, 30). My research shows that a third proposal to found a liberal organization for the post-war world was also circulating among some of those who would form the Mont Pelerin Society. This was a suggestion to found a "Liberal International", and its opening congress in Oxford ended up overlapping with the first meeting of the Mont Pelerin Society. This was of little concern for the neoliberals however, as the organization in question, which also exists to this day, ended up being an umbrella organization for political parties, many of a more social liberal bent, and not a closed society for intellectuals.[20] Hayek's ideas concerning his society were laid out in a letter to Hunold dated 9th of October 1946, where he attached a memorandum, and added that he would be more than happy to write more fully about his plans and whom he wanted to invite, should Hunold want any further information.[21]

In that letter, Hayek said he did not have sufficient funds yet, and would suggest a "preparatory meeting for prospective members, on neutral ground, preferably Switzerland". This is how the strong neoliberal connection to Switzerland was cemented and how Hunold became the organizer of the first Mont Pelerin Society meeting, as well as its secretary for a decade to come. Hayek was also very eager to have a strong American presence at the meeting, as he had met so many promising recruits to his neoliberal cause when lecturing in the USA. At one point he was approached by Harold Luhnow, the head of the William Volker fund, who had offered

---

[18]Hoover Institution Library and Archives, Mont Pelerin Society, Box 5, Folder 3, "Mont Pelerin Correspondence".

[19]Hoover Institution Library and Archives, Mont Pelerin Society, Box 5, Folder 15, "Mont Pelerin Report".

[20]Friedrich Naumann Stiftung für die Freiheit, Archives of the Liberal International: "Oslo 1946" and "Oxford 1947".

[21]Hoover Institution Library and Archives, Friedrich Hayek Collection, Box 61, Folder 9, "Cover letter to Albert Hunold".

Hayek funds to set up "a study of the conditions for a competitive order in the United States". Luhnow had offered \$25.000 per year for three years, and Hayek suggested it be located at Chicago University (this is what would become known as the "Free Market Study") (Van Horn and Klaes 2011, 293). Luhnow also offered \$5.000 in order for Hayek to have an administrative secretary at the LSE. Hayek was thrilled by this, stating in his reply on May 3, 1945 that "only with such help shall I be able to combine continued research work with the various public activities and engagements into which I have been drawn by the book". With Luhnow's money, Hayek was on his way to becoming a full-time neoliberal activist. In the same letter, Hayek mentioned to his benefactor the idea of an "International Academy of Social Political Philosophy", stating

> I personally am so convinced that the tasks such an institution would have to perform are so important that I mean to devote a considerable part of my time to it if there is any chance of getting such an institution started. I do not know whether that will be possible, but I am convinced that if it is started it will require very considerable funds and it is one of those purposes where the funds can only come from private sources.[22]

Hayek enclosed his draft article on the subject, and by 11th of January 1947, he wrote to Hunold to tell him he had succeeded through his American contacts in getting costs covered for 16 people travelling from the US to the conference (Hartwell 1995, 31). The funding came from Luhnow's Volker Foundation, which had been set up by Kansas City furniture magnate William Volker at the bequest of Loren Miller, a libertarian activist who would also join the conference (Blundell 2001, 67). Invitations had been pouring out for some time, and five days later, the 16th of January, Hayek had received forty replies and twenty-eight acceptances.

Primary Sources

Hoover Institution Library and Archives, Stanford University, Palo Alto, California, USA:
- Friedrich Hayek Collection
- Mont Pelerin Society Collection
- Fritz Machlup Collection

Special permission to quote from the papers of Friedrich Hayek has been given by the estate, courtesy of Professor Bruce Caldwell, Duke University.

Yale University Library, New Haven, Connecticut, USA:
- Walter Lippmann Collection

Friedrich Naumann Stiftung für die Freiheit, Archiv des Liberalismus, Gummersbach, Germany
- Archives of the Liberal International

---

[22] Hoover Institution Library and Archives, Fritz Machlup Collection, Box 43, Folder 16, "Radio Script".

Secondary Literature

Bedeleem, M. (2017). *Fighting for the mantle of science: The epistemological foundations of early neoliberalism 1931–1951*. Montréal: Université de Montréal.

Bell, D. (2014). What is liberalism? *Political Theory, 42,* 682–715.

Blundell, J. (2001). *Waging the war of ideas*. London: The Institute of Economic Affairs.

Bockman, J. (2011). *Markets in the name of socialism: The left-wing origins of neoliberalism*. Stanford: Stanford University Press.

Burgin, A. (2012). *The great persuasion: Reinventing free markets since the depression*. Cambridge, Mass: Harvard University Press.

Caldwell, B. (2004). *Hayek's challenge: Intellectual biography of F.A. Hayek*. Chicago: University of Chicago Press.

Caldwell, B. (2011). Hayek on socialism and on the welfare state: A comment on Farrant and McPhail's "Does F.A. Hayek's Road to Serfdom Deserve to Make a Comeback?" *Challenge*.

Congdon, L. (1997). Between brothers: Karl and Michael Polanyi on fascism and communism. *Tradition and Discovery* XXIV, 7–13.

Dekker, E. (2016). *The viennese students of civilization—the meaning and context of Austrian economics reconsidered*. Cambridge: Cambridge University Press.

Dunning, W. (1904). A century of politics. *North American Review, 179,* 801–814.

Farrant, A., & McPhail, E. (2010). Does F.A. Hayek's "Road to Serfdom" Deserve to Make a Comeback? *Challenge, 53,* 96–120.

Fawcett, E. (2014). *Liberalism: The life of an idea*. Princeton: Princeton University Press.

Foucault, M. (2008). *The Birth of Biopolitics: Lectures at the Collège de France, 1978–79*. New York: Palgrave Macmillan.

Gerken, L. (2000). *Walter Eucken und sein Werk: Rückblick auf den Vordenker der sozialen Marktwirtschaft*. Mohr Siebeck.

Gieryn, T. (1983). Boundary-work and the demarcation of science from non-science. *American Sociological Review, 48,* 785–795.

Gleason, A. (1995). *Totalitarianism: The inner history of the cold war*. New York: Oxford University Press.

Hall, P. A. (1989). *The political power of economic ideas—Keynesianism across nations*. Princeton: Princeton University Press.

Hartwell, R. M. (1995). *A history of the mont Pelerin society*. Indianapolis: Liberty Fund.

Hayek, F. (1948). *Individualism and economic order*. Chicago: The University of Chicago Press.

Hayek, F. (1998). *Law, legislation and liberty: A new statement of the liberal principles of justice and political economy*. London: Routledge.

Hayek, F. (2007). *The road to serfdom—the definitive edition*. The University of Chicago Press.

Losurdo, D. (2011). *Liberalism: A counter-history*. London: Verso.

Mirowski, P., & Plehwe, D. (Eds.). (2009). *The road from Mont Pèlerin: The making of the neoliberal thought collective*. Cambridge, Mass: Harvard University Press.

Mises, L. (1990). *Economic calculation in the socialist commonwealth*. Auburn, Alabama: Ludwig von Mises Institute.

Mitchell, M. T. (2006). *Michael polanyi*. Wilmington, Delaware: ISI Books.

Pinder, J. (1998). *Altiero Spinelli and the British Federalists: writings by Beveridge, Robbins and Spinelli, 1937–1943*. London: Federal Trust : Marketing and distribution by Kogan Page.

Polanyi, M. (1997). *Society, economics, and philosophy*. Transaction Publishers.

Popper, K. (2003). *The open society and its enemies: Volume two: Hegel and marx*. Routledge Classics.

Robbins, L. (1939). *The economic basis of class conflict and other essays in political economy*. London: Macmillian and Co., Limited.

Robbins, L. (1968). *The economic causes of war*. New York: Howard Fertig Inc.

Robbins, L. (2007). *The economic problem in peace and war—some reflections on objectives and mechanisms*. United Kingdom: Read Books.

Rodrigues, J. (2013). The political and moral economies of neoliberalism: Mises and Hayek. *Cambridge Journal of Economics, 37,* 1001–1017
Röpke, W. (1935). Fascist economics. *Economica*: 85–100.
Röpke, W. (1950). *The social crisis of our time*. Chicago: The University of Chicago Press.
Skidelsky, R. (2000). *John Maynard Keynes: Fighting for Britain*. London: Macmillan.
Slobodian, Q. (2018). *Globalists—the end of empire and the birth of Neoliberalism*. Cambridge Massachusetts: Harvard University Press.
Tribe, K. (1995). *Strategies of economic order—german economic discourse, 1750–1950*. Cambridge: Cambridge University Press.
Van Horn, R., & Klaes, V. (2011). *Intevening in Laissez-Faire Liberalism: Chicago's Shift on Patents*. In *Building Chicago Economics*, 180–208. Cambridge: Cambridge University Press.
Walpen, B. (2004). *Die offenen Feinde und ihre Gesellschaft*. Hamburg: VSA-Verlag.
Wapshott, N. (2011). *Keynes Hayek: The clash that defined modern economics* (1st ed.). New York: W.W. Norton & Co.
White, L. H. (2012). *The clash of economic ideas: The great policy debates and experiments of the last hundred years*. Cambridge University Press.
White, R. J. (1950). Review. *The Economic Journal, 60,* 575–577.
Zmirak, J. (2001). *Wilhelm Röpke—Swiss Localist, Global Economist*. Wilmington, Delaware: ISI Books.

Part II
The First Meeting (1947)

Chapter 5
An Army of Fighters for Freedom

> … we live in the long shadow of a debate with which most people are altogether unfamiliar. If we ask who exercised the greatest influence over contemporary Anglophone economic thought, five foreign-born thinkers spring to mind: Ludwig von Mises, Friedrich Hayek, Joseph Schumpeter, Karl Popper, and Peter Drucker.
>
> Tony Judt in "What is Living and What is Dead in Social Democracy? (Judt 2009)

The first thing you would notice is the smell. The year is 1947. It is the 1st of April in the Swiss Alps. Spring is in the fresh mountain air, but we are inside a smoke-filled room at the Hotel Du Parc, a grand building overlooking Lake Geneva below and the French Alps on the other side. Some forty people are gathered here, almost all of whom are middle-aged, suit-clad men. The rich smell of pipe smoke lies heavily in the air. Perhaps none of them even noticed this particular fact. How utterly normal the scent must have been then, the very odour of indoors. To us, however, observers from a future world of strict smoking laws, the fragrant combination of fresh smoke, arising from the pipes of the serious-looking men, and old smoke, emanating from the curtains and tapestries, might have been the first thing to catch our attention. This is a sensory reminder that although similar and relatable, the world of 1947 was not quite the same as our world. Stacks of paper are everywhere in the room. On tables, in hands and resting in laps are notes and manuscripts, later to be stored in economists' archives all over the world. To this day, those pieces of paper still smell like old pipe smoke.[1] Behind a typewriter, which holds a fresh sheet of thin paper, sits one of the only two women in the room. She is a 19-year-old economics student from the London School of Economics named Dorothy Hahn. She has been given the job of writing the minutes of this very important conference. Surrounded by distinguished professors and luminaries, she feels nervous. To make things worse, the French typewriter she has been assigned to has some of the keys put in a different

[1] I can confirm that this is the case at least with the archives after Friedrich Hayek, Fritz Machlup, Lionel Robbins, Milton Friedman, Trygve Hoff and Maurice Allais.

O. Innset, *Reinventing Liberalism*, Springer Studies in the History of Economic Thought,
https://doi.org/10.1007/978-3-030-38885-0_5

order than what she is used to back home in England.[2] Rays of sunshine make their way in through the windows, illuminating the rising smoke in mid-air and forming geometrical shapes on the floor and on the walls.[3] A man gets up from his chair. In three weeks from now, he is to turn 64. His name is William Rappard, and he has been tasked by Friedrich Hayek with the important mission of chairing the very first session of the very first meeting of what was some days later to be named the Mont Pelerin Society.

This second part of the book zooms in on the proceedings of the Mont Pèlerin conference, and its main source are the minutes typed up by Mrs. Hahn on that unfamiliar typewriter. The documents now exist in various incomplete forms both at the Hoover Institution Library and Archives at Stanford University in Palo Alto, California, and at the Liberal Archive in Ghent, Belgium. In addition, I have visited the personal archives of some of the men present: Friedrich Hayek, Milton Friedman, Lionel Robbins, Fritz Machlup, Maurice Allais and Trygve Hoff. The first part of this book charted the road *to* Mont Pèlerin for some of the most important conference attendees and developed the notion of the dual argument as a central tenet of early neoliberal thought. This analysis of the intellectual and organizational efforts that went into the neoliberal thought collective *before* their founding meeting will be crucial to gain a wider appreciation of the discussions undertaken at this fascinating ten-day event. The conference itself eventually counted ten full sessions with introductions, two excursions and several meetings on the future of the organization. If I was to report in detail on every single session of the meeting in addition to my own analysis, this book would be very long and something of a difficult read.[4] I have therefore chosen to focus attention on the sessions and discussions that I judge to be the most important ones. In doing so, I am aided by the previous section's analysis of the dual argument, which guides my judgement regarding which of the sessions should be seen as essential to the political project of neoliberalism, and which could be better understood as side issues. The difficult task of selection and framing is also helped by the sources themselves, and the main organizer, Friedrich Hayek's, repeated insistence that the early sessions introduced by him were "by far the most important ones". Hayek pre-programmed the first week of sessions, and so they will be the main focus in Chaps 6 and 7. The second week of sessions was programmed by the attendees in situ, and as was perhaps to be expected (but much to Hayek's dismay), the conference veered somewhat off-topic, as the attendees went on to organize sessions discussing everything from trade unions and agricultural policy to the geopolitical role of the Soviet Union and the possibility of nuclear war. The content of these sessions and discussions will be summarized and referred to in Chap. 8, but due to the before-mentioned need for focus, they will cede into the background in this narrative of early neoliberal thought as a new way of thinking about markets as

[2]Interview with Dorothy Hahn 18.10.2016.

[3]This description is based on photos from the meeting, found in the archives of Lionel Robbins. London School of Economics Library Archives, Lionel Robbins Collection, Box 10, Folder 2.

[4]I would know, because in one of the early drafts I did precisely that.

mediators of modernity, and a new way of thinking about modern states as active facilitators of these devices.

The programme of the first week of sessions was the following:

Tuesday, April 1st:
Morning: Report on aims and organization of Conference by Hayek
Afternoon and Evening: "Free" Enterprise or Competitive Order

Wednesday, April 2nd:
Morning: Modern Historiography and Political Education
Afternoon and Evening: The future of Germany

Thursday, April 3rd:
Morning and Evening: The Problems and Chances of European Federation
(The afternoon was occupied by an excursion to Chateau de Coppet)

Friday, April 4th:
Morning: Liberalism and Christianity
Afternoon: General discussion of aims and purposes of a permanent organization
April 5th and 6th (Saturday and Sunday) were taken up by excursions to Schwyz and Einsiedeln.

The following chapter will go into the demographics of the conference attendees, and the introduction held by William Rappard. An important point will be the rather homogenous character of this group of people. Despite their diverse national backgrounds, they were almost exclusively privileged white men, and I will argue that this has to be taken into account when contextualizing their ideas, although this fact of course holds little explanatory power in and of itself. Chapter 6, "Using the state", will focus on Hayek's introduction and the key session he had entitled "'Free Enterprise' or Competitive Order". It was in this session that Hayek was hoping to advance the discussion embodied in the dual argument's simultaneous attack on economic planning and laissez-faire liberalism: what sort of state interventions could be considered to help rather than hinder market mechanisms, and therefore not be a form of economic planning? Chapter 7 focuses on the context of post-war Europe and the sense of a new beginning. I will argue that the sessions on the possibility of a European federation and the future of Germany can be seen together with the excursions to Chateau de Coppet and Schwyz as indicative of what kind of new Europe these intellectuals were envisioning. Chapter 8 summarizes the chaotic second week of sessions and the efforts to create a lasting organization. Special attention is paid to a session on agricultural policies, in which a conference attendee claimed that the dual argument was in fact contradictory, and that the other neoliberals had been arguing for a variety of interventions whose sum could only be considered to be economic planning.

Previous Scholarship

The first meeting of the Mont Pelerin Society has been referred to in a number of books and journal articles, and described in some detail in Ronald M. Hartwell's *A History of the Mont Pelerin Society* (Hartwell 1995), Angus Burgin's *The Great Persuasion* (Burgin 2012) and to a certain extent Daniel Stedman Jones' *Masters of the Universe* (Jones 2012). In German, Bernhard Walpen's *Die offenen Feinden und ihre Gesselschaft* offers a convincing study through the lens of Gramscian theories of hegemony, but this volume is now out of print. Chapter 4 of *Wandlungen des Liberalismus* by Phillip Plickert also describes the first meeting. Ronald M. Hartwell was himself a member of the society (Jones 2012, 73), and even served as president between 1992 and 1994 (Mirowski and Plehwe 2009, 4). His volume was commissioned and supported financially by the society itself, and as he writes himself: a "formidable group of members, including past and present officers of the Society, subjected a final draft of the history to detailed and effective criticism" (Hartwell 1995, xviii). The political influence of the Mont Pelerin Society has been judged to be considered by a variety of scholars and commentators. It is obvious therefore that we must do more than to simply take their own celebratory retelling of their history at face value.

The main problem with previous work on this meeting by independent scholars is the degree to which this early phase of neoliberalism and the context of Europe in the interwar and early post-war years tends to be written off, implicitly or explicitly, as largely irrelevant for the subsequent development of neoliberalism, which is the main focus of all these narratives. It is my contention that by not taking this period and this context seriously enough, scholars like Burgin and Stedman Jones tend to miss the true importance of the dual argument and the neoliberals' new notion of markets as mediators of modernity. As far as the work of Angus Burgin is concerned, it should be clear from the introduction and Part I that I am in some disagreement with his tendency to portray neoliberalism as a return to laissez-faire. This interpretation of the neoliberal project forms the arch of his narrative about the reinvention of "free" markets (Burgin 2012, 5). Burgin does write that "An exploration of the rhetoric of the society's members in its early years reveals a movement far less doctrinaire than the conventional narrative would indicate", and even that "The financial crisis and subsequent political instability left them broadly convinced of the need for a social philosophy that transcended the abstract dictates of laissez-faire" (Burgin 2012, 9). However, both Burgin and Daniel Stedman Jones seem to see this as some sort of passing pragmatism, which ended with the rise of Milton Friedman as a public figure and president of the Mont Pelerin Society from the 1960s onwards (Burgin 2012, 11; Jones 2012, 98–99). The guiding assumption seems to be that neoliberalism is ultimately about "free markets" and laissez-faire, and so all the evidence to the contrary is taken to be deviations from the norm. This seems to me to be a reading of the early years of neoliberalism too heavily influenced by presuppositions from the 2000s about what neoliberalism really is. Stedman Jones does write:

> The specifically European problems and traditions central to the intellectual formation of Hayek, Popper and Mises should not be understated despite their subsequent "Anglicization" or "Americanization". These influences – for example the fear of Nazi totalitarianism and the bundling together of diverse opponents, progressive, liberal, socialist and social democratic politics, under the label 'collectivism' – had a bearing, sometimes indirectly, on how neoliberalism was developed later by American theorists such as Friedman and Buchanan. (Jones 2012, 14–15)

Despite this, both Burgin and Stedman Jones appear to see the years between 1920 and 1947 as little more than an interesting European background for what later developed into a transatlantic free market project. These studies therefore contribute to the ongoing confusion about what the prefix *neo* in neoliberalism actually signified. Taking the left and right of contemporary American and British politics as their starting points, these analyses seem to miss the real novelty of early neoliberalism: it was much more than a pragmatic middle ground between social liberalism and laissez-faire. It was a theory of modernity, combining a new conceptualization of markets as mediators of modernity with a will to use modern states in their service.

The three chapters of Part I uncovered the dual argument in early neoliberal thought and traced the organizational efforts leading up to the 1947 meeting. In Part II we will see the dual argument in action and focus special attention on key sessions in which the attendees tried to map out ways of using states in the service of markets. Some of the attendees, however, resisted and claimed that the whole approach was fraught with contradictions. The chapters of Part II can be seen partly as a work of microhistory, as they go into some detail to describe not only the content of the discussions held, but also the surrounding atmosphere, including excursions and meals, and the demographic of the conference attendees. As mentioned in the introduction, this is meant as an aid to the task of *contextualization*, which has been high on the agenda of intellectual historians since the famous interventions of Quentin Skinner several decades ago (Skinner 2002). Microhistory is not usually connected to intellectual history, so the theoretical apparatus for conducting enquiries in intellectual history in this way is rather underdeveloped. In the history, philosophy and sociology of science there is a large literature on scientific communities, but this often focuses more on the sociology of knowledge and how various "thought collectives" arrive at their findings; and less on customs, habits and the specific modes of interaction that exist within academic communities (Sismondo 2010). There is a growing anthropological literature on how performance of rituals inform politics and even international diplomacy, but to my limited knowledge it has yet to take on the very specific milieu of more academically inclined, activist communities like the one in question in this book (Cole 2009; Alexander 2010). The following in-depth study of the first meeting of the Mont Pelerin Society is therefore more empirically based than it is grounded in any hitherto developed theoretical notions.

Introducing Neoliberalism

The point of this chapter is to introduce the context of the meeting and the thirty-seven attendees. The frame is provided by the before-mentioned William Rappard, and the introductory remarks he gave that April morning in the smoke-filled room overlooking Lake Geneva. He began his short address, delivered some three weeks before his 64th birthday, by extending thanks: "First and foremost they are due to our eminent colleague Hayek, without whose constructive imagination, tenacious courage and unflagging efforts over a number of months and even of years, this international meeting of academic liberals would have remained an idle dream".[5] Rappard was born in America, but had become a naturalized Swiss citizen, making a name for himself on the burgeoning scene of international diplomacy. There were three Swiss nationals at the conference in total: Rappard, Hunold and the economist Hans Barth. Rappard was an influential figure, not only because he founded the Graduate Institute of International Studies and became professor and later rector of the University of Geneva, but also because he was a former director at The League of Nations. He took part in the peace talks at Versailles in 1919 and is said to have made a strong impression on President Woodrow Wilson, convincing him to locate the League of Nation Headquarters in Rappard's adopted hometown of Geneva in 1920. The organization may have ended in failure, but in the new post-1945 world of international cooperation, Rappard would become the Swiss representative both to the UN, the International Labour Organization (ILO) in Geneva, and the United States Embassy (Ebeling 2000). As mentioned in Chap. 3, Rappard's Graduate Institute in Geneva had hosted many important neoliberals, and a certain mythology of Switzerland as a liberal utopia already loomed large for some of the conference attendees (Franc 2016a). Wilhelm Röpke, who was based at the institute, saw the federated Swiss state as a model society, in which small land-holding families governed themselves in accordance with rural traditions of strict property rights and minimal central government (Franc 2016b). We noted this traditionalist streak in early neoliberal thought in the previous chapter, and it is especially strong in the work of Röpke. Due to his idealization of Swiss society, John Zmirak's biography of Röpke has the subtitle *Swiss Localist, Global Economist* (Zmirak 2001). Andrea Franc has written about neoliberalism in Switzerland as a form of what she calls "cultural nationalism" (Franc 2016c), and as we will see, Switzerland and its history was indeed held up as a model several times during the conference. Chapter 3 referred to the interwar years' scene of international diplomacy and American funded research institutes as an important context for the early neoliberal movement. Similarly, the concept of

[5]The quotations from Rappard's opening address are taken from a manuscript and not from notes made by Dorothy Hahn. They can therefore be considered to be rather accurate. The top of the first page of the archival document in question states: "PRIVATE Not for publication (It is specially requested not to quote from this document except with the express permission of the person concerned)". I have, however, taken the liberty of the historian to make some quotations, as I read the disclaimer to relate to more short-term use of the manuscript. Liberaal Archief, Mont Pelerin Society, Box 1, Folder 1: "Mont Pèlerin, 1947".

"summits" bringing together leaders from around the world could be seen as something of a post-war phenomenon. However, unlike, for instance, the 1944 Bretton Woods Conference or the 1955 Bandung Conference, the Mont Pèlerin conference in 1947 was distinctly less publicized and of a less diplomatic nature. The people gathered met as like-minded individuals representing only themselves, and so any rituals in which they engaged had the internal function of binding the group together, more than any external display.

In 1938, Rappard had also given a series of lectures at the University of Chicago which were later published in book form under the title *The Crisis of Democracy*. Much like other neoliberals, he saw modern democracies as inefficient, easy prey for various "interest groups", and carrying in them the seeds of totalitarian rule. According to him, the Swiss version of democracy was what offered hope for the future of humankind, notably because Switzerland had a long history of various forms of democratic rule. Echoing both Edmund Burke and Hayek's theories of the organic, slow evolution of social orders, Rappard's lecture in Chicago claimed that totalitarianism had been the result of a rapid transition to democracy: "… it is not in the states in which democracy was an inheritance of the past, but those in which it was merely a programme or a hope for the future, that have until today succumbed to the onslaught of authoritarian violence" (Rappard 1938, 69). Rappard highlighted the dangers of democracy seen as a tool to change the world; instead it had to be a continuation of the traditional social order. According to Rappard, Switzerland's constitutions had, since the 1830s, "extended to all the fundamental principles of political liberalism" (Rappard 1938, 67). This was a curious thing to say in 1938, since at least half the adult population of Switzerland did not get the right to vote until some thirty-three years later, in 1971. It would take another full twenty years before all Swiss cantons had granted women the right to vote also in local elections. As was indicated in Part I, however, liberal thinkers had for centuries used words like "all" to mean only people like themselves: privileged white males (Losurdo 2011). Rappard did concur in his 1938 speech that it might seem odd to not grant women the right to vote, but he referred to what seemed to be a widely held opinion in Switzerland at the time that the majority of women did not actually want the vote, so "it would hardly be democratic on the part of the men to impose it upon them" (Rappard 1938, 67).

The Attendees

The following section will show that the attendees of the first Mont Pèlerin conference were indeed people very much like William Rappard: male, white, middle-aged, highly educated and materially comfortable. In a treatise arguing against one or more aspects of neoliberal philosophy, this sort of observation could be considered an *argumentum ad hominem*. As emphasized in the introduction, however, this book is not meant as a work of social theory in itself, and I make no normative arguments relating to the content of neoliberal doctrine. This is a work of intellectual history, meant to untangle and explain the arguments made by the actors, and to use the benefit of hindsight and historical analysis to show patterns and commonalities hitherto unnoticed. An important aspect of the task of contextualizing these utterings is to understand the *homines* who made the utterings, in order to gain a further appreciation of who they were and the *intentions* they might have had in saying what they did. Before moving on to the content of Rappard's introduction, we will therefore take a brief look at the biographies of the thirty-seven attendees, and then break down some of the key demographics of the group gathered at Mont Pèlerin in 1947. This will be done in the main body of the text and not in a separate annex, since this information is important in achieving the goal of contextualizing early neoliberalism. It is my contention that the class, gender and racial background of these thinkers have to be taken into account when we analyse both their ideas and the culture out of which they grew. This is not to suggest that their ideas can be easily discarded as merely a reflection of their social standing; only that when attempting to understand their ideas and where they came from, we will do well to not discard the social background of the thinkers in question either. It is perhaps unlikely that, for instance, a group of underprivileged women of colour from the same countries would have gotten together to discuss economic theory at this point in time; but it is likely that people from different cultural and economic backgrounds than the neoliberals would have seen recent economic developments in a very different light. The neoliberals argued intellectually against socialism, organized labour and most forms of social programmes, and it would be sloppy to not also consider their social backgrounds when contextualizing their arguments. As we will see, their view of the world was from a position of great privilege, from which they were mainly able to see "economic planning" as inefficient, and the rise of mass democracy as a threat to freedom.

List of Attendees

Carlo Antoni (1896–1959)—was an Italian philosopher and a historian. A student of Benedetto Croce (who had also been invited to the conference), he specialized in German philosophy, and his main work, published in 1942, was called *La lotta contra la ragione*—the fight against reason. He was given the chair of philosophy of history at the University of Rome in the same years as the first Mont Pelerin Society meeting (Biscione and Carlo 1961).

Hans Barth (1904–1965)—was a Swiss professor of philosophy and journalist. He was the son of Hans Barth, a famous historian. He wrote for the *Neue Züricher Zeitung* and became professor of philosophy, political science and ethics at the University of Zürich in 1946 (Cattani 2002).

Karl Brandt (1899–1975)—was born in Essen in 1899 and became professor at the *Landwirtschaftlichen Hochschule* in Berlin in 1929. He was an economist and emigrated to the US in 1933, where he first worked at the New School of Social Research, before moving to Stanford University in 1938. His main interests as an economist were agriculture and food production (Campbell et al. 1975).

Orval Watts (1898–1993)—was an American economist working for the Foundation for Economic Education, a brand new think tank in 1947. Watts had worked with its president, Leonard Read earlier, when the former was the head of the Los Angeles Chamber of Commerce. Along with his work for the think tank and other interest groups, he taught economics at various American universities (Rothbard 1995, 450–452).

Cicely Veronica Wedgewood (1910–1997)—was a British historian who had graduated from Oxford. She had published a biography of Thomas Wentworth, 1st Earl of Strafford at the age of only 25; a large work entitled *The Thirty Years War* only three years later; and a book on Oliver Cromwell the year after that (1939). She held no university position at the time, but was made "special lecturer" at the University College in London in 1962 (The Associated Press 1997).

John Davenport (1905–1987)—graduated as an economist from Yale in 1926, but worked as a journalist. He would become editor of the financial weekly Barron's in 1949 and of Fortune magazine in 1954. He had published a book about Winston Churchill in 1945, and one about the work of Chicago economist Henry Simons and the field of law and economics in 1946 (Davenport 1987).

Stanley Dennison (1912–1992)—was a British economist, at the time a fellow at Caius College in Cambridge (Cairncross 1996, 48). Ralph Harris, who later became president of the Mont Pelerin Society, described Dennison as having been a "powerful exponent of economic freedom in the tradition of Alfred Marshall" while at Cambridge in 1945 (Matthews 1984, 219), and he was later considered amongst the forbearers of Margaret Thatcher's economic policies (Letwin 1992, 80).

Aaron Director (1901–2004)—was an American economist, who had recently obtained a position as professor at the University of Chicago Law School. Director came to be known as the founder of the field "Law and Economics", which uses economic models and reasoning to make legal arguments. Director's family had emigrated from present-day Ukraine in 1913, and he was one of the few attendees with former affiliations with left-wing politics from his youth days. Director graduated from Yale in 1924 and changed his politics after becoming a graduate student at the University of Chicago under Frank Knight (Arbeiter 2004).

Walter Eucken (1891–1950)—was a German economist born in Jena. He was the son of Nobel prize-winning author Rudolf Eucken and did his habilitation in Berlin in 1921. Since 1927 he had been professor at Albert-Ludwigs-Universität in Freiburg, and together with amongst others the political scientist Franz Böhm and the lawyer Hans Grossman Doerth, he formed a strand of thought known as the Freiburg School, later to be called *ordoliberalism*, from the name of the journal *ORDO* they would establish in 1948 (Gerken 2000).

Erich Eyck (1878–1964)—was a German lawyer and historian. He was from a bourgeois, Jewish family in Berlin, and went to Freiburg to complete his studies. Amongst other works he wrote a three-volume biography of Otto von Bismarck before going into exile in Great Britain in 1938, where he completed a biography of William Gladstone (Eyck 2004).

Milton Friedman (1912–2006)—was the son of Jewish immigrants to Brooklyn and one of the very few original Mont Pelerin Society members who came from a reasonably humble background. He earned a BA from Rutgers University in 1922, an MA from Chicago the year after and then a PhD in Economics from Columbia University in 1946. He joined the faculty of the University of Chicago the same year (Milton Friedman (1912–2006) 2008).

Harry Gideonse (1883–1966)—was an American economist who had served as president of Brooklyn College since 1939. He had also taught and studied at the University of Chicago, Columbia University, and the Institute for Graduate Studies in Geneva (Waggoner and Walter 1985).

Frank D. Graham (1890–1949)—was a Canadian-born American economist. He had been Walker Professor of economics and international finance at Princeton University since 1945. He was best known for his work on international trade and international monetary institutions (Professor Graham).

Floyd Arthur Harper (1905–1973)—was an American economist who had graduated from Michigan State University. He had been a professor of marketing at Cornell University, but left his position in 1946, allegedly because he was not allowed to put works by Hayek on the curriculum. He had recently been employed by the newly founded Foundation for Economic Education (Wilkinson et al. 1905–1973).

Friedrich August von Hayek (1899–1992)—was an Austrian economist who had been working in London at the London School of Economics since 1930. He was from a wealthy, aristocratic family in Vienna—his father was a botanist and Ludwig Wittgenstein was his cousin. In the mid-1930s Hayek more or less retreated from economics into political philosophy and gained worldwide fame with his 1944 book *The Road to Serfdom* (Wapshott 2011, 110–123).

Henry Hazlitt (1894–1993)—was an American journalist working as the editor of *Newsweek*, having previously been at *The New York Times* and *The Wall Street Journal*. He was born in Philadelphia, and like Milton Friedman he was not from a rich family. His book *Economics in One Lesson* was published in 1946 to great acclaim, and it was his review of *The Road to Serfdom* that lead to it being published in *Reader's Digest* in 1944 (Rockwell 2007).

Trygve J. B. Hoff (1895–1982)—was a Norwegian economist and businessman. He earned his PhD from the University of Oslo in 1938 with a thesis repeating some of Mises and Hayek's arguments about socialism from the socialist calculation debates. The Oslo School of Economics was highly Keynesian and mathematical, so Hoff was unable to launch a career as an economist. Instead he sets up consulting companies and the right-wing journal *Farmand* (Mjøset 2015). He was also involved in setting up the Liberal International at the same time, but later remarked that the attendees of that conference did not understand the meaning of the word "liberal", something which indicated his strong aversion to social liberalism.[6]

Albert Hunold (dates unknown)—was a Swiss businessman, among other things a dealer in fine Swiss watches, who was instrumental in organizing the first meeting of the Mont Pelerin Society. He later caused a great stir when he fell out with Hayek in what has been known as "The Hunold Affair", which lead to Wilhelm Röpke

[6]Riksarkivet, Oslo, Trygve Hoff/Farmand, Box 16.

having to take over the presidency of the organization from Hayek. Hunold did not speak on matters political during the conference (Hartwell 1995).

Carl Iversen (1899–1978)—was a Danish economist and professor of political science and national economy at the University of Copenhagen since 1939. In the 1960s he would become head of the Danish Economic Council (Toftg et al. 1979).

John Jewkes (1902–1988)—was professor of economic organization at Merton College at Oxford University. His main work *Ordeal by Planning* was published the year after the conference and contained both elements of the dual argument. In 1962 he would become the third president of the Mont Pelerin Society (Fonseca and Jewkes (1902–1988).

Bertrand de Jouvenel (1903–1987)—was a French philosopher, aristocrat, political economist, futurist and nobleman from the Champagne region. From a very young age, he caused much stir in high society with his love life. In the 1930s he was editor of the journal of the French fascist party, and in 1945 he published the book *Du Pouviour*. After the war he moved to Switzerland (Knegt 2015).

Frank Knight (1885–1972)—was an American economist and one of the founders of the Chicago School. He was born in Illinois and came to Chicago from the University of Iowa in 1929. His most famous work was *Risk, Uncertainty and Profit* from 1921. He famously argued with A. C. Pigou over social costs and also contributed to the argument for toll roads based on analyses of "traffic equilibrium" (Knight 1991).

Fritz Machlup (1902–1983)—was an Austrian economist, a student of Mises, who had worked in the USA since 1933. It was he who secured Hayek a publication deal in the USA for *The Road To Serfdom*, and in the absence of Hayek or international telephone calls, he made several decisions on his behalf regarding condensed versions, cartoons and radio shows in the US.[7] In 1947 he had recently moved from the University of Buffalo to Johns Hopkins in Baltimore.

François Trevoux (dates unknown)—was a French law professor based in Lyon (White 2012, 212), of whom little is known.

Henri de Lovinfosse (dates unknown)—was a Belgian businessman of aristocratic descent, of whom little is known. He published a book called *Solution sociale* with the philosopher Gustave Thibon in 1951, in which they claimed that a more harmonious society could be reached because of a great convergence of interests between all people (Solución social—primer libro editada por Fenareta 17. aug).

Loren Miller (dates unknown)—considered himself a civic reformer, and one of his main contributions to the political project of neoliberalism was persuading the furniture magnate William Volker to set up the William Volker fund in 1932. The Volker fund paid the expense of all the American attendees of the first Mont Pelerin Society conference. Miller ran the foundation until 1942, and after some time as an executive at the Kansas City Civic Research Institute he became the head of the Bureau of Governmental Research in Detroit (Blundell 2001, 38).

Ludwig von Mises (1881–1973)—was an Austrian economist based in New York City at the New School for Social Research. He was born to Jewish parents who

[7] HLA, "Fritz Machlup Collection", Box 43, Folder 15, "Friedrich Hayek 1933–1944".

had been raised into nobility in what is now Ukraine. He had started the socialist calculation debates, which this book argues was foundational for neoliberalism, and had inspired a whole generation of anti-socialists with books like *Socialism* and *Bureaucracy* (Powell 2000).

Herbert Tingsten (1896–1973)—was a Swedish publisher and political scientist. He was the son of a high-ranking public servant and had held a chair as professor of political science at Stockholms högskola since 1923. In 1946 he took up the post as editor in chief of the daily newspaper *Dagens Nyheter* (Herbert Tingsten 1961).

Felix Morley (1894–1982)—was an American and the son of a famous mathematician; he won a Rhodes scholarship to study at Oxford. He later obtained a Guggenheim scholarship to work at the League of Nations in Geneva and got his PhD from the Brookings Institution. He was the editor of *The Washington Post* from 1933–1940 and won the Pulitzer Prize in 1936 for his critique of Franklin D. Roosevelt's National Industrial Recovery Act. In 1944 he founded the conservative magazine *Human Events* (Weil 1982).

Michael Polanyi (1891–1976)—was Austro-Hungarian of Jewish descent and had held a chair as professor of chemistry in Manchester since 1933. He was a polymath and also a trained doctor who had written extensively on the philosophy of science and economic planning (Mitchell 2006).

Karl Popper (1902–1994)—was an Austrian philosopher of upper-middle-class background. He emigrated to New Zealand in 1937, where he wrote the manuscript for his magnum opus *The Open Society and its Enemies*. It was published in 1944 with the help of Friedrich Hayek, who also helped him obtain a chair at the London School of Economics (Karl Popper 1997).

William Rappard (1883–1958)—was born in New York City to Swiss parents and moved to Switzerland as a young man. He spent most of his life in Geneva, working for the League of Nations, the University of Geneva and the Institute of Graduate Studies, which he helped found. The headquarters of the World Trade Organization in Geneva are named after him (Ebeling 2000).

Leonard Read (1898–1993)—was a former businessman who had made a career in various chambers of commerce in California. In 1946 he had decided to dedicate himself to the cause of "free" markets, and so he sets up the Foundation for Economic Education, one of the world's first neoliberal think tanks (Boudreaux and Slepko Boudreaux et al. 2008).

Maurice Allais (1911–2010)—was both a physicist and an economist. Like Friedman and Hazlitt, he was among the few Mont Pelerin members from a modest background, born in the Haute-Seine area. He was director of the *Bureau de documentation et de statistique minière* until 1948, but would go on to win a Bank of Sweden award as one of the world's most renowned economists (Aujard 2002).

Lionel Robbins (1898–1984)—was a British economist, credited with bringing "continental economics" to the United Kingdom and shifting Anglo-Saxon economics from its Marshallian direction. He was based at the London School of Economics and was involved with several government agencies during and after the Second World War (Lionel Robbins (1898–1984) 2008a).

Wilhelm Röpke (1899–1966)—was a German economist born in Hannover. He was professor in Jena, Graz and Marburg before leaving Germany for Istanbul and Geneva. By 1947 he was a member of Germany's currency reform council, and he enjoyed great influence with Ludwig Erhard, another founding member of the Mont Pèlerin Society, who became finance minister and later chancellor of West Germany (Zmirak 2001).

George Stigler (1911–1991)—was an American economist of German descent. He had studied economics at Chicago under Knight and Director, where he had become close friends with Milton Friedman. In 1947 he had just been given a position of professor at Columbia University (Stigler (1911–1991) 2008).

Some of those who could not attend the conference included Antony Fischer, who would later start the Institute of Economic Affairs, Arnold Plant, the Italian economist Costantino Bresciani-Turroni, the Swedish economist Eli Heckscher and the Italian president Luigi Einaudi (Hartwell 1995, 32–33).

Demographics

As we can see from Fig. 5.1, the crowd addressed by William Rappard that April morning in 1947 included nationals from all over Europe and the USA. As Hagen Schulz-Forberg and Niklas Olsen have recently shown, the League of Nations and various other international organizations funded by foundations like the Rockefeller Foundation and the Carnegie Endowment were an important backdrop for early neoliberal organization in the interwar years. These connections have led Quinn Slobodian to focus attention on how neoliberalism was a *transnational* project from

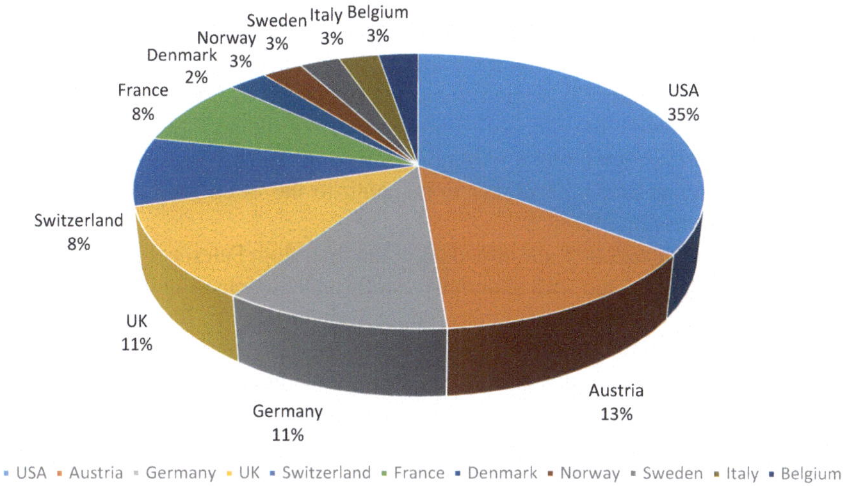

Fig. 5.1 Attendees of first MPS meeting by nationality

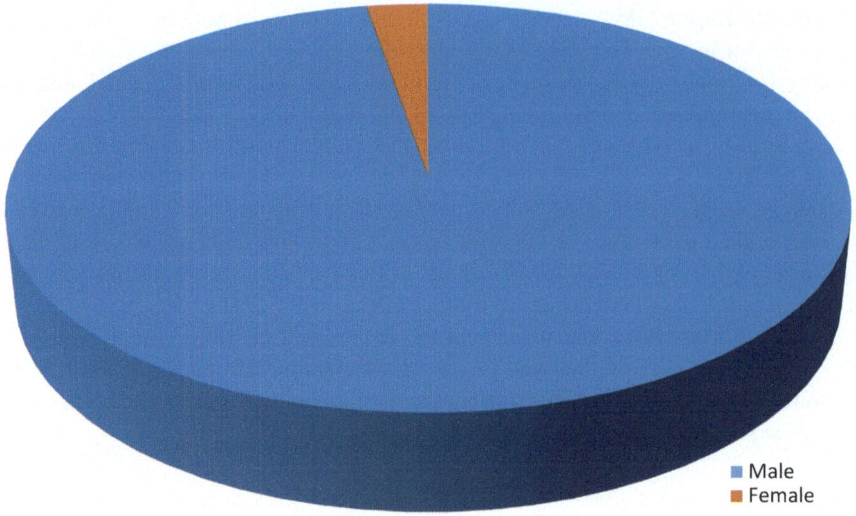

Fig. 5.2 Attendees of first MPS meeting by gender

the very beginning: both in its intellectual outlook and in its novel organizational form through the transnational organizations and institutes that provided the institutional framework for early neoliberalism (Slobodian 2015). The early neoliberals were very much part of a new, international elite emerging in the interwar years which connected academic research in the social sciences with international diplomacy and the world of business.

Being so international, they must have felt like quite a diverse group of people, but as Figs. 5.2 and later 5.5 will reveal, it was mainly their passports and languages which made them so. Apart from Mrs. Hahn, the secretary, the only woman in attendance was the British historian Cecily Wedgewood, who shared lodgings and train compartments with Mrs. Hahn on the journey from London down to Mont Pèlerin. In a later recollection, the Norwegian attendee Trygve J. B. Hoff wrote: "While at the first meeting there were few women—only interpreters and secretaries—later years have seen an increase in spouses joining the meeting (many of which have shown a surprising interest and faithfulness in listening to the often long and strenuous lectures and discussions)".[8]

Almost without exception, the attendees of the first Mont Pelerin conference were white men with PhDs,[9] and with materially comfortable lives hailing from materially comfortable backgrounds. This is not to detract from the value or logical consistency of their arguments, but when contextualizing their intellectual efforts, it is worth noting at the very outset of this narrative what a homogenous group the attendees of the first Mont Pèlerin meeting really were. Especially so since they were discussing

[8]Riksarkivet, Oslo, Trygve Hoff/Farmand, Box 16 (translated from the Norwegian).

[9]The only ones who might not have had PhDs were the American journalists Felix Morley and Henry Hazlitt and libertarian activists Loren Miller and Leonard Read.

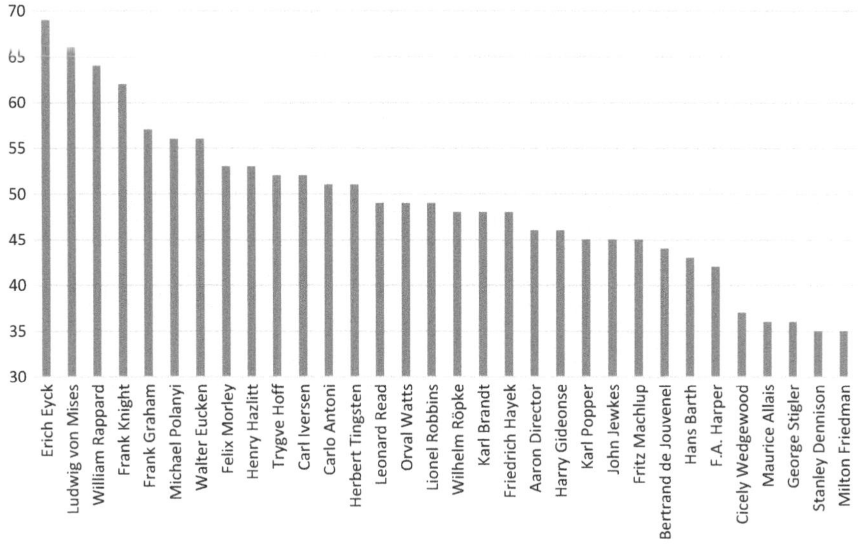

Fig. 5.3 Age of founding MPS members in 1947

matters pertaining to all of humankind, and the way in which modern society was to be organized. Their view was one located in a very specific social stratum. As Corey Robin notes in his book *The Reactionary Mind,* however, placing conservative thinkers in the upper social strata of society is the beginning of an analysis, not the end of it (Robin 2011). The neoliberals' view of the growth of state power and government expenditure was that of a privileged elite, something which is highly visible, for instance, in Wilhelm Röpke's 1947 text "International crusade against luxuries", which was circulated to all members of the society just after the meeting. In the midst of what we will later read was a starvation crisis of catastrophic proportions, Röpke found it opportune to write a long article complaining about the difficulty of obtaining luxury goods, like fine leather satchels, and he blamed this horrid state of affairs on taxation and illiberal government intervention.[10]

As visible in Fig. 5.3, the attendees' age ranged from 35, Milton Friedman and Stanley Dennison, to 69, Eirch Eyck. However, only nine people out of 37 fell outside of the age group 42–57, so also in this respect they were a rather uniform group. They were not particularly young, nor very old, but men in their so-called "prime". Their average age was 47,5.

Looking at their life spans in the "Biographies" section, one is also struck by how long almost all of them lived for (see Fig. 5.4). Friedrich Hayek made it to 93, Milton Friedman to 94 and his brother-in-law, Aaron Director, lived to be 102. Ludwig von Mises lived until 92 and Maurice Allais became 109, the list goes on. A few of them, like Frank Graham, Walter Eucken and Wilhelm Röpke, died in their 60s or just before, but the vast majority lived way past 80. 11 of them lived to be over 90, which

[10]Hoover Archives, Mont Pelerin Society Collection, Box 28, Folder 5: "R-W".

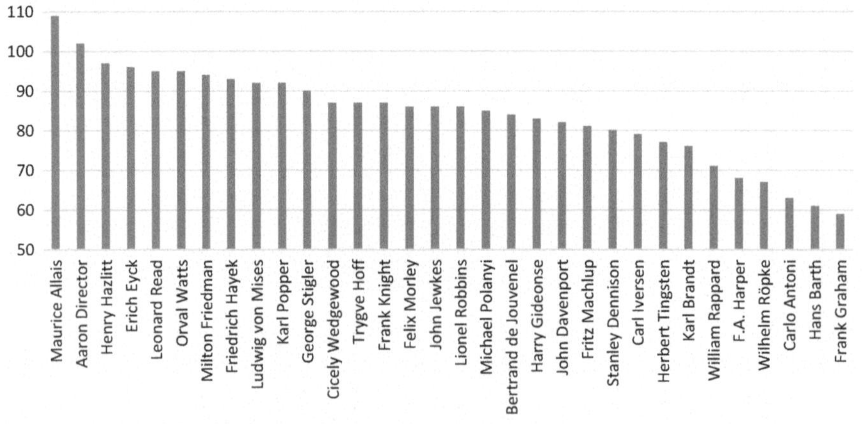

Fig. 5.4 Age at death of founding MPS members

constitutes 34%. This group of people would attempt to influence society for a long time.

This adds more weight to the argument that these intellectuals saw modern society and its history in a very particular light. The average life expectancy for those born in 1900 in both Germany and the United Kingdom was 45,6 years.[11] This low number obviously had a lot to do with the world wars and economic downturns this generation would endure, but it is worth pausing to note that amongst the attendees of the Mont Pelerin conference, who all hailed from pretty much the same generation, the *average* life lasted a staggering 84 years. It is fair to say that the Mont Pelerin Society members lived a good deal longer also than those who died of natural causes. Life expectancy is closely linked to social class, where those in comfortable material circumstances, on average and for a multitude of different reasons, live much longer than those with less financial freedom (Pickett and Wilkinson 2009). It could be argued that the early neoliberals wanted to extend that fabled "freedom in economic affairs" to more people than themselves, but arguments pointing in a different direction could also be posed. Either way, it is certainly beyond discussion that the early neoliberals' own position within the social order they wanted to save was one of great privilege.

Liberalism, Economics and Science

This brings us back to William Rappard's opening address. After thanking Hayek especially, Rappard went on to extend further thanks also to "the anonymous benefactors in the United States and in Switzerland", and "my compatriot Dr. Hunold, from Zurich", who had made the Swiss funds available and organized the stay at Mont Pèlerin. As mentioned at the end of Chap. 4, the anonymous benefactors in the

[11] http://ourworldindata.org/life-expectancy/.

US were the William Volker Foundation, and in Switzerland they were Swiss banks like Credit Suisse and the Swiss business confederation. Rappard then remarked on the use of English as lingua franca of the conference, alluding to the history of English liberalism and what he called the "preponderance of Anglo-Saxondom in what remains of liberalism in the world today".

Rappard used this linguistic point to segue into the more specific content of his address, a remark on liberalism and economics: "The term of economics I cannot help finding dangerously ambiguous in that it refers both to a science and to a policy or a possible variety of policies", said Rappard, setting the tone for a conference that was to probe deeply into the philosophical and political implications of being "liberal" in a modern, post-war world. Rappard noted that in French, one differed between *science* économique and *politique* économique, whereas German did the same with the distinction between Volkwirtschafts*lehre* and Volkwirschafts*politik*. Rappard claimed that they were two "entirely different things" and that this created confusion of which "economists as men of science are the chief victims". "Science cannot be liberal or illiberal. In a sense it cannot be anything but liberal", he exclaimed. For Rappard, liberalism was a science-based policy, but: "Most policies all over the world today are in fact illiberal and it is because we believe that they should be liberal that we are assembled here today". Rappard went on: "The distinction is absolutely fundamental. It alone explains why our friend Hayek, in setting up his list of guests, has not included therein many economists who are not liberals, but has to our great joy admitted certain liberals who are not economists". As we have seen from the list of attendees there were indeed many prominent economists who had not been invited, and a certain number of historians, philosophers and journalists not specializing in economics among those gathered. Rappard noted that many economists had been liberals in both the scientific and the political sense of the term, but then took care to make a different point in stating that Adam Smith, "The greatest of all", had placed his liberal doctrine "not only on scientific findings, but on two assumptions" which according to Rappard "could lay no claim to scientific validity". The first assumption was that men and nations were engaged in labours of production with the main purpose of enriching themselves, and the other "was the assumption of the homo economicus, of the economic man". The question then posed by Rappard was: "Is the economic man necessarily a liberal?" a "foe of restrictive policies"?

To illustrate this conundrum, Rappard told the story of how he had "happened to be" in Algiers at the time of the landing of the allied forces in November 1942, and had been "impressed by the sight of countless Arabs seated on the curb of the sidewalks in all the streets of the city. They seemed quite indifferent to what was going on and they certainly were absolutely idle", said Rappard, who had questioned a French friend about "this striking fact". It had been explained to him that "Arabs in Algiers never did any more work than was absolutely necessary..." A General Weygan who had been Governor General of Algeria had reportedly attempted to double the wages and rations of Arabs (so that they would have the same as Algerians of European origin), but to no avail as their productive efforts had been even further reduced: "... the Arabs apparently got more enjoyment out of life by working less than they would have secured by producing and consuming more".

Fig. 5.5 Attendees of first MPS meeting by ethnicity

I have noted the relative homogeneity of the conference attendees (see also Fig. 5.5), and as far as one is able to tell from Rappard's text, his statements would have been considered appropriate within this circle. The society discussed liberation of colonies in their St. Moritz meeting ten years later, and the historian Kim Priemel has written that its "main thrust was an embarrassingly simplistic and brazenly racist justification of European imperialism" (Priemel 2016, 388), indicating that the plight of the world's people of colour was not a very pressing issue for the society's members. Rappard went on to remark that in conversation with British colleagues the night before, he had heard that "the absenteeism of some of the Welsh miners called for a similar explanation". The question for Rappard was then: "Can these Arabs and these Welsh philosophers be denied the right to call themselves economic men?" Rappard's answer was no, and he went on to describe Adam Smith as "a Scot who preferred to work and to save", noting that "For the Scotch brand of the homo economicus, work was a virtue first because the sturdy Nordic mountaineer loved freedom, secondly because he did not shirk effort and thirdly and finally because he was not averse to wealth…".[12]

It is hard to know exactly what to make of Rappard's musings on Algerian and Welsh national character as a different sort of homo economicus than the one upon which Adam Smith had based both liberal philosophy and the field of economics. Due to his connections to international diplomacy, Rappard was most likely one of the few of those gathered at Mont Pèlerin who had set foot in what was then known as "the colonies", but whose name would soon change to "the developing world" or even "the third world". In a later recollection, the Norwegian attendee Trygve Hoff wrote

[12]Hoover Institution Library and Archives, Mont Pelerin Society, Box 5, Folder 12: "Minutes".

that although there were no "colored" or "crooked-eyed" attendees at the meeting (he expressed hope that there would be some at later conferences), he still noted a certain division along racial lines. "Neither dark eyes, curly hair or a bent nose" was a "certain proof of Jewish lineage", he wrote, but he still suggested that sub-groups within the society were being formed along ethnic lines, presumably between Jews and non-Jews.[13] These comments certainly suggest a rather limited knowledge of other cultures, and perhaps Rappard was mainly reporting to the conference attendees from the outside world. It is possible to see his remarks in relation to the emerging paradigms of development and aid in the early postcolonial world. Recent studies from 1950s Algeria reveal the importance of ideas similar to Rappard's about Arabs as not quite *homo economicus* or entrepreneurial enough for a modern world, also in early development aid efforts (Davis 2011).

Rappard's differentiation between economic science and economic policies seems to have been rather slippery, as he then went on to conclude that:

> Modern economic liberalism ... is the legitimate off-spring of the union between two first cousins: Adam Smith's penetrating and essentially sound scientific analysis of the economic world of his day, and Adam Smith's inborn love of freedom, constructive effort and wealth.

Thus the conclusion appears to have been that liberal economic theory was scientific, and that liberal economic policies were the logical conclusion drawn from these scientific facts by those who love freedom, constructive effort and wealth (a category excluding both Arabs and the Welsh). In his work on *Liberal Languages*, Michael Frieden has written that "The scramble for the mantle of scientific authority is frequently a facile and flawed route to legitimacy pursued by the ideological producers themselves" (Frieden 2005, 12). Rappard did not appear to think so, however, and it seemed clear to him that the political conclusions drawn from scientific facts eluded only those people believed by Rappard to be very different from those gathered at the Mont Pèlerin. One is reminded of Hayek and other early neoliberals' constant claims that politicians and policymakers were ignoring the truths of economics and liberalism in moving towards socialism and other forms of collectivism. Indeed, Rappard ended his address by stating: "Unless the world has become completely mad, it must sooner or later come to realize and to admit the productive superiority of a society based upon the principle of free enterprise". Finishing off, Rappard argued that "The socialism of Europe" was "the policy of a tired race", and said, perhaps privy to the Marshall Plan, which would be announced some two months later, that it was largely being subsidized by capitalism from America ("a still energetically youthful continent"). Before leaving the word to Hayek, Rappard concluded to both American and European listeners: "May it prove to be for both continents the starting point of an intellectual, economic and political renaissance without which it would seem well nigh impossible not to despair of the future".[14] Thus the very first conference of what was to become the Mont Pelerin Society had begun.

---

[13]Riksarkivet, Oslo, Trygve Hoff/Farmand, Box 16 (Translated from the Norwegian original).

[14]Hoover Institution Archives, Mont Pelerin Society, Box 5, Folder 12: "Minutes".

Primary Sources

Hoover Institution Library and Archives, Stanford University, Palo Alto, California, USA:
Mont Pelerin Society Collection

Het Liberaal Archief, Gent, Belgium
Mont Pelerin Society Collection

London School of Economics Special Collections, London, UK:
Lionel Robbins Collection

Riksarkivet, Oslo, Norway
Papers of Trygve Hoff/Farmand.

Secondary Literature

Alexander, J. C. (2010). *The performance of politics—Obama's victory and the democratic struggle for power*. Oxford: Oxford University Press.

Arbeiter, L. (2004). *Aaron director, founder of the field of law and economics*. The University of Chicago News Office, September 13.

Aujard, H. (2002). *Un savant méconnu: portraits d'un autodidacte: sur l'œuvre de Maurice Allais, Prix Nobel de sciences économiques*. Paris: C. Juglar.

Biscione, M., & Carlo, A (1961). *Dizionario Biografico degli Italiani*. Roma: Istituto dell'Enciclopedia Italiana.

Blundell, J. (2001). *Waging the war of Ideas*. London: The Institute of Economic Affairs.

Boudreaux, D., & Slepko, N. (2008). Read, Leonard E. (1898–1983). *The Encyclopedia of Libertarianism*. Thousand Oaks, CA: Cato Institute.

Burgin, A. (2012). *The great persuasion: Reinventing free markets since the depression*. Cambridge, Mass: Harvard University Press.

Cairncross, A. (1996). *Economic ideas and government policy—Contributions to contemporary economic history*. London–New York: Routledge.

Campbell, G., Falcon, W. P., Jones, W. O., & Brandt, K. (1975). *Stanford University historical society*. California: Palo Alto.

Cattani, A., & Barth, H. (2002). *Historischen Lexicon der Schweiz*. Bern: Historischen Lexicon der Schweiz.

Cole, C. (2009). *Performing South Africa's truth commission: Stages of transition*. Bloomington: Indiana University Press.

Ebeling, R.M., & Rappard, W. E. (2000). An international man in an age of nationalism. *Foundation for Economic Education*.

Eyck, F., & Eyck, E. (2004). In *Nationalismus in den Kulturwissenschaften. Band 2: Leitbegriffe—Deutungsmuster—Paradigmenkämpfe. Erfahrungen und Transformationen im Exil*, 545–548. Göttingen: Vandenhoek & Ruprecht.

Fonseca, G. L., & Jewkes, J. (1902–1988). *History of economic thought website*. New York: Institute for New Economic Thinking.

Franc, A. (2016a). The importance of Switzerland for the neoliberal movement in World War II and the postwar years 2014. In WZB, Berlin.

Franc, A. (2016b). Wilhem Röpke's utopia and Swiss reality: from neoliberalism to neoconservatism. In WZB, Berlin.

Franc, A. (2016c). Neoliberalism as cultural nationalism: The "Swiss group" in the Mont Pelerin Society. In WZB, Berlin
Knight, F. H. (1991). *The University of Chicago centennial catalogues*. Chicago: University of Chicago.
Frieden, M. (2005). *Liberal languages*. Princeton and Oxford: Princeton University Press.
Stigler, G. J. (1911–1991). (2008). *The concise encyclopedia of economics*. Indianapolis: Liberty Fund.
Gerken, L. (2000). *Walter Eucken und sein Werk: Rückblick auf den Vordenker der sozialen Marktwirtschaft*. Mohr Siebeck.
Davis, M. H. (2011). Algeria as Postcolony? Rethinking the colonial legacy of post-structuralism. *Journal of French and Francophone Philosophy, 19*, 136–152.
Hartwell, R. M. (1995). *A history of the Mont Pelerin society*. Indianapolis: Liberty Fund.
Herbert, T. (1961). *Vem är det 1961*. Vem Är Det—Svensk Biografisk Handbok. Stockholm: Norstedt förlag.
Davenport, J. (1987). *New York times*, June 12.
Jones, D. S. (2012). *Masters of the Universe: Hayek, Friedman, and the birth of neoliberal politics*. Princeton: Princeton University Press.
Judt, T. (2009). *What is living and what is dead in social democracy?* New York University.
Popper, K. (1997). *Stanford encyclopedia of philosophy*. Palo Alto, California: Stanford University.
Knegt, D. F. (2015). *A new order for France and Europe? Bertrand de Jouvenel and Alfred Fabre-Luce between Liberalism, Fascism and Europeanism (1930–1954)*. Florence: European Unviersity Institute.
Henderson, D. R. (Ed.) (2008) Lionel Robbins (1898–1984). In *The concise encyclopedia of economics*. Indianapolis: Liberty Fund
Losurdo, D. (2011). *Liberalism: A counter-history*. London: Verso.
Matthews, R. C. O. (1984). *Economy and democracy*. London: Macmillan.
Henderson, D. R. (ed.) (2008). Milton Friedman (1912–2006). In *The concise encyclopedia of economics*. Indianapolis: Liberty Fund.
Mirowski, P., & Plehwe, D. (Eds.). (2009). *The road from Mont Pèlerin: The making of the neoliberal thought collective*. Cambridge, Mass: Harvard University Press.
Mitchell, M. T. (2006). *Michael Polanyi: The art of knowing*. Wilmington, Delaware: ISI Books.
Mjøset, L. (2015). Nyliberalisme, økonomisk teori og kapitalismens mangfold : noen historiske linjer og en norsk kasusstudie. *Agora* 29.
Pickett, K., & Wilkinson, R. (2009). *The spirit level: Why more equal societies almost always do better*. London: Allen Lane.
Powell, J. (2000). *The triumph of liberty*. New York: Free Press.
Priemel, K. C. (2016). *The Betrayal—The Nuremberg trials and German Divergence*. Oxford: Oxford University Press.
Professor Graham. *Princeton IES*. Princeton, New Jersey: Princeton IES.
Rappard, W. E. (1938). *The crisis of democracy*. Chicago: University of Chicago Press.
Robin, C. (2011). *The reactionary mind: Conservatism from Edmund Burke to Sarah Palin*. New York: Oxford University Press.
Letwin, R. (1992). *The anatomy of thatcherism*. London: Transaction Publishers.
Rockwell, L. H. Jr. (2007). Biography of Henry Hazlitt (1894–1993). *Articles of Interest—Mises Institute*, August 1.
Rothbard, M. N. (1995). *Making economic sense*. Auburn, Alabama: Ludwig von Mises Institute.
Sismondo, S. (2010). *An introduction to science and technology studies*. Chichester: Wiley-Blackwell.
Skinner, Q. (2002). *Visions of politics, volume 1, regarding method*. Cambridge: Cambridge University Press.
Slobodian, Q. (2015). World Federation against the Welfare State: Hayek and Röpke Think Global before 1945. In Hitotsubashi University, Tokyo, Japan.
Soluci6n social—primer libro editada por Fenareta. 17. aug. *Fenareta*.

The Associated Press. 1997. C.V. Wedgwood, 86, Storyteller of History. *The New York Times*, March 11.

Toftg, J., Banke, N., & Iversen, C (1979). *Dansk Biografisk Leksikon*. Köbenhavn: Gyldendal.

Waggoner, W. H., & Harry, D. R. (1985). Gideonse Dead; Ex-Head of Brooklyn College. *New York Times*, March 14.

Wapshott, N. (2011). *Keynes Hayek: The clash that defined modern economics* (1st ed.). New York: W.W. Norton & Co.

Weil, M. (1982). Felix Morley, Scholar, Educator and Journalist, Dies at 88. *The Washington Post*, March 15.

White, L. H. (2012). *The clash of economic ideas: The great policy debates and experiments of the last hundred years*. Cambridge University Press.

Wilkinson, W. Harper, Floyd Arthur "Baldy" (1905–1973). In *The Encyclopedia of libertarianism*, 217–218. Thousand Oaks, CA: Cato Institute.

Zmirak, J. (2001). *Wilhelm Röpke—Swiss localist, global economist*. Wilmington, Delaware: ISI Books.

Chapter 6
Using the State

'The state' is one of the most elusive concepts in social and political theory and major writers often demonstrate this by using the term differently…" (Mayo 2011, 57–71)

Peter Mayo in "The Centrality of the State in Neoliberal Times: Gramsci and beyond" (2011)

Although I hold that the dual argument should be seen as a whole, it obviously consists of two rather distinct parts. In the years before 1947, which was the topic of Part I, it could be argued that one part of the dual argument was given more weight than the other. In their books, articles and lectures, the early neoliberals focused primarily on their theory of totalitarianism as a result of economic planning. As we have seen, the attack on laissez-faire was present before 1947, yet it was not as obvious as was the campaign against "economic planning" as the root of all society's ills. In the discussions at Mont Pèlerin, however, almost the opposite was the case. The supposed totalitarian nature of both the Soviet Union in the East and the rise of social democracy in the West was remarked upon and functioned as an important backdrop, but as we will see, the specific discussions focused more on the futility of laissez-faire and the need to change liberalism. I argue that part of the reason for this is that these were internal discussions, whereas the works published between 1920 and 1947 were meant to persuade an external audience.

When discussing amongst each other, it was not as necessary for the neoliberals to repeat their claim that socialism and social liberalism led to totalitarianism and dictatorship. On the other hand, actually coming to grips with the contradictions embodied in the dual argument and defining what sort of state actions were needed in a modern, liberal society was of the upmost importance. This is evident in the approach of Friedrich Hayek, the main organizer, who emphasized this aspect of the dual argument both in his introductory speech and in his introduction to the first session of the meeting, which he claimed was the most important of them all. This chapter focuses on these two introductions by Hayek and the following discussion on the use of the state to ensure a functioning market society. As will become clear, neoliberals of all stripes, members of the Chicago school, the ordoliberal school and

O. Innset, *Reinventing Liberalism*, Springer Studies in the History of Economic Thought,
https://doi.org/10.1007/978-3-030-38885-0_6

other factions of the group, supported Hayek's idea that states had to be used to ensure a more competitive society. Conflict arose, however, when Hayek's mentor Mises weighed in with his criticism of the neoliberal approach and his arguments favouring the old-fashioned notion of laissez-faire. The project to discuss a liberal form of interventionism in more detail thus derailed, and the attendees ended up arguing with Mises about whether or not states could have a positive function at all.

Hayek's Welcome

After Rappard's short introduction, the floor was given to the man of the hour: Friedrich Hayek.[1] The beginning of the Mont Pèlerin Society was in some ways also the end of a long journey for him. Ever since his arrival in London in 1931, and his 1933 memo "Nazi-Socialism", written to Sir William Beveridge (quoted in Chap. 4), Hayek had wanted to fight collectivism in all its forms. He had come to think that the way to do this was to *reinvent* liberalism, purge it of "false individualists" and use this new ideological clarity to advocate for a different world order. After the publication of *The Road to Serfdom* in 1944 he became famous, travelled to the US, and saw a window of opportunity open for him. His plan to put together a society of like-minded, frustrated liberals had been developing and coming ever closer to reality since he had first discussed it at a meeting in Cambridge only three years before. Now he was there, stating bluntly: "(…) the moment has arrived to which I have so long looked forward". Hayek expressed feelings of both gratitude and "real alarm about the responsibility I have taken on me". He went on to declare that if liberal ideas were to have any chance of revival, "a great intellectual task" lay ahead:

> This task involves both purging traditional liberal theory of certain accidental accretions which have become attached to it in the course of time, and facing up to certain real problems which an over-simplified liberalism has shirked or which have become apparent only since it had become a somewhat stationary and rigid creed.

Readers will recognize this as a compressed version of the dual argument, attacking both laissez-faire liberalism and social liberalism with the aim of creating a new form of liberalism. Hayek's "purge" would have mainly referred to the "constructivist" tendencies that he had argued perverted the social liberal tradition. Many years later Hayek would claim that this type of liberalism was a "pacemaker for socialism" (Hayek 1972, 398). The "facing up to certain real problems which an over-simplified liberalism has shirked" was the second part of the dual argument: the attack on laissez-faire, as a "somewhat stationary and rigid creed" which did not correspond to the realities of the modern world and the crucial importance of state

[1]Hayek's address is another one whose manuscript has been saved for posterity. Again there is a disclaimer at the top saying "It is specially requested not to quote from this document except with the express permission of the person concerned." Again, I have taken the liberty of the historian to make some quotations, as I read the disclaimer to relate to more short-term use of the manuscript. Hoover Institution Library and Archives, Mont Pelerin Society, Box 5, Folder 12: "Minutes".

power in enforcing a neoliberal world order. I have argued that this dual argument and the challenges bound up in it is the most important background for early neoliberal thought, and we see here how Hayek expressly framed the first meeting of the Mont Pelerin Society in precisely these terms.

If it indeed was a desperate situation for liberalism, Hayek told the attendees of this historical conference that he did not despair. In his travels over recent years, he had found people from different fields and in different parts of the world who had been "rediscovering the basic principles of liberalism … hard at work to reconstruct a liberal philosophy which can fully meet the objections which in the eyes of most of our contemporaries have defeated the promise the earlier liberalism offered." Hayek emphasized how everywhere he had found "isolated men … working on essentially the same problems and on very similar lines." The tentatively called Acton-Tocqueville society was now finally bringing these people together, and Hayek went on to defend his choice of not inviting socialists of any kind to the discussion, something for which Karl Popper had already criticized him: (Mirowski 2013, 71) "… common work on the more detailed outline of a liberal order is practicable only among a group of people who are in agreement on fundamentals…", he stated. Hayek then implicitly questioned William Rappard's claim that "tired" European socialism was living off the dynamism of American capitalism. Instead, he noted that the further one travelled west "to countries where liberal institutions are still comparatively firm, and people professing liberal convictions still comparatively numerous, the less are these people yet prepared really to re-examine their own conviction…" Contrary to Rappard's claims, Hayek found that "in those countries which either had actually experienced a completely totalitarian regime or closely approached it, a few men had through their experiences gained a clearer conception of the conditions and value of a free society." Thus Hayek offered a somewhat different view to Rappard on the question of which liberals from which geographical contexts would have the most to offer in the coming reinvention of their creed: "… the wisdom is not all on one side and the observation of the actual decay of a civilization has taught some independent thinkers on the European Continent lessons which I believe have yet to be learnt in England and America if these countries are to avoid a similar fate".

Erwin Dekker has argued that Viennese intellectuals based their response to the volatile situation of the interwar years on the experience of seeing the Habsburg empire dissolve, and their dreams of a liberal empire with it (Dekker 2016, 132). Austrian economists felt they were witness to the same development happening twice, and here we see Hayek claiming that the same things that had happened in Europe could happen in America, and that European liberals were thus well equipped to council their American allies.

The dominance of economists over other professions and background must have been obvious to everyone attending, yet Hayek waxed lyrical on the importance and fruitfulness of discussions between economists like himself and lawyers, historians and political philosophers. Referring to the first aspect of the dual argument, he contended that economists had learned how to "discover all the beliefs which are part and parcel of that movement that leads to totalitarianism". Nonetheless, he was quick to add that they could not be sure that they did not "as uncritically as any one else accept, under the influence of the atmosphere of our time, ideas in the field of history or philosophy, morals or law which belong to the same movement which we oppose in our field." The lesson seemed to be that scholars of history and philosophy might be able to detect aspects of collectivism, rationalism, false individualism constructivism or any of the other diseases Hayek had analysed as leading to totalitarianism, that economists might miss and even incorporate into their own thinking without even being aware of it.

Hayek then apologized for the "embarrassing nature" of having to decide who was to be invited to the conference. He nonetheless stressed that: "it is not sufficient that our members should have what used to be called 'sound' views'", alluding to some assumedly well-known standard of right-leaning political orientation with the implication that this was no longer sufficient: "What we need are people who have faced the arguments from the other side, who have struggled with them and fought themselves through to a position from which they can both critically meet the objection against it and justify their views." This was a time to be highly analytical, critical and innovative if the reinvention of liberalism was to be successful.

Hayek then went on to acknowledge and apologize for the imbalance between economists and other professions, blaming in part his personal contacts, but also suggesting yet again that "economists are perhaps more generally aware of the immediate dangers and of the urgency of the intellectual problems which we must solve if we are to have a chance to direct the movement in a more desirable direction." Hayek wanted to expand neoliberalism, but to his mind there was no doubt that his creed grew out of the field of economics: the critique of socialism developed through the socialist calculation debates and the underlying notion of markets as mediators of modernity. According to Hayek "not a single one of all those to whom I sent invitations did not express his sympathies with the aim of the Conference", and he then went on to list 26 people who had not been able to attend. The list included Walter Lippmann, Alexander Rüstow and Jaques Rueff, who were all present at the 1938 colloquium in Paris. He then expressed sorrow at the deaths of Chicago economist Henry Simons, who it is now known committed suicide in the summer of 1946; (Van Horn 2014) Sir John Clapham, who preceded over the meeting at Cambridge in 1944 in which Hayek first laid out his plans for a transnational organization to reinvent liberalism; and the young French economist Etienne Mantoux who was killed in action only eight days before the German capitulation on 7 May, 1945. Continuing with housekeeping items, Hayek noted that although some journalists were in attendance, "I think this should be regarded as a private meeting and all that is said here in the discussion as "off the record" as the American term is."

Hayek then laid out the programme of the first week, noting first that the same evening's session entitled "'Free Enterprise' or Competitive Order", "seems to be much the biggest and in some ways the most important… It is the field where it is most important that we should become clear in our own minds, and arrive at an agreement about the kind of programme of economic policy which we should wish to see generally accepted." This was the key session as far as Hayek was concerned, and he continued: "Its ramifications are practically endless, as an adequate treatment involves a complete programme of a liberal economic policy." It seems clear that

Hayek was perfectly aware that the dual argument as an attack on both new liberalism *and* laissez-faire liberalism implied a serious reconceptualization of liberal thought for the modern, post-war world. This *reinvention* was the most important topic of debate, and he wanted to set the conference off on this path by discussing it in the very first session that same evening.

After alluding to the session on historiography, Hayek segued into a comment on how the liberal creed had "contained many elements which on the one hand led many of its adherents directly into the folds of socialism or nationalism and on the other hand antagonised many who shared the basic values of individual freedom…" This was part of Hayek's attack on social liberalism and his purging of the false individualism he thought led to collectivism and socialism. He referred to it as the "false rationalism, which gained influence in the French Revolution and which during the past hundred years has exercised its influence mainly through the twin movements of Positivism and Hegelianism." According to Hayek, this had led to a "breach between true liberal and religious convictions…" and he claimed there would be "no hope for a revival of liberal forces" if this breach was not healed by a more epistemologically modest reinvention of liberalism. This alluded to the following Wednesday's session on "Liberalism and Christianity", and Hayek then made only brief remarks on the importance of Thursday's sessions on the future of Germany and the prospects of European federation: "problems of such immediate urgency that no international group of students of politics should meet without considering them…" Before turning to his final remarks, Hayek regretted not having been able to organize a session on the meaning of the Rule of Law, a theme dear to his heart in his subsequent work on the proper legal framework for a modern, market society (Hayek 1972; Hayek 1998).

There followed some remarks on the formal organization of the meeting. Dorothy Hahn would be keeping minutes of what Hayek referred to as "the business part of our discussions" and English would be the main language. This indicated its rising status on the international scene, but also the simple fact that Hayek himself did not speak French. He also commented on the societies future efforts at recruitment, insisting that a future, permanent organization "must remain a closed society, not open to all and sundry, but only people who share with us certain common convictions… whatever permanent body we form (it) must be a closed society." If membership could be acquired by election, it would give the organization the character of "Academy", Hayek thought, and to this day applications to join the Mont Pelerin Society must be supported by two current members of the society.[2] Hayek then commented on possible difficulties of getting financing for a permanent transnational organization without "any strings or conditions of any sort being attached to the offer", expressing gratitude to Hunold for making the Swiss funds available and to Luhnow of the William Volker Charities Trust in Kansas City. Finally, he expressed that he would wait until the group had become better acquainted with any further practical tasks and "any attempt to justify the name which I have tentatively suggested." He finished:

[2]The application is then considered by a Membership Committee, which makes a recommendation to a Board of Directors. https://www.montpelerin.org/montpelerin/join.html.

"For now we are just the Mont Pèlerin Conference to which you will have to give your own laws and whose procedure and destiny is now entirely in your hands."

Hayek Peeling Oranges

After Rappard's and Hayek's welcome speeches, there was a break until 2.30 pm for the afternoon and evening session. The catering at the conference was remembered by Dorothy Hahn as being "very fancy" for a young woman arriving from bombed out London. There was still rationing in much of England and continental Europe, and the latter was badly affected by famine. Mrs. Hahn remembers vividly how, in the luxurious Hotel du Parc, there were oranges for lunch one day, but that she was unable to peel them as she had never in her life had one before. Hayek peeled two oranges for her at the table, something which caused Dorothy Hahn great embarrassment.[3] I believe that this brief image of the famous Austrian economist peeling oranges for his embarrassed English secretary tells us quite a lot. Hahn was a bright student of Hayek, and as a woman she was therefore singled out to become his secretary. Later in life she would work as the secretary of her husband, the famous economist Frank Hahn, and do secretarial work for other economists.[4] The "girlish" embarrassment she felt, and her position at the conference as a secretary instead of as a bright young economist speaks volumes about gender relations at the time. The orange[5] also speaks of Europe in 1947, where devastating war had made something as simple as oranges, which had been imported to England for over a century, (Choi 2009) a rare delicacy that a nineteen-year-old woman had never tasted. In the Swiss alps in 1947, Dorothy Hahn's forty-eight-year-old Austrian boss of aristocratic descent must have seemed simultaneously like a ghost from the past and a guide to the new world in which she found herself. As we will see in Chap. 7, 1947 was very much seen as a new beginning, and the neoliberals at Mont Pélerin were eager to create a new liberalism for a new time. Yet they kept referring to past thinkers, and a certain aristocratic privilege and nostalgia for things past always stayed with them in their conflicted attempts to reinvent liberalism.

"Free" Enterprise or Competitive Order

Hayek began his second address of the day with a strong attack on his own political camp, the political right. The movement towards planning, he claimed, was "due, more than anything else, to the lack of a real programme, or perhaps I had better say, a

[3]Interview with Dorothy Hahn, Cambridge, 21.12.2015.

[4]Ibid.

[5]More extensive attempts at studying history through foodstuffs include (Spary 2012) And Steven Shapin's musings on "the epistemology of the pineapple" in (Shapin 2011).

consistent philosophy of the opposition groups".[6] Conservatives were guilty of double standards he thought, since groups that pretended to oppose socialism also gave support to policies of government intervention when this was believed to be to their own advantage. "… the pretending defenders of 'free enterprise' are in fact defenders of privileges and advocates of government activity in their favour rather than opponents of all privilege", he said. Here Hayek was rehearsing an argument he would repeat for the rest of his life: the insistence that his ideas from *The Road to Serfdom* were not intended to defend the privileges of big businesses, but instead a principled attack on *all* government planning and state involvement in economic affairs. The great danger in what he saw as business conservatives' misinformed embrace of his ideas was that "once the principle is admitted that the government undertakes responsibility for the status and position of particular groups, it is inevitable that this control will be extended to satisfy the aspirations and prejudices of the great masses." He was of course referring to the welfare states that had developed in the US and Europe during the interwar years, and were now being expanded significantly (Rodgers 1998). This fear of "the masses" demanding a decent life from modern states is a recurring and very important theme in the arguments of early neoliberals from various camps. The ordoliberals largely agreed with the analysis of Carl Schmitt, and argued that a state which starts to feed "special interests" would become a weak state. That afternoon, however, Hayek's spirited attack was also launched against conservatives and capital interests: "There is no hope of a return to a freer system until the leaders of the movement against state control are prepared first to impose upon themselves that discipline of a competitive market which they ask the masses to accept." Hayek claimed that "no organized political group anywhere is in favour of a truly free system", and urged his allies to think beyond "fixed limits of practicability imposed by public opinion."

Hayek then went on to claim that "Public opinion on these matters is the work of men like ourselves", quoting from Keynes' famous words on the power of economic ideas. The paragraph from Keynes' *General Theory* on how men in power are merely reproducing ideas of "some economic scribbler decades earlier" was reproduced by Hayek both in this speech, and in a famous 1949 essay entitled "The Intellectuals and Socialism". It has gone on to inspire the narrative structure of a great number of books and articles on neoliberalism (Burgin 2012; Jones 2012). The full quote referred to by Hayek is as follows:

> Practical men who believe themselves to be quite exempt from any intellectual influence, are usually the slaves of some defunct economist. Madmen in authority, who hear voices in the air, are distilling their frenzy from some academic scribbler of a few years back. I am sure that the power of vested interests is vastly exaggerated compared with the gradual encroachment of ideas. Not, indeed, immediately, but after a certain interval; for in the field of economic and political philosophy there are not many who are influenced by new theories after they are twenty-five or thirty years of age, so that the ideas which civil servants and politicians and even agitators apply to current events are not likely to be the newest. But, soon or late, it is ideas, not vested interests, which are dangerous for good or evil (Keynes 1965, 383–384).

[6]Liberaal Archief, "Mont Pelerin Society", Box 1, Folder 1 "Mont Pèlerin, 1947".

Hayek claimed that it was from this "long run point of view, that we must look at our task", a remark which lends some credibility to the idea that the men gathered at Mont Pèlerin really did succeed in changing the world, however slowly. Although heavily funded by capital interests, their ideas were out of favour in policy circles in their own time. As we will discuss in the conclusion, however, they were later embraced and adopted in a variety of conflicting ways in several different places across the world (Ban 2016). Hayek hinted at the long road ahead by exclaiming that the general public at his time of speaking was "to some extent entirely beyond the scope of reasoning"—a remarkable comment indicating just how little faith Hayek had in popular democracy. Nonetheless, Hayek said that the hard task ahead needed "to show that the aims which our generation has set itself are incompatible or conflicting, and that the pursuit of some of them will endanger even greater values…. I believe very careful distinctions will have to be drawn between the sense in which security and equality can and cannot be provided in a free society." Once again, we see very clearly that it was the rise of democracy, socialism and the welfare state which caused such momentous concern for Hayek and his fellow neoliberals. By "security" and "equality" he would have been referring to popular policies of economic redistribution and social security, but he claimed that these goals were simply not compatible with neoliberal ideals of a free and open society.

Then came the second, often overlooked aspect of the dual argument: the attack on laissez-faire. Hayek called it "the most fatal tactical mistake of many nineteenth century liberals" to have "given the impression that the abandonment of all harmful or unnecessary state activity was the consummation of all political wisdom…" and "that the question of how [Hayek's emphasis] the state ought to use those powers nobody denied to it offered no serious and important problems on which reasonable people could differ." This was where laissez-faire had failed miserably: the state existed, and it was powerful. *Too* powerful for Hayek's liking, yet that did not mean that liberalism was only about fighting the state. Instead it had to become a theory also of how to best *use* the state for liberal ends. He then quoted John Stuart Mill's *Political Economy*, written while Mill was what Hayek referred to as "still a true liberal". There, Mill had claimed that the principle of private property had never had a fair trial in any country, and Hayek went on to lament how Mill in becoming a socialist, himself had given up on private property. Instead turning "his attention to schemes involving its restriction or abolition rather than its more effective use, thus abandoning the noble cause of making pure private property the basis of a modern society." Hayek later developed what John Gray has called "an obsession" with John Stuart Mill and his relationship with Harriet Taylor. He collected their letters to each other and concluded in an article that it must had been Taylor who turned Mill away from "true liberalism" (Gray 2015).

Within a few minutes then, Hayek had both stated that this new creed was a principled creed not to be mistaken for a defence of privileges, but also that the principle of private property was what lay at its heart. Hayek further claimed that liberalism was not the absence of state activity, rather:

> a policy which deliberately adopts competition, the market and prices as its ordering principle and uses the legal framework enforced by the state in order to make competition as effective and beneficial as possible – and to supplement it where, and only where, it cannot be made effective.

The question Hayek wanted to discuss then, was the principles behind exactly when competition needed to be "supplemented", and how – what kind of legal framework should be adopted to make it as efficient as possible? "Competition can be made more effective and more beneficent by certain activities of government", he stated. The laissez-faire or "Manchester-liberal" notion of a night-watch-man state was thus incomplete, he thought, claiming that "Where the traditional discussion becomes so unsatisfactory is where it is suggested that with the recognition of the principles of private property and freedom of contract, which indeed every liberal must recognise, all the issues were settled… It is only after we have agreed on these principles that the real problems begin." Hayek referred to his title for the session "'Free' Enterprise or Competitive Order", venturing that "The two names do not necessarily designate the same system and it is the system described by the second which we want". Interestingly however, when this lecture was printed as part of the publication *Individualism and Economic Order* (1948), Hayek changed the title from "Free Enterprise or Competitive Order", to a less provocative "Free Enterprise and Competitive Order" (Hayek 1948, 107–119). In its original form however, Hayek's lecture clearly stated that "free" enterprise and a competitive order were not necessarily the same thing. The attack on laissez-faire was obvious.

In a striking example of how different the general view on government provided services was in 1947 from what it is now, Hayek then went on to state that "in a modern community (a) considerable number of services which are needed, such as sanitary and health services… could not possibly be provided by the market for the obvious reason that no price can be charged to the beneficiaries." Part of his attack on laissez-faire did include the admission that some services would have to be run by the public, and Hayek seemed unable to imagine that there could be a market in something like health services. Little did he know that people like Milton Friedman, who was present, and later society members and presidents would go on to promulgate the very view that markets were indeed also much better than governments at providing virtually *any* service, including sanitary and health services. There is a growing tendency to describe Hayek as some sort of *soft* neoliberal, or to describe early neoliberalism as a moderate third way between laissez-faire and social democracy (Sloan Wilson 2015). I will argue in the conclusion that this would be a mistake, as it is the very logic of state enforced efficient markets that Hayek and the early neoliberals pioneered which made subsequent attacks on public financing and the marketization of public services a possibility. In 1947, it was impossible for Hayek to even imagine how successful this new way of thinking about the role of markets and states in the modern world would actually be. Thus his repeated claims in the 1940s that some services must be public and that a social safety net must be provided was not a matter of Hayek being moderate; rather it shows the degree to which his view was on the defensive at the time, so that some concessions had to be made to the opposing view. Hayek insisted: "At some stage or other we shall certainly have to consider which services of this kind we must always expect the governments to provide outside the market [Hayek's emphasis] and how far the fact that they must do so will also affect the conditions on which the market economy proceeds." Public services paid for through taxation, but operated for profits by private companies competing in specially designed markets was well beyond even the neoliberal imagination in 1947.

Hayek went on to urge the participants again to "above all beware of the error that the formulae 'private property' and 'freedom of contract' solve our problems." Hayek wanted more nuance, stating that "Our problems begin when we ask what ought to be the contents of property rights", and made specific reference to the issues of land ownership and modern cities:

> the simple rules which are adequate to ordinary mobile 'things' or 'chattel' are not suitable for indefinite extension... Unless we can provide some guidance in fields like this about what are legitimate or necessary government activities and what are its limits we must not complain if our views are not taken seriously when we oppose other kinds of less justified 'planning'.

He proceeded to talk about the prevention of monopoly, and wanted specifically to talk about "inventions, copyright, trademarks and the like". To Hayek it was "beyond doubt that in these fields a slavish application of the concept of property as it has been developed for material things has done a great deal to foster the growth of monopoly and that here very drastic reforms may be required if competitions is to be made to work". Note again the core idea that competition can be "made to work" by drastic reforms. As we have seen, this was a line Hayek very much shared with the German ordoliberals (Van Horn 2009). Hayek thought of patents as "particularly interesting from our point of view because they provide so clear an illustration how it is necessary in all such instances not to apply a ready made formula but to go back to the rationale [Hayek's emphasis] of the market system and to decide for each class what the precise rights are to be which the government ought to protect." This is another key formulation of Hayek's project: trying to restate liberalism for a new world that was very different from that out of which "classical liberalism" grew. The way to do this for Hayek involved trying to understand what he called the *rationale* of the market system and thus somehow channel how these thinkers would have thought had they been alive, and how they would have applied their principles to radically different circumstances.

Hayek then went on to talk of freedom of contract. Echoing Walter Lippmann's remarks from *The Good* Society, he stated that "'Freedom of contract' is in fact no solution because in a complex society like ours no contract can explicitly provide against all contingencies... the precise content of the permanent legal framework, the rules of civil law, are of the greatest importance for the way in which a competitive market will operate", he said, lamenting also that "little intellectual effort has been directed to the question in what way this legal framework should be modified, to make competition more effective." Stefan Kolev's contention that Hayek at this point was in the midst of a second phase of his intellectual development, in which he was an ordoliberal philosopher focused on the "traffic rules" of the market system, seems to hold true for his interventions at the 1947 meeting (Kolev 2010). Hayek proclaimed that corporation laws regarding limited liability had "greatly assisted the growth of monopoly", to the point where "size of enterprise has become an advantage beyond the point where it is justified by technological facts". Unlike the American Supreme Court, who in the landmark 2010 ruling *Citizens United versus FEC* awarded corporations the same rights as individuals, (Brown 2015, 154–173) Hayek stated "It seems to me that in general the freedom of the individual by no means need be extended to give all these freedoms to organised groups of individuals".

So far, Hayek had "spoken only of what is required to make competition effective on the side of employers…" in order for them "to put their own house in order". However, he was quite clear that that "we must not delude ourselves that in many ways the most crucial, the most difficult and the most delicate part of our task consists in formulating an appropriate programme of labour or trade union policy". Here liberals had failed and ended up legalizing "violence, coercion and intimidation", by which he presumably meant unions and organized labour. "If there is to be any hope of a return to a free economy the question how the powers of trade unions can be appropriately limited in law as well as in fact is one of the most important of all the questions to which we must give our attention." Hayek was, however, running out of time at this point and had to abandon his broadside against labour power and hurriedly moved on to taxation, stating that there were two serious consequences of what he called present societies' "extreme egalitarian ends". One being that it was "practically impossible for the successful man to rise by accumulating a fortune", the other being one related to inheritance tax. Hayek would later pen philosophical treaties defending inheritance, (Hayek 1972, 85–102) but for now he had to conclude that "there are many other important problems which I have not even mentioned", acknowledging that it was indeed "too wide a field to treat the whole of it adequately even if we could devote the whole of these ten days to its discussion."[7]

Support from Freiburg and Chicago

Professor Aaron Director gave a second introduction,[8] where he stated that there had been a steady shift from individualism to authority in economic life for over two generations. At first it had been gradual, and state interference had mainly been a response to the humanitarian tradition of liberalism. Director was here referring to the

[7] The version of Hayek's manuscript kept at The Liberal Archive in Gent is different from the one kept at the Hoover Institution Library and Archives. In the former, there are long sections entitled "ASSOCIATIONS", "MONETARY STABILIZATION" and "EQUALITY" before the speech closes off. This version is also gathered from somewhere at the Hoover Institution, albeit not in the box related to the archives of the Mont Pelerin Society, which contains the shortened version. It seems reasonable to assume that the shortened version was the one Hayek presented at the conference and thus I have limited my treatment to that. Liberaal Archief, Mont Pelerin Society, Box 1, Folder 1: "Mont Pèlerin, 1947".

[8] There is no manuscript available for Director's intervention and it was not recorded exactly verbatim by Mrs. Hahn. I have therefore chosen to paraphrase the various interventions, instead of writing them as quotations in quotation marks, even though parts of the minutes appear as full sentences. Liberaal Archief, Mont Pelerin Society, Box 1, Folder 1: "Mont Pèlerin, 1947".

rise of social liberalism, described in Chap. 3, and it could be argued that it was this "humanitarian tradition of liberalism" that the neoliberals sought to purge. Director said that he found that the shift was now part of a definite design to adopt an entirely different type of economic organization, in many ways reprising Hayek's argument about the collectivist nature of social liberalism, and pointing to the overlaps between socialism and social liberalism in the preceding century. Director offered three explanations for this. One was a change in what he called "basic beliefs", where individual freedom no longer commanded the support it once did, and order security and fixed status in life had become prevailing objectives. In this sense, Director argued, the free competitive market was being abandoned because it did its task *too* well, and thus yielded results incompatible with new moral values. The second explanation offered by Director was the widespread opinion that competitive markets were no longer suited as an organizing principle, this referred to the argument put forward by those who claimed that socialism was simply a more rational and efficient form of social organization. The third explanation was the one Director took as the basis of discussion: that the destruction of the competitive order was a direct consequence of the incomplete character of the theory of liberalism as developed in the nineteenth century, which provided no role for the state in economic life beyond that of enforcing contracts. Here Director was completely in line with Hayek, claiming that liberals had had no solution to offer derived from their fundamental philosophy since the middle of the nineteenth century. Director said he had no wish to minimise the harms that had been caused by current state intervention, but he also wanted to emphasise that the intervention had its root in real problems that could be eliminated only by offering better solutions. Thus Director, like Hayek, advocated that the theory of liberalism had to be extended to include a prescription of the role of the state. He then went on to draw three lessons that this reinvented theory of liberalism needed to be based on. Firstly, Director said it was apparent that free enterprise was indeed consistent with monopoly power. Secondly it was apparent that a competitive system would allocate resources effectively, but that it was not able to do so in the absence of stable and suitable monetary rules. The third lesson was that a competitive system appeared to fall short of meeting what he called the democratic standards of equality. Director thus seemed to favour regulations to secure competition, monetary stability and a certain form of social equality. After this, he claimed that the founders of 19th century liberalism served the cause of freedom by promoting free enterprise, and that the task ahead of modern day liberals would be to promote freedom by promoting the dispersion of power necessary for a competitive order. The founders of liberalism endeavoured to minimize the coercive powers of the state, he said, but the task of Director's day would be to redefine the role of the state in order to prevent the assumption of this power by organized minority occupational groups, referring presumably to labour unions. Director then went on to establish three fields in which he thought state action was required to make the competitive order work: the prevention of monopolies, the control of combinations among either business concerns or workers and the provision of monetary stability. In addition, he mentioned the problem of inequality and distress and the possible scope for state activity in the redistribution of income, but on this topic he was more ambiguous.

Walter Eucken also held what was intended to be an introduction, but after Hayek's lengthy intervention and a slightly shorter one by Director, his brief remarks appeared more as a comment. Eucken's intervention centred on two remarks about monopoly. The content of his intervention is not clear from the minutes I have found, but in a section in the article "Reinventing Monopoly and the Role of Corporations", Robert Van Horn reads Director's introduction at the 1947 meeting based on the minutes quoted above, and he also makes reference to Eucken's reply. According to Van Horn, "Eucken pointed out that Director erroneously presumed that the government should directly address the monopoly problem" (Van Horn 2009, 212). Van Horn further writes:

> Eucken based his comment on a key premise of ordoliberalism: The autonomous monopoly office, the enforcer of competition law should be immune from political influence and should be guided in assessment with established legal strictures. (Van Horn 2009, 213)

The definition of "government" is what is at stake in Eucken's disagreement with Director. The ordoliberal view holds that the enforcers of competition law should be outside of political control. Crucially, it would still be a structure formed by the state and meant to support markets, but it would be "immune from political influence". Eucken was thus chastising Director for assuming that liberal state interventions to ensure a competitive market society would somehow be at the mercy of democracy. That was not the point of the strong, ordoliberal state. Rather its purpose was the precise opposite: to shield markets from the pressures of democracy. The main point of Van Horn's article is to show that "despite the fact that Director did not support an economic constitution and an independent monopoly office, he shared Eucken's disdain for concentrated power because it undermined freedom" (Van Horn 2009, 213). Despite the issue of whether the "monopoly problem" should be addressed "directly" by government, members of both the Freiburg and the Chicago school shared common ground on the importance of competition law and using the state to make markets more competitive. With the later rise of Chicago Law and Economics, however, the Chicago school approach to this would change considerably (Van Horn 2009). The subsequent shifts in neoliberal doctrine will be discussed briefly in the conclusion, but for now we can observe that in 1947, the schools of Chicago and Freiburg were largely united in support for Hayek's revamping of liberalism based on what I have called the dual argument.

Discussion[9]

In the following discussion, Frank Graham said he found himself almost in complete agreement with Professor Eucken, but wondered whether he was correct to have said that natural monopolies would be handled worse when taken over by the state.

[9]There seems to have been two separate parts to the discussion—one immediately following Hayek's introduction, and one evening session. The collection of minutes at the Hoover Archives holds the minutes of one of these and the collection at The Liberal Archive in Gent has the other. The latter have the time signature 4.30, whereas the former has the time signature 8.30, so I will therefore assume that this is the order in which the discussion took place, although the fragmentary nature of the minutes leave something to be desired for those seeking to establish absolute clarity.

According to him, the right place for a natural monopoly was in the state; the significant thing being that the profits would go to the state, something which he thought justified the existence of a monopoly price as opposed to a market price. Hayek then took the floor again, attempting to clarify the difference between a competitive order and ordered competition: the former being a system to make competition work, the latter something which on the contrary restricted competition from working. His main concern would be to make the market work where it can work, once again noting that there were some services that could not be made subject to the market mechanism. He then raised the issues of monetary and financial policy, asking how monetary policy may be automatic and outside the range of politics, and the existence of provision for the unemployed and unemployable. He thought it taken for granted that this had to exist, but that the issue was how to make it interfere as little as possible with the market mechanism. The key questions of course were which outcomes and processes to define as part of the mechanism, but Hayek did not go into that, and as we will discuss in the conclusion, neither did anyone else. He then repeated some of his general outlines of the difficulties of market policy proper, including property and contract law; how to deal with monopolies; corporations and associations; problems of taxation and problems of international trade.

The next page of minutes has the time signature 8.30 on it, indicating that quite some time, and most likely a break for dinner, had passed since the session began with Hayek's introduction at 4.30. As the bright April night grew dark, the civilized discussions seemed to increase in temperature as Ludwig von Mises soon weighed in with his more dogmatic laissez-faire attitude. First, however, Professor Carl Iversen suggested, rather heretically, that the rules being laid down by liberals could be the rules to be adopted by state monopoly. This prompted Walter Eucken to say that if it were the question of placing a single monopoly in the hands of the government, it would be one thing, but that to transfer a number of monopolies to the government would be very different. The American conservative activist Loren Miller, one of the very few who was only referred to only as *Mr.* Miller in the minutes, stated his disagreement, but he was rather alone. John Jewkes even claimed that everyone present was ready to accept that it is one function of the state to provide some services. He was, however, immediately turned on by Ludwig von Mises. The others accused Mises of defending orthodoxy of the 18th century with his laissez-faire dogmatism, but he would not budge. Mises claimed that interventionists had always wanted different types of interventionism, and therefore had thought that they were in opposition—indicating that intervention would always be intervention, no matter how it was conceptualized. This was completely at odds with Hayek and the other neoliberals grand idea of finding ways to use the state in the service of markets, and so the amicable spirit and general sense of agreement was challenged by Mises stance.

We noted in Chap. 3 that whatever Hayek's interventions in the 1938 Walter Lippmann Colloquium really were, Alexander Rüstow perceived him as sharing Mises' "paleo-liberal" views. This does not correspond to our close reading of Hayek's work at the time; however Bruce Caldwell has remarked that although Hayek departed significantly from Mises, he always treated him very carefully and avoided confrontation with his former mentor, (Caldwell 2004, 144–145) who had a reputation for being a difficult person (Leeson 2013, 17). After Mises' outburst, Hayek therefore offered some more diplomatic words, affirming that any proposal to redistribute income was in itself an interference. He asked rhetorically if there was a point, once you start towards redistribution of income by taxation, where you can stop short of a totally planned economy, referring to the slippery slope argument which both he and Mises had been making. According to Hayek, however, it was important to distinguish between interfering with wages and with fixing minimum wages in a market economy, and he claimed that the latter was an interference that left relative scales unchanged.

Lionel Robbins then continued the diplomatic mission towards Mises, saying that everyone agreed with him that *most* interventions of the state in regards to the workings of the market mechanism had been bad, and that he hoped Mises would agree that the main task of the society's members would be to re-educate the world to understand the functions performed by the market and by free enterprise. However, Robbins' stated that it was an essential principle of a competitive society that the "freedom of contract should not be allowed to destroy freedom of contract". By this he was referring to the argument that the freedom of the powerful, in this case large corporations with monopolies, could easily interfere with the freedom of others, in this case smaller companies. Robbins then argued that what he referred to as "the people's reply to economists' recommendation of free market forces" was a claim that free enterprise tended to coagulate into monopoly. To this, Robbins suggested that the neoliberals gathered in the room ought to reply that many manifestations of monopoly had in fact been deliberately fostered by the state and that they should like these manifestations to disappear.

Chapter 2 of this book began with Mises' interventions in the socialist calculation debates, and there is no doubt that his ideas about markets were of the upmost importance for the birth of the neoliberal movement. In this session of the 1947 meeting, however, we see very clearly that the younger members of the group were desperate to move beyond Mises' laissez-faire stance and to find ways to use the power of modern states for liberal ends. Unlike the other neoliberals, Mises seemed to not see the distinction between what Hayek in *The Road to Serfdom* had called planning for competition, and planning against it (Hayek 2007, 90). The mythology surrounding Mises holds that he once stormed out of a room with other neoliberals, presumably on the ship from the US to Europe in 1947, calling them "a bunch of socialists" (Rockwell and Llewellyn 1998). The other neoliberals on the other hand, were eager to make Mises understand that theirs was not a social liberalism, and Hayek stated explicitly that income redistribution was a form of interference that did lead onto a slippery slope towards totalitarianism. Although they seemed to accept the need for some public services, the neoliberals' focus was on using states to make markets more competitive and certainly not to achieve any form of social equality. The point was to use the state to avoid power concentrations and monopolies which hampered the working of markets, but Mises again argued that all the trouble with monopoly sprang from government policy. Criticizing Mises dogmatism, Frank Graham argued that perfect freedom existed only in the jungle, where there is no law, and that if Mises' suggestions were carried out, everyone would find themselves in said jungle. Graham ventured that the people gathered at Mont Pèlerin were there to find the middle road between the jungle and the jail, something which involved very careful consideration of what government ought to do and how much it ought to do it. He further claimed that unless government took the active role to maintain competition, it would not be maintained. Thus Graham too, along with Hayek and Director, seemed to follow the ordoliberals' idea about the importance of a strong state to ensure a competitive market society. I would therefore argue that this was a central neoliberal idea, with which everyone apart from Mises and Loren Miller seemed to agree. In another defence, Mises asked rhetorically whether society should be based on public or private ownership, and declared himself in favour of private enterprise. So too were the other neoliberals, of course, but what they had been able to do was to turn Mises critique of socialism into a critique which also struck at laissez-faire liberalism. They argued that the problem with monopolies and large corporations were that they inhibited the proper workings of the market mechanism. In a sense, this was also the central problem with socialism (although they obviously held that the two were very different). Theirs was a pro-market critique of laissez-faire. Making market mechanisms the mediators of modernity enabled the neoliberals to criticize laissez-faire not for being an anti-social creed, but for corrupting the market mechanism and making society less competitive. This was not a development Mises had foreseen, and he maintained his laissez-faire views.

At the end of the discussion Aaron Director concluded that they would never get anywhere in defining what the rules of the game should be, if they did not even know whether there should be any rules at all. It was an apt summary of the first day of discussions, where the development of neoliberalism had been arrested by the man who first set the train in motion.

Primary Sources

Het Liberaal Archief, Gent, Belgium:
Mont Pelerin Society Collection

Hoover Institution Library and Archives, Stanford University, Palo Alto, California, USA:
Mont Pelerin Society Collection

Interview with Mrs. Dorothy Hahn, Cambridge, 21.12.2015.

Secondary Literature

Ban, C. (2016). *Ruling ideas—How global neoliberalism goes local*. Oxford: Oxford University Press.

Brown, W. (2015). *Undoing the Demos—Neoliberalism's stealth revolution*. Cambridge Massachusetts: Zone Books.

Burgin, A. (2012). *The great persuasion: Reinventing free markets since the depression*. Cambridge, Mass: Harvard University Press.

Caldwell, B. (2004). *Hayek's challenge: Intellectual biography of F.A. Hayek*. Chicago: University of Chicago Press.

Choi, J. Y. (2009). *The introduction of tropical flavours into British cuisine, 1850-1950*. AP European History Class: In Research Paper.

Dekker, E. (2016). *The Viennese students of civilization—The meaning and context of Austrian economics reconsidered*. Cambridge: Cambridge University Press.

Gray, J. (2015). How Friedrich Hayek became fascinated with the romance of Harriet Taylor and J S Mill. *New Statesman*, May 28.

Hayek, F. (1948). *Individualism and economic order*. Chicago: The University of Chicago Press.

Hayek, F. (1972). *The constitution of liberty*. Chicago: Gateway.

Hayek, F. (1998). *Law, legislation and liberty: A new statement of the liberal principles of justice and political economy*. London: Routledge.

Hayek, F. (2007). *The road to Serfdom—The Definitive Edition*. The University of Chicago Press.

Jones, D. S. (2012). *Masters of the universe: Hayek, Friedman, and the birth of neoliberal politics*. Princeton: Princeton University Press.

Keynes, J. M. (1965). *The general theory of employment, interest and money*. Hinsdale: Dryden Press.

Kolev, S. (2010). F.A. Hayek as an ordo-liberal. *HWWI Research Paper* 5.

Leeson, R. (2013). *Hayek: A collaborative biography—Part I: Influences, from Mises to Bartley*. New York: Palgrave Macmillan.

Mayo, P. (2011). The centrality of the state in neoliberal times: Gramsci and beyond. *International Gramsci Journal*: 57–71.

Mirowski, P. (2013). *Never let a serious crisis go to waste: How neoliberalism survived the financial meltdown*. London: Verso.

Rockwell Jr., & Llewellyn, H. (1998). Mises and liberty. In Auburn, Alabama.

Rodgers, D. T. (1998). *Atlantic crossings: Social politics in a progressive age*. Cambridge, Mass: Belknap Press of Harvard University Press.

Shapin, S. (2011). Changing tastes: How foods tasted in the Early modern period and how they taste now. In Uppsala University.

Sloan Wilson, D. (2015). The road to ideology. How Friedrich Hayek became a monster. *Evonomics*.

Spary, E. C. (2012). *Eating the enlightenment: Food and the sciences in Paris, 1670–1760*. Chicago: University of Chicago Press.

Van Horn, R. (2009). Reinventing monopoly and the role of corporations: The roots of Chicago law and economics. In *The Road from Mont Pelerin* (pp. 204–238). Cambridge Massachusetts: Harvard University Press.

Van Horn, R. (2014). Henry Simons' death. *History of political economy, 46*, 525–535.

Chapter 7
A New Europe

> ...the federation will have to possess the negative power of preventing individual states from interfering with economic activity in certain ways, although it may not have the positive power of acting in their stead. (Hayek 1948, 267).
>
> Friedrich Hayek in "The Economic Conditions for Interstate Federalism", (1939).

The next morning's sessions were opened by Cecily Wedgwood, the only female attendee of the conference. She opened by saying: "I understand that after the animated argument of last night, this morning's session is to be a cooling off process". She continued: "I do not know whether that hope, expressed yesterday evening, has anything to do with what I take to be my status at this conference". Wedgwood appeared to make reference to her being the only woman at the conference, but in elegant fashion she instead went on to discuss her status as the only *historian* at the conference, arguing: "it would be a mistake to get the idea that history cannot generate as much passion as economics. It can generate as much, or even more". Although I certainly agree with Wedgwood on a general level, this particular session on historiography was largely a forgettable one. Both Hayek and Popper had been especially critical of "historicism" in their wartime publications, and Dekker notes that for them, "historicism is not mainly associated with the German historical school and its aversion to theory, but rather to the Hegelian tradition of universal historical laws". It was "the prophetic character" (Dekker 2016, 139) of Marxism and other forms of socialism that was feared by the neoliberals, and so the session on historiography had little to do with previous concerns of Austrian economics and their famous *Methodenstreit* with the German historical school (Caldwell 2004, 64–83). The introductions by Wedgwood and Carlo Antoni instead focused on how to fight what they perceived as the growing trend of fatalism, and the notion that economic planning and socialism were inevitable historical developments. The following discussion included a debate regarding whether there was such a thing as a market for

O. Innset, *Reinventing Liberalism*, Springer Studies in the History of Economic Thought,
https://doi.org/10.1007/978-3-030-38885-0_7

historical narratives, and what liberal historians might do to gain more traction for their (correct, it was assumed) version of history.[1]

This once again points to the interesting interplay between past, present and future in the ideological work carried out by the early neoliberals in their historical context. The reason for choosing "A New Europe" as the title of this chapter is to draw attention to the social, political and geopolitical concerns of the particular moment in time in which neoliberalism was first institutionalized. The years following the cataclysmic Second World War were a time of great misery, but also of great optimism and vision for the future. The neoliberals had visions too, and these visions rested on their conceptualization of markets as mediators of modernity, analysed in Part I, and on their corresponding belief that states had to be put to use to create the modern market society, discussed in the previous chapter. The epigraph to this chapter is taken from Hayek's 1939 essay "The Economic Conditions for Interstate Federalism", in which he argued that federations could be used to limit the extent of economic planning in a modern world post empire, dominated by independent nation states. In *The Road to Serfdom*, he had argued that economic planning presupposed the existence of a complete ethical code that all people could ascribe to, the existence of which was an impossibility in a diverse, modern world. His essay on federalism argued in a similar fashion that economic planning was only possible under conditions of "the comparative homogeneity, the common convictions and ideals, and the whole common tradition of the people of a nation state" (Hayek 1948, 264). A federation could thus be an opportunity to curb economic planning and instigate a rule-based system in which democratically elected national governments could no longer interfere with market mechanisms. Some scholars understand neoliberalism to be a project of US domination of the rest of the world, beginning in the 1970s (Blyth 2007), at times supplemented with the introduction of the United Kingdom as an additional national subject with some agency in the "transatlantic project" of neoliberalization (Jones 2012). In contrast to this interpretation, other scholars challenge both the periodization and the geographical limitation of this narrative. Pierre Dardot and Christian Laval, for instance, are eager to show that neoliberalism does not only have European roots, but that the political organization of post-war Europe is far from the reverse image of neoliberalism that we are sometimes lead to believe (Dardot and Laval 2013).

The degree to which the European integration project is neoliberal, and if so for how long this has been the case, has been the subject of much recent debate (Streeck 2011; Biebricher 2015). It is not an issue this book to address directly, but I hope this chapter can contribute to a broadened understanding of neoliberalism as something more than an Anglo-American policy programme put into place from the 1970s and onwards. The main focus of this chapter will thus be the context of post-war Europe, with important issues such as the beginning of the Cold War and the process of denazification in Germany. I will pay special attention to the conference sessions entitled "The Future of Germany" and "The Problems and Chances of European Federation", and also the neoliberals' excursions. Their visits to the liberal haven

[1] Liberaal Archief, Mont Pelerin Society, Box 1, Folder 1: "Mont Pèlerin, 1947".

of Chateau de Coppet and the birthplace of Swiss federalism will tell us something about how their visions for Europe's future were influenced by past liberal thinkers, the history of Switzerland and a wish to unite liberalism with Christianity. Although they wanted a new liberalism, it is clear that tradition and a conservative approach to social order also played an important part in early neoliberalism (Cooper 2017). I will argue at the end of the chapter that the early neoliberals' theory of modernity in this respect shares some similarities with the desire of fascism to create a modernity based on tradition and hierarchies (Griffin 2007).

Post-war

The end of the Second World War is merely 70 years ago. It was a cataclysmic event that profoundly changed the world as a whole, and Europe in particular. Some of this is attempted captured in Tony Judt's history of Europe since 1945, which is entitled simply *Postwar* (2005). So much of what has happened in the second half of the twentieth century needs to be seen in relation to this enormously destructive event, which killed some 60 million people, left 50 million homeless (Kershaw 2016, 471) and changed the balance of world power forever. In *Goodbye To All* That, Dan Stone writes that "memory of the Second World War is the key to understanding European affairs since 1945" (Stone 2014, xi). The Second World War is what lies between the early beginnings of the neoliberal group, as described in Part I, and the founding meeting of their lasting organization, which is described in this part of the book. Stone further claims that "in order to understand the post-war years one needs to know not just what happened ('event history'), but what people at each point in time thought about what had happened in the past (…)" (Stone 2014, x). This is highly relevant for the present investigation, because the question we are grappling with is not only how the war may have changed neoliberal ideas, but also how neoliberals would use the memory of the war to advance ideas they had held also before the war took place.

Nothing was ever the same after 1945, especially with regard to the main topic of this book and indeed of the first meeting of the Mont Pèlerin Society: the role of the state in modern social life. The historiography of this period describes the rise of welfare states in both Europe and the US. The Scandinavian welfare states are famous, and so are those of France, Italy and the Benelux countries. Germany built its own version of this, based less on Keynesian ideas about macroeconomic policy, and more on compromises between powerful ordoliberal policymakers and the German unions (Allen 1989). John Ruggie has famously called the era one of "embedded liberalism" (Ruggie 1982), alluding to the role that liberalism and capitalism played in a history that is sometimes construed as purely social democratic. According to Tony Judt, "it was in Britain that the most ambitious efforts were made to build from scratch a genuine 'Welfare State'" (Judt 2005, 74), but various piecemeal welfare provisions were turned into full-blown redistributive welfare states all over Europe at this time. Variations on the phrase "the war changed everything" (Judt 2005, 73) are commonplace in the historiography covering the rise of these. To an economist and economic historian like Thomas Piketty, the post-war years were *les trentes glorieuses* of democratic capitalism (Piketty 2014), but I follow Timothy Shenk's insistence that "even capitalism's golden age was mixed with baser metals" (Shenk 2013). The time in which the welfare states were first implemented also holds the key to understanding what can be seen in the present as their demise and undoing. "The Second World War transformed both the role of the modern state and the expectations placed upon it", writes Judt (Judt 2005, 73). But there were already forces at work in the interwar years, resisting this newfound "faith in the state", and plotting for this transformation to be something quite different from the post-war welfare state, and perhaps something closer to our current impasse.

The Beginning of the Cold War

1947 was a year of crisis in Europe. A few days after the Mont Pèlerin conference opened, France's minister of National Economy, André Phillipe, stated bluntly: "We are threatened with total economic and financial catastrophe" (Judt 2005, 94). Some parts of France had bread rationing and large strikes erupted at Renault factories, prompting fears of a Communist takeover (Evans and Godin 2005). Agricultural production in Europe had been nearly halved during the war (Kershaw 2016, 470), and malnutrition was still widespread some two years after its end. On top of all this, the winter of 1947 had been the worst since 1880, and all countries except Switzerland and Sweden suffered from food shortages. In Germany there was no functioning currency, and cigarettes were the accepted medium of exchange (Judt 2005, 86). In this atmosphere of crisis and despair, the burgeoning Acton-Tocqueville Society was far from being the only Euro-American cooperation project. By the spring of 1947, "Washington's bilateral approaches to Europe's economic troubles had manifestly failed" (Judt 2005, 91), and by June the same year, secretary of state George Marshall would launch his famous European Recovery Programme, later to be called the Marshall Plan. Dan Stone calls this the moment when the Cold War began in earnest (Stone 2014, 30). According to Judt too, 1947 was a major turning point for Europe, the beginning of prosperous years to come. All this, however, was far from obvious at the time.

As many as thirteen of the thirty-seven attendees at the conference were US nationals (see Fig. 5.1), and sixteen of the participants, that is almost half of them, were based in the US and had to travel what was then an exceptionally long way to get to Mont Pèlerin. 1947 was also the year in which the Norwegian explorer Thor Heyerdahl took 101 days crossing the Pacific Ocean on his Kon-Tiki raft. The voyage across the Atlantic Ocean on a steamship was certainly not as slow as that, but it did take up to four days. Of the American-based attendees, nine were located in the East Coast area, four in the Midwest and one on the West Coast.[2] With the sea journey itself lasting at least four days, it is reasonable to assume that if the US-based attendees travelled by ship, like Keynes did when he participated in the Bretton Woods conference in 1944 and read *The Road to Serfdom*, they would have had to leave their homes at least a week prior to April 1. Thus they were sure to have heard the news of President Harry S. Truman's recent speech to a joint session of Congress in Washington DC on March 12, in which he laid out what was later to be called "The Truman Doctrine". Together with the Marshall Plan, it signalled the beginning of a new geopolitical era.

The pretext for Truman's speech had been the burgeoning civil war in Greece, and a Great Britain verging on bankruptcy that had officially asked the US to take over its responsibilities in the Aegean region (Hobsbawm 2000, 229). In his speech, President Truman asserted that the USA would help "democracies" all over the world to "maintain their free institutions and national integrity against aggressive movements that seek to impose on them totalitarian regimes" (Gleason 1995, 265). This was obviously a reference to the Soviet Union, because relations between the world's new superpowers had been steadily deteriorating for some time. Just months earlier, the Soviet Union had announced, much to the surprise of the USA, that it would not be joining the Bretton Woods institutions, which had been conceived at the conference in 1944 and included the International Monetary Fund and the World Bank (Judt 2005, 108). Later the same year, a council of foreign ministers held in New York had failed to agree a German peace treaty, and tensions were mounting (Stone 2014, 29). The Cold War was about to begin, and the concept of totalitarianism was right at the heart of it. Tony Judt has been one of many to claim that "The years 1941–45 had just been an interlude in an international struggle between Western democracies and Soviet totalitarianism" (Judt 2005, 104). But "Soviet totalitarianism" was not really the totalitarianism that the attendees of the first meeting of the Mont Pelerin Society were worried about. The totalitarian threat they feared the most was not an external, but an internal threat to western democracies if they did not abandon "economic planning".

The remaining twenty-one attendees of the conference all arrived from various locations in a Europe shattered by war. The UK-based attendees travelled by ship to the continent, and then by train overland. It is likely that they travelled through France, which was now one of the occupying powers of Germany. The French occupation zone consisted of the historically and economically very important Ruhr area, and the French disagreed with the other Allied nations over how to handle the occupation. There were accusations that France was obstructing reconstruction efforts in order to wind down Germany into several smaller states. However, these tensions within the Allied Control Council were of little importance compared to those between the Soviet Union and the three other countries. Just a few months before the Mont Pèlerin conference started, on 1 January 1947, USA and Great Britain had joined

[2]Most of this information this is based on is acquired from Hoover Archives, Mont Pelerin Society Collection, Box 1, Folder 1: "Booklets".

their zones together into the bizone, and the Allied Control Council was considered more or less defunct.

The Post-war Right

The contested retrospective distribution of blame and honour for the events that took place during Second World War has quite recently become the subject of renewed historical enquiry (Priemel 2016). Our understanding of neoliberalism has much to gain from these new perspectives on the political nature of history-writing in the post-war years. The painstaking efforts made by post-war European nation states to draw clear lines between heroes and villains during the preceding upheaval have been charted by Tony Judt, who remarks that this was an impossible task after such a long and all-encompassing war, which included so many other conflicts within it. This problem was not only confined to Germany, but included issues of collaboration all over Europe. "Having assigned the blame for the recent past, and punished those whose cases were the most egregious or psychologically satisfying, the majority of people in the lands recently occupied by Germany were more interested in putting uncomfortable memories behind them and getting on with their fractured lives", Judt writes (Judt 2005, 52). It was of the utmost importance for the neoliberal movement to be able to portray themselves as active resistors of Nazism and fascism. After all, they had argued that fascist dictatorship would be the dreaded endpoint of societies *not* following their advice on economic planning. The various European countries all had different experiences of war, occupation, neutrality and collaboration. Carl Iversen from Denmark, Herbert Tingsten from Sweden and Trygve Hoff from Norway represented a Scandinavian country each. Of these, Sweden had claimed neutrality and Denmark and Norway had been occupied. In the latter country, Hoff's liberal journal *Farmand* later claimed to have been one of the first media outlets to be banned by the Nazi occupation regime (Nordbakken 2017, 139). Italy and Belgium also had one representative each at the conference, Carlo Antoni and Henri de Lovinfosse, respectively. Of these, Belgium had been occupied, whereas Italy had originally formed part of the Axis forces, only to switch sides towards the end of the war after the allied invasion and the toppling of Benito Mussolini. Germany had four representatives, including Brandt and Eyck who travelled from the US and the UK, and of course Wilhelm Röpke and Walter Eucken. Of these, it was only Eucken who had lived in Germany during the war, and as described in Chap. 4, despite being able to reinvent themselves as anti-totalitarians, the ordoliberals of the Freiburg School had indeed been working with the Nazi authorities on designing economic policies during the war (Ptak 2009). Figures like Gustav Schmölders (Priemel 2016, 387), Alfred Müller-Armack and Heinrich von Stackelberg had indeed been active Nazis (Tribe 1995).

The five exiled Austrians—Machlup, Popper, Hayek, Mises and Polanyi—together made up the second largest national contingent (Stone 2014, 45). We saw in Chap. 3 how Ludwig von Mises initially praised fascism, but was later forced to leave Vienna for a post at Rappard's Graduate Institute in Geneva and then to make way for the US via Spain and Portugal around the time of the outbreak of war (Hülsmann 2007, 753–757). In Austria, a law was passed in 1947 which distinguished between more and less incriminated Nazis, and gave the latter category, some 500,000 people, amnesty. By 1956, the former group, some 42,000 people, would also be given amnesty, and Judt remarks that "After that, Austrians simply forgot about their involvement with Hitler altogether" (Judt 2005, 51–52). Stone has called the attempted settling of accounts from the war years "a process that involved not asking too many questions about precisely who had done what or suffered what during the war years".

For obvious reasons, Germany was in a special position, and in 1947, the Allied powers were, rather unsuccessfully, attempting to carry out so-called "denazification programmes". The Nuremberg trials had finished some five months before the conference at Mont Pèlerin, during which Konrad Adenauer, the future chancellor, had spoken out against them, claiming that Nazi fellow travellers had to be left in peace and that "Denazification was lasting much too long and doing no good" (Judt 2005, 53). Both in the Allied and in the Soviet occupation zones, denazification remained a shallow process, as it was simply not practically possible. Both the population and the leaders were too deeply embedded in the crimes of the past for a complete purge to be feasible. At the end of it all, "the search for serviceable myths of anti-Fascism—for a Germany of anti-Nazis, a France of Resisters or a Poland of victims—was the most important invisible legacy of World War Two in Europe". According to Judt: "Without such collective amnesia, Europe's astonishing post-war recovery would not have been possible" (Judt 2005, 61). The birth of neoliberalism as an anti-totalitarian creed is part of this myth. And as we will see, the men gathered at Mont Pélerin strongly implied that the horrors of World War II were due to the things they had been fighting all along: "economic planning" and "collectivism".

If the German members of the neoliberal movement, even those with ties to the Nazi administration, were able to fall down on the right side of history when judgement was passed in post-war Europe, this was not the case with Louis Rougier. Although he was responsible for the Walter Lippmann Colloquium and a key organizer of the nascent movement, he was not invited to the Mont Pèlerin conference at all. Instead, he was ousted from the neoliberal thought collective due to his connections to the Vichy regime, described in greater detail in Chap. 4. Curiously, no such fate befell his fellow national, Bertrand de Jouvenel, a former fascist sympathizer who had taken up residency in Switzerland, and who made up the French delegation along with Maurice Allais and Francois Trevoux. Indeed, the ordoliberals were not the only neoliberals whose sympathies during the war had been less impressive than certain hagiographic accounts of the Mont Pelerin Society would suggest (Hartwell 1995; Nordbakken 2017). Jouvenel had been the editor of *L'Émancipation nationale*, the journal of *Partie Populaire Français*, France's fascist party (Kestel 2007). Fascism has traditionally been construed as fundamentally anti-liberal, but there were also points of great convergence between some variants of fascism and neoliberalism, notably with regard to the question of democracy. In an intense and revealing correspondence from 1944, to which we will return, Wilhelm Röpke and Bertrand de Jouvenel found each other in mutual distrust of democracy and a longing for an elite of enlightened aristocrats (Knegt 2015, 219–226). In 1944, an enthusiastic reviewer in *Economic Journal* wrote about Wilhelm Röpke's book *Civitas Humana* of the same year: "He asks us to put away 'democratic prudery' and acknowledge frankly that not only private property, but also unequal property, is a pre-requisite to moral civilised living" (White 1950). As described in Part I, early neoliberalism was in many ways defined by this distrust of popular democracy. In their reinvention of previous liberal critiques of democracy and universal suffrage, it was argued that the rise to prominence of mass politics was what lay behind the turn towards economic planning and subsequent totalitarian dictatorships. The fascist past had severely discredited Europe's political right, however, and this is an important backdrop for the Mont Pèlerin conference. In some ways, it was not possible to be much further to the right than the neoliberals in 1947, and neoliberalism should be understood as a thoroughly right-wing appropriation of liberalism.

I noted in Chap. 3 that the Lippmann Colloquium was not only the first conference of neoliberalism, but also its most social liberal moment. Although they spoke up against social liberalism and claimed state interference led to totalitarianism, many of the men gathered at the Lippmann Colloquium also seemed to take social questions more seriously than what was the case at Mont Pèlerin in 1947. Although it lost to "neoliberalism", "left-wing liberalism" was in fact one of the suggested names discarded at the colloquium (Jones 2012, 35). The subsequent rightward turn of early neoliberalism might have been what led to the absence in 1947 of yet another key figure of the Lippmann Colloquium, Walter Lippmann himself. He was listed as a founding member of the society, but never attended any of the conferences. Before becoming a critic of Roosevelt's New Deal programme, Lippmann had been considered a progressive liberal, and at the outbreak of world war, Lippmann's politics had changed once again (Lippmann 1997, introduction). Already on 28 October 1938, a few weeks after Edvard Beneš resignation as president of Czechoslovakia following Germany's invasion, Lippmann wrote in a letter to Rougier: "In many ways I feel that the immediate problem in Europe is no longer how to save liberty, but how to save the national independence of the people who would like to preserve their liberty. It may be that to preserve their independence they may have to sacrifice for the time being much of their liberty".[3] Lippmann proceeded to break off contact with most of the neoliberals, and his change of attitude towards the movement whose first meeting was named after him is summed up in a short reply to Hayek many years later, on 2 January 1960. The latter had sent Lippmann the manuscript for his *The Constitution of Liberty* on 18 December 1959, writing:

> It is the final outcome of many years of thought on the principles of a free society – indeed of a trend of thought which may be said to have started twenty-two years ago when I read

[3]Yale University Library, Walter Lippmann papers, Selected correspondence 1931–1974, Folder 1848: Louis Rougier.

> The Good Society. I have put into this volume everything I have on the subject and I rather hope that the argument will appeal to you.[4]

Lippmann wrote back that he had not read it, but:

> I have, however, been browsing in it and I am puzzled to find that you have one reference to corporations and nineteen to labor unions. Does this mean that the index is at fault or can it mean that you believe the corporation and its problems rates less than a page in a treatise of this kind? I should really like to know before I read the book what you say about this.[5]

As far as we know there was never any answer to this letter, as Hayek must have taken the hint and realized that Lippmann's mildly progressive politics were no longer compatible with neoliberalism. Instead, he would be remembered by biographer Crauford Goodwin as a "life-long Keynesian" (Goodwin 2014, 51).

The Future of Germany

Cold War issues like the Truman doctrine and the Marshall Plan, and the many attempts to deal with the recent past in a variety of national contexts through denazification and similar processes, were the backdrop of the session dedicated to "The Future of Germany". Introductions were held by Wilhelm Röpke and Walter Eucken. Röpke was the first speaker and declared that the problem of Europe was Germany, and that the problem of the world was Europe. The man who in a recent paper had rallied against "the war on luxuries" still insisted that the problem had to be seen in terms of the most elementary needs, and added: "We may therefore be forced to define liberalism, for Germany, purely as being the state of non-totalitarianism".[6] Röpke then continued with a reference to US Secretary of State James Byrnes' famous "Stuttgart speech" held a year and a half earlier in September 1946. The speech was entitled "Restatement of Policy on Germany", and was notable mainly due to the signal being sent to Moscow regarding continued US military presence in Europe. A second goal was to prevent desperate Germans from turning to communism, and the speech also signalled the replacement of previous economic policies in the US-occupied areas, known as the Morgenthau plan. The new policies put in its place were meant to indicate a change of policy towards economic *reconstruction*, but Röpke claimed it had not brought about the expected results, and that this was partly due to the merger of the American and British occupation zones, which had taken place only three months earlier. Röpke made reference to the last of four Moscow Conferences, which was held between Byrnes and his counterparts Bevin

---

[4]Yale University Library, Walter Lippmann papers, Selected correspondence 1931–1974, Box 10, Folder 11: Hayek.

[5]Yale University Library, Walter Lippmann papers, Selected correspondence 1931–1974, Box 10, Folder 11: Hayek.

[6]There is no manuscript for Röpke's introduction, so again I will paraphrase his remarks based on the minutes kept by Mrs. Hahn. Liberaal Archief, Mont Pelerin Society, Box 1, Folder 1: "Mont Pèlerin 1947".

and Molotov in the Christmas of 1945, and claimed there was a danger it was "just one big red herring". He did not elaborate on this, but according to the memoirs of George Kennan, an American diplomat who was present at the Moscow conferences, Byrne cared only about the political effect of the peace treaty "at home". Kennan later wrote: "The Russians know this. They will see that for this superficial success he pays a heavy price in the things that are real" (Kennan 1967, 267–268).

According to Röpke, the cost of reviving the German economy was "increasing in geometrical progression". If Germany was allowed to produce, Röpke thought the situation would be much better, "but without industrial Germany being allowed to produce, the situation is disastrous". Röpke thought that Western Germany would have no further problems if it was allowed to produce, but that the question was whether to re-integrate Western Germany with the Eastern zones controlled by the Russians: "Is it necessary or not. My answer is that it is not necessary". Röpke argued that Germany would still need help for a long time, but that "this help should now be put on a sound basis". For Röpke this meant "Drastic monetary reform, in the form of a drastic deflation".

The floor was then given to Walter Eucken who was to focus even more on economic theory, and stated that he saw his introduction as a supplement to Röpke's remarks. "It was very surprising that the occupation did not mean the end of the Nazi system", he said, referring not to the unsuccessful denazification process, but instead to the first part of the dual argument: the notion that Nazism first and foremost had to do with economic planning. According to Eucken, the Nazi's price and production system "was preserved in all detail and with only little change in personnel". The only change was the division into zones, and Eucken argued that the present development showed how a planned economy of the separate states was so inefficient that it decayed. According to him, the rations were so small that "nobody, literally nobody" could live on them. In consequence, side by side with the planned economy, a separate unofficial economic structure was growing up. According to Eucken this separate economy had three main features: the general growth of barter, the use of products like brandy or cigarettes as money, and the home production of potatoes and vegetables. He argued that "the German economy is undergoing a progressive primitivisation [sic] and now corresponds rather to the economic system of the 6th and 8th centuries". Eucken claimed that there was full employment and that an enormous amount of work was being done, but with very little result. He referred to a meeting he had had with the before-mentioned Lord Beveridge, who had been active in British wartime planning. Eucken had told him about the low productivity of the barter economy, where a "thousand people thus achieve in a day what a single trader could do in a few hours".

Eucken then paraphrased Lenin by asking: "What is to be done? The planned economy is evidently collapsing", he concluded, and the "only hope is to restore the market economy". Like Röpke he advocated currency reform, since according to him, there could be "no division of labour without a functioning currency system". The new money had to be linked up with foreign currencies, so that credit from abroad could be made available. Eucken did concede that a new currency would bring steep rises in the prices of agricultural products, something which would lead to starvation. Still he stated unequivocally: "I believe prices must be allowed to rise but only if at the same time a free market and international trade are resumed. This is admittedly a risky policy". A market economy had to be constructed, even if it lead to starvation. Eucken finally referred to a "small point of difference from Röpke", relating the issues of the Eastern zone: "it is very important, politically and economically, that the East not be written off or abandoned for good", he said. Eucken's final words are worth quoting at length (Mrs. Hahn's transcription appears to be accurate), both because of the interesting invocation of classical economic theory, but also for the degree to which Eucken's sentiments were to be repeated in George Marshall's groundbreaking speech at Harvard University when launching the Marshall plan only two months later:

> The classical economists regarded it as a weakness of the individual that he does not always regard his true interests. They do not recognise their common interest of regaining Germany to the Western system. The present tendency to keep Germany going for charitable reasons is very unhealthy. The Western powers ought to act on their own self-interest. That presupposes however that German industry is allowed to do something on its own initiative. And that she should not be dependent for everything on permits. At the moment Germany is half a corpse.[7]

It was precisely the realization that an economically strong (albeit militarily weak) Germany (and Europe) was in the best interest of the US that lay behind the Marshall plan. It is a widely held view that this was a lesson learned from the Versailles process after World War I, and that it helped the international community avoid a third outbreak of war in Europe. More importantly for the development of neoliberalism was Eucken's insistence that Germany's problems were due to economic planning and the lack of functioning market mechanisms. Keith Tribe has claimed that the "bleak picture" painted by ordoliberals of the rise of a barter economy in Germany was "at best partial, at worst wildly exaggerated". According to him, "There were certainly shortages of food and energy, but this cannot be directly blamed on the absence of a proper market mechanism; it was instead linked to the general problems of resource allocation in Europe and the politics of occupation and reconstruction" (Tribe 1995, 234). Eucken thus presented a rather partial theory of what the problems in Germany really were, based on his deeply held belief that market mechanisms were the only possible foundations for a modern society. Based on this neoliberal belief, the horrors of Nazism and the subsequent descent of Germany into poverty and disarray were blamed on economic policies that interfered with the market mechanism.

Discussion

The ensuing discussion was opened by Karl Brandt, a German economist exiled to Stanford University. He began his lengthy intervention by stating that "If we were to go in to Germany, we would all be shocked at what we saw". Brandt did not refer

[7]Liberaal Archief, Mont Pelerin Society, Box 1, Folder 1: "Mont Pèlerin, 1947".

to human misery, but instead to the "Decay of the liberal economy in which we are all interested". In the neoliberal view, the most shocking thing about post-war Germany was the lack of market mechanisms. Brandt spoke of the influx of people being repatriated bringing "nothing in the way of material goods. Only disease". He estimated it would take eight to ten years to replace lost capital equipment and, echoing Keynes' *The Economic Consequences of the* Peace, he argued that it was now important to prevent a recurrence of war due to the public sentiment "still smouldering in those parts of the world". The German calorie consumption had fallen from 3000 to 1000 calories per head and Brandt claimed that "The catastrophe which has befallen the industrial country of Germany has no equal whatever in history". He then referred to the denazification process, but claimed it was instead leading to a renazification. The tribunals were very slow, he claimed, saying that "Germans talk of 'Hitler's 1000 years' Reich, 14 years of Nazism, 986 years of denazification". At that rate you would never get rid of the Nazis, said Barth, their children would suffer, and the result would be a hatred of the Allies and their methods. Barth suggested giving amnesties, possibly levying an extra tax on those who did not have to pass through the tribunals. Speaking of the currency question, Barth disagreed with Eucken, saying that Germany also needed food, textiles and raw materials. He finished by asking Eucken what he thought was the right time for the removal of price controls, a move we now know happened only months later, on explicit advice from Röpke and Eucken.

Lionel Robbins, who had been central in the British war effort, then took a more moderate stand than his German colleagues, and defended price controls and rationing in Britain. He said inflation had been on the way when they were put into place, and that they could not be removed at that time. Brandt agreed, and said that establishing a "free price market system" in Germany would lead to starvation. Milton Friedman and George Stigler made some theoretical comments, and after an unclear intervention by Hayek, Eucken then re-entered the discussion and claimed that the central problem was the effect of production, which had no direction and therefore did not produce a fix amount of goods to distribute. He restated his claim that the lack of a free market economy lead to a most senseless use of resources and to an intense misdirection, a central point from the socialist calculation debates. Milton Friedman again made a highly theoretical comment, reporting that he thought it a fallacy for a free market to be something that rich nations could afford and poor nations had to do without. Rappard, on the other hand, argued that if the reports of food shortages were true, then "liberalism should not be prejudiced by trying to establish a free market economy".

In summary, we may say that the discussion offers a fascinating glimpse into this moment in time, when the founders of the neoliberal movement argued about how to economically reconstruct Germany along neoliberal lines and whether or not starvation would be a logical outcome of their faith in markets; and if so whether that was to be deemed necessary. In particular, Eucken's introductory speech contained many of the ideas which would influence reconstruction in West Germany, as the ordoliberals went on to play an important role in policymaking. A great number of German ordoliberals would become members of the Mont Pelerin Society in the following years, and the historian Kim Priemel has argued that the society played an important role in rehabilitating German intellectuals to international circles in the post-war years (Priemel 2016, 387). The most prominent of these was Ludwig Erhard, who was not present but nonetheless listed as a founding member. He would go on to become finance minister of West Germany and later chancellor. Under clear guidance and advice from the ordoliberals, West Germany would begin abolishing price controls as early as 1948, the year after the conference. The news of this was delivered to the German public by Erhard with this statement: "only a state that establishes both the freedom and the responsibility of its citizens can legitimately speak in the name of the people". Michel Foucault saw this as a way in which neoliberal economic policy also played a part in absolving the German people for the sins of the Nazi state, since the ordoliberal redefinition of what gives a state legitimacy implied that the Nazi state could not be considered a legitimate state acting on behalf of its people (Foucault 2008, 80).

In redefining the legitimate role of states, the ordoliberals were thus engaged not only in economic policymaking *per se*, but in the complex process of dealing with the Nazi past. Röpke's statement that liberalism in Germany could be defined purely as the state of non-totalitarianism speaks volumes about the complex processes of reinvention involved in making neoliberalism the opposite of "totalitarianism". The pre-war idea that economic planning was the essence of totalitarianism was still touted by Röpke, Eucken and his colleagues, and this was certainly part of the reason why German post-war economic policy was decidedly less Keynesian than that of many other European countries (Allen 1989). However, the "social" aspect of West Germany's famous *soziale Markwirtschaft* is hard to gauge from Eucken's intervention, and indeed, as Tribe has observed, from ordoliberal theorizing in general. Tribe claims that the popular post-war idea of a "social market economy" was nothing less than a "political slogan", which had very little to do with the actual theoretical work of the ordoliberals (Tribe 1995, 203–205), who had focused more on the price mechanism and often rather aggressively opposed welfare systems and popular democracy (Tribe 1995, 240). When writing of the social policies launched by the ordoliberal Alfred Müller-Armack (1901–1978), who had coined the phrase "social market economy" and later joined the Mont Pelerin Society, Tribe writes:

> The comprehensiveness of this programme of reform is no less striking than the complete absence of its discussion and elaboration by Müller-Armack himself or by any of his colleagues; discussion which might be thought necessary given the potential conflict between many of the proposals (for example that concerning a 'market-based equalisation of incomes to remove harmful differences in income and wealth') and the usual strictures on the impairment of the price mechanism. (Tribe 1995, 236)

The analysis is supported by several other scholars, who see the idea of a social market economy in post-war West Germany as something of a PR campaign. The welfare state measures introduced in West Germany could thus be seen largely as against the ideas of the ordoliberal thinkers and a result of compromise with other forces. This is an important admission, because it counters the notion that ordoliberalism and early neoliberalism was a form of social liberalism, when it was actually framed as an attack on the ideas of social liberalism.

The Problems and Chances of European Federation

Thursday, April 3rd was the third day of the conference, and unlike the previous days, only one session was scheduled: a discussion on the problems and chances of European Federation, following on from Hayek's 1939 essay on federation in general and the very fluid political situation in Europe in particular. The discussion took place in the morning and was introduced by Bertrand de Jouvenel, the aristocrat and former fascist, who was able to rebrand himself as a liberal in the years immediately after the war. As mentioned, one of the main common points between the liberals and an upper class fascist sympathizer like de Jouvenel was distrust of democracy. Another point in common was Europeanism and the goal of European federation, and the two are not completely unconnected. In *A New Order for France and Europe?* Daniel Knegt discusses the Europeanist character of the fascism of the two French intellectuals Alfred Fabre-Luce and de Jouvenel. Fabre-Luce remained on the extreme right after the war, whereas Jouvenel found a new home in the organization meeting in his newfound Swiss neighbourhood. Knegt writes:

> Thanks to his Swiss exile, Jouvenel was quickest to adapt to the new circumstances. In his influential magnum opus *Du Pouvoir*, he adopted a sceptical form of right-wing liberalism, convinced that both state power and the essentially irrational character of the masses could easily lead to tyranny. Outside France, this analysis caught the attention of neoliberal academics such as Friedrich Hayek and Wilhelm Röpke, who were equally sceptical of democratic society's potential of survival. Jouvenel was quickly integrated in these international circles and became a founding member of the neoliberal Mont Pèlerin Society in 1947. At the same time, he continued to associate himself with extreme- rightist and even royalist newspapers and reviews. (Knegt 2015, 42)

Du Pouvoir appeared in 1945, and in it, Jouvenel wrote of "totalitarian democracy" (Jouvenel 1962, 254–281) and claimed that liberty instead had "aristocratic roots" (Jouvenel 1962, 317–336). Jouvenel and Röpke apparently met for lunch at the conference venue, the Hotel du Parc, several times during and after the war, and they corresponded intensely from around 1944. The two found each other in mutual despair over the rise of mass democracy, and in a review of Röpkes *Deutsche Frage*, Jouvenel wrote: " (…) certain poisons are capable of a prodigious effect on the modern masses. Vast crowd movements can be caused, not by appealing to reason, but through a stimulation of anger and hope that truly is a demonic art". Jouvenel argued that those who were "motivated by generous intentions" and wanted to extend the state apparatus for social means should ask themselves "if they are not preparing a prodigious dungeon for other madmen" (Knegt 2015, 219). It was its anti-democratic character that attracted De Jouvenel to the neoliberal project, and Knegt writes:

> Just how much Jouvenel and Röpke agreed on the dangerous irrationality of the masses is illustrated by another long article in *Curieux* in which Jouvenel introduced Röpke's work to a French-speaking audience. Citing Röpke, Jouvenel deplored that the introduction of democracy in the nineteenth century had coincided with the decline of aristocratic individualism and the rise of the hordes. From that moment, it had become useless to 'reason with individual common sense' but one had to 'excite collective fever' instead. "Citizens want laws and magistrates, the masses want myths and heroes: they tend towards totalitarianism

> with a movement required by their nature as masses. Whoever wants to fight this has to study the phenomenon of swarming [grégarisme]. (Knegt 2015, 221)

This was indeed the same argument that Hayek and Röpke made, but it was also an echo of Benjamin Constant's writings on "modern freedom"; Gustave Le Bon's (1841–1931) writings on "mob rule"; José Ortega y Gasset's (1883–1955) writings on "the rebellion of the masses"; Tocqueville's idea of the tyranny of the majority and a whole host of liberal critiques of democracy discussed in Chaps. 1 and 3 of this book. "We have got a long way to go intellectually before we shake liberalism free from Ricardianism", wrote Jouvenel to Röpke on 28 November 1946 (Knegt 2015, 221). It is somewhat unclear what he meant by "Ricardianism", but it is clear that early neoliberals like De Jouvenel were engaged in a project to *change* liberalism.

Unfortunately, de Jouvenel did not give a manuscript for his introduction, and we are thus left with the very short opening remarks by Maurice Allais and the discussion following Jouvenel's remarks. Allais opened the proceedings by claiming it was a great error not to realize that liberalism implies an international outlook. According to Allais, federalism could not be accomplished in a single blow, and there would still be separate states for some time to come. He claimed that the main obstacle to federalism was what he referred to as "the irrational attitude" of people who themselves were federalists but assumed that other people were not. He thus seemed to think there was actual support for federalism, but inferred that it was impossible to envisage a federated system based on the existing national systems. Unlike in the USA, this was a question of fundamental difficulty for the issue of a federation in Western Europe. He claimed that the nineteenth century had been a century of growth for monopolies of power, something he claimed could not have happened if not for the growth of nationalist feeling. We see that it was also clear to Allais that powerful (democratic) nation states were a problem, and he saw this problem as connected to nationalism.

Discussion

The Belgian industrialist Henri de Lovinfosse was the first to speak in the discussion, and he ventured that two types of unions were possible, an economic union and a political one. According to him, Belgium's road was the economic one, something he thought would show the way to international development. He envisioned a European union with common laws in two phases: the first was economic and would make separate economies interdependent, and the second phase would be political. Lovinfosse considered this a practical suggestion, and in hindsight it was not very far from the actual attempted process of European integration—from economic cooperation to a steadily closer legal and political union. Allais then claimed that there were enormous difficulties involved in an economic union between industrial and agricultural states, but suggested a sort of quota system. Lovinfosse agreed that there were difficulties, especially because the monetary and capital situation of the different countries had been very badly affected by the war. He suggested that a Belgium–Holland union might be the first step and that France and Denmark might later join in—first economically, then politically. The Dane, Carl Iversen, then noted that there would be an enormous economic advantage in abolishing trade walls between the different countries, but that he did not feel convinced about insisting on a complete union for purely economic reasons. Felix Morley then suggested that there was a parallel to the development of a customs and political union in the USA. While the American colonies may have had a common language and what he, interestingly, referred to as a "common racial basis", Europe had an enormous advance in communications. According to Morley, it was all about will, and he claimed that the Americans at the meeting had more unity than the Europeans seemed to realize. Morley believed it was possible to achieve a union if the will was there, but asked "why start from the economic union and not grasp the whole nettle firmly?"

François Trevoux then said that there were two sorts of international ideas, communism and liberalism, and the weakness of liberalism lay in its lack of a mystique—a point similar to that made by Louis Rougier. Hayek then entered the debate making the key point that federalism required a transfer of power to the federal level. In that way, federalism implied a necessary restriction on the powers any of the governments can exercise. According to him, federation was only practicable in a liberal society, and he made it quite clear what he meant by "liberal" by quoting Lord Acton:

> Of all checks on democracy, federation has been the most efficacious and the most congenial.... The federal system limits and restrains the sovereign power by dividing it and by assigning to Government only certain defined rights. It is the only method of curbing not only the majority but the power of the whole people.

For Hayek, federalism was the perfect way to curb democracy and arrive at a liberal, rule-based society. This was precisely the point he had made in his 1939 essay, where he argued that the members of a diverse federation would only be able to agree on the most general of policies (Hayek 1948, 255–272). Thus the very structure of a federation could be designed to avoid democratic interference with market mechanisms, something which makes quite clear why federation and close European cooperation were so high on the neoliberal agenda. The distrust of democracy also explains why an aristocratic former fascist sympathizer like Jouvenel was attracted to a neoliberalism, which also chimed well with his pan-Europeanism. The idea of a future European federation to ensure a liberal society not hampered by popular democracy was already present in the writings of Lord Acton, and as we will see, also in the federated Swiss republic.

Exploring Roots

A new Europe was in the making, and the neoliberals wanted to influence this process. They were clear about the need for a new liberalism, but it is also clear that they built on previous forms of elitist liberalism and critiques of democracy. An interesting case in point is the choice of excursion for the afternoon of the day of the discussion on European federation. The neoliberals travelled some 75 kilometres to the Castle of Coppet, just outside Geneva.[8] The castle had once been the home of Jacques Necker, the Swiss-born finance minister to Louis XVI, and the main attraction of the castle is the tomb of Necker and his wife, whose remains have been preserved in alcohol (Berger 2000, 24; Boon 2016, 128). Another resident of the castle was Necker's daughter, Germaine de Staël, better known as Madame de Staël. She had gone into exile at Coppet as early as 1793, and in 1802, after the publication of her critical novel *Delphine*, she was officially expelled from Paris by Napoleon. She started the famous *Coppet group*, whose most famous member was Staël's lover, none other than the previously mentioned liberal critic of democracy and universal suffrage Benjamin Constant (Winegarten 2011). At the castle by the lake, the Coppet group were not only happy to enjoy the "modern liberty" as theorized by Constant, but also engaged themselves politically through discussion, writing and the shaping of political opinion in France and Germany. There were indeed lineages from this grand building along the Geneva Lake to the slightly less grand one in which the first members of the Mont Pelerin Society had gathered. Their meeting in 1947 provides a fascinating example of the many-layered, intertwined processes of history-making through history-writing. The members of the Mont Pelerin Society sought to *reinvent* liberalism and preserve western civilization and liberal ideals in a modern world. While doing so, they paid homage to those liberal thinkers who had to escape the "tyranny of the majority" in order to write their tracts on the dangers of the masses from secluded chateaus in Switzerland. It was this branch of liberalism, which condemned universal suffrage and mass democracy as dangerous perversions of the ideals of liberty, that the neoliberal economists and philosophers of 1947 sought to build on in making markets the prime mediators of modern society.

The following day was reserved for a discussion on "Liberalism and Christianity". Hayek had signalled early on that much like Röpke, he wanted to unite his new liberalism with Christian thought, and he was followed in this by the deeply religious Walter Eucken, who chaired the session. Despite wanting to create a new liberalism, these three thinkers shared a very traditional outlook and feared the rise of what Röpke called "proletarianization" (Ancil 2012). Like the Austrians, the German ordoliberals felt they were living through a crisis of civilization and were confronting "the problems of modernity" (Dekker 2016, 89). Their conservative outlook made them look to Christianity, but in the session their plans were somewhat derailed by Chicago economist Frank Knight, who struck a provocative, anti-religious note in his introduction, claiming that liberalism was scientific and that religion had proved itself to be anti-liberal. This lead to a confused discussion on the relationship between science, liberalism, socialism and religion, which ended with Eucken claiming that from his Christian viewpoint, he regarded the competitive order as essential. The theological connection between Christianity and the ordoliberal conception of a competitive order remained unclear. Eucken further claimed that the main victims

[8]London School of Economics Library and Archives, Lionel Robbins Collection, Box 10, Folder 2, "Excursions".

of the Nazi oppression had all been liberals, but at the same time Christians. In the wake of the mass extermination of Jews and also various forms of communists and social democrats undertaken by the Nazis, it is somewhat difficult to comprehend this rather stunning statement, but, as noted earlier, it was of vital importance for the German ordoliberals to present themselves as the victims of Nazi rule. Eucken's comment suggests that he truly saw things in this way, although my analysis has sketched a different picture.

The attendees used the rest of the Friday to discuss the possibility of forming a permanent organization, an ongoing discussion of the meeting that will be addressed in the next chapter. The weekend was spent on an excursion to the canton of Schwyz, some 250 km away from Mont Pèlerin.[9] This visit serves as another insight into the ways in which the neoliberals wanted a new Europe to embody some of the things they cherished the most about its past, namely, Christianity and Swiss federalism. The canton is named after the town of Schwyz, and together with Uri and Unterwalden it was one of the founding cantons of Switzerland. In fact, the federation's German name, *Die Schweitz*, is derived from Schwyz, and the famous Swiss flag is modelled after its coat of arms. The canton held a leading role in the unification, and the Swiss Federal Charter from 1291, the *Bundesbrief*, had been on display in the Bundesbrief museum since 1936 (Landoldt 2017). Yet again, it was a fitting destination for the neoliberals, both in light of the fetishizing of Switzerland as a liberal Utopia that especially Röpke, Rappard and to a certain extent Hayek were responsible for, but also in light of their discussions on federation as a means of keeping democracy in check and stopping centralized economic planning and redistribution. The attendees travelled by train and stayed overnight. They also visited the famous abbey of Einsiedeln, north-west of the town of Schwyz. It was the day before Easter Sunday, and the conference attendees took part in a famous resurrection ritual and listened to choral and organ music.[10] In light of the proclaimed desire by the ordoliberals, Hayek and people like Frank Graham, that liberalism needed to ally itself with Christianity, this too seems perfectly apt. In Hayek's planning of the sessions and Hunold's planning of their setting, little was left to coincidence.

The question of a new Europe was very much the backdrop of the first meeting of the Mont Pelerin Society. Part I and the previous two chapters have shown that their main ideas were embodied in the dual argument, and the quest to find a new liberalism where state intervention was used not to redistribute wealth or cure capitalism's ills, but rather to make markets more competitive. In this chapter, we have seen that neoliberal ideas about the future of Europe also included ideas of a federation to curb the powers of popular democracy, and a desire to unite their creed with Christianity. The degree to which the early neoliberals were grappling with the issues posed by the rise of mass democracy and modernity is clear. Scholars who see fascism as a phenomenon related to modernism claim that it included a desire to

[9]London School of Economics Library and Archives, Lionel Robbins Collection, Box 10, Folder 2, "Excursions".

[10]London School of Economics Library and Archives, Lionel Robbins Collection, Box 10, Folder 2, "Excursions".

channel the energies of modernity into paths defined by tradition. Like socialism and communism, fascism was a modern creed for a "brave new world", but it was also one explicitly wanting to maintain or reinstate traditional forms of hierarchies (Griffin 2007). The neoliberals' appeals to Christianity and property show that they were engaged in a parallel project, fuelled by a similar animosity towards socialism, and a similar recognition that things would have to change in a modern world. Fascism offered corporatism and submission to strong leaders as a non-socialist solution to the problems of modernity, whereas neoliberalism favoured market mechanisms and a strong state charged with their protection and maintenance. These are very different, non-socialist solutions, and I am in no way claiming that fascism and neoliberalism are the same thing. The two did, however, arise from the same context, and the analysis of this chapter, along with that of Chap. 3, has shown that some of the analysis on which they rested is more similar than what is suggested by the binary opposition between liberalism and "totalitarianism" that we are sometimes offered.

Primary Sources

Hoover Institution Library and Archives, Stanford University, Palo Alto, California, USA:
Mont Pelerin Society Collection

Yale University Library, New Haven, Connecticut, USA:
Walter Lippmann Collection

Het Liberaal Archief, Gent, Belgium
Mont Pelerin Society Collection

London School of Economics Special Collections, London, UK:
Lionel Robbins Collection

Secondary Literature

Allen, P. S. (1989). The Underdevelopment of Keynesianism in the Federal Republic of Germany. In *The Political Power of Economic Ideas—Keynesianism Across Nations*, 263–291. New Jersey, United States: Princeton University Press.

Ancil, R. (2012). Roepke and the restoration of property: The proletarianized market. *The Imaginative Conservative*, October 9.

Berger, M. (Ed.). (2000). *Germaine de Staël—politics, literature and national character*. New Jersey: Transaction Publishers.

Biebricher, T. (2015). Neoliberalism and democracy. *Constellations, 22,* 255–266.

Blyth, M. (2007). One ring to bind them all: American power and neoliberal capitalism. In *Growing Apart? America and Europe in the 21st Century*, 109–135. Cambridge: Cambridge University Press.

Boon, S. (2016). *The life of madame necker*. New York: Routledge.

Caldwell, B. (2004). *Hayek's challenge: Intellectual biography of F.A. Hayek*. Chicago: University of Chicago Press.

Cooper, M. (2017). *Family values—between neoliberalism and the new social conservatism*. Brooklyn, NY: Zone Books.

Dardot, P., & Laval, C. (2013). *The new way of the world: On neoliberal society*. Brooklyn, NY: Verso.

Dekker, E. (2016). *The viennese students of civilization—The meaning and context of austrian economics reconsidered*. Cambridge: Cambridge University Press.

Evans, M., & Godin, E. (2005). The great fear of 1947: Could France have gone communist? *History Today* 55.

Foucault, M. (2008). *The Birth of Biopolitics: Lectures at the Collège de France, 1978–79*. New York: Palgrave Macmillan.

Gleason, A. (1995). *Totalitarianism: The inner history of the cold war*. New York: Oxford University Press.

Goodwin, C. D. (2014). *Walter lippman: Public economist*. Cambridge Massachusetts: Harvard University Press.

Griffin, R. (2007). *Modernism and fascism—The sense of a beginning under mussolini and hitler*. London: Palgrave Macmillan.

Hartwell, R. M. (1995). *A history of the mont pelerin society*. Indianapolis: Liberty Fund.

Hayek, F. (1948). *Individualism and economic order*. Chicago: The University of Chicago Press.

Hobsbawm, E. J. (2000). *The age of extremes: A history of the world, 1914–1991*. Incorporated: Peter Smith Publisher.

Hülsmann, J. G. (2007). *Mises: The last knight of liberalism*. Auburn, Alabama: Ludwig von Mises Institute.

Jones, D. S. (2012). *Masters of the universe: Hayek, Friedman, and the birth of neoliberal politics*. Princeton: Princeton University Press.

de Jouvenel, B. (1962). *On power*. Boston: Beacon Press.

Judt, T. (2005). *Postwar—A history of europe since 1945*. London: Vintage Books.

Kennan, G. (1967). *Memoirs 1925–1950*. Boston: Little Brown.

Kershaw, I. (2016). *To hell and back—Europe 1914–1949*. New York: Viking.

Kestel, L. (2007). L'engagement de Bertrand de Jouvenel au PPF de 1936 à 1939, intellectuel de parti et entrepreneur politique. *French Historical Studies*, 105–125.

Knegt, D. F. (2015). *A New Order for France and Europe? Bertrand de Jouvenel and Alfred Fabre-Luce between Liberalism, Fascism and Europeanism (1930–1954)*. Florence: European Unviersity Institute.

Landoldt, O. (2017). Schwyz (Kanton). *Historisches Lexicon der Schweiz*. Bern: HLS.

Lippmann, W. (1997). *Public opinion*. New York: Simon & Schuster.

Nordbakken, L. P. (2017). *Liberale tenkere for vår tid*. Oslo: Civita.

Piketty, T. (2014). *Capital in the twenty-first century: The dynamics of inequality, wealth, and growth*. Cambridge Massachusetts: The Belknap Press of Harvard University Press.

Priemel, K. C. (2016). *The betrayal—the Nuremberg trials and german divergence*. Oxford: Oxford University Press.

Ptak, R. (2009). Neoliberalism in Germany: Revisiting the Ordoliberal foundations of the social market economy. In *The Road from Mont Pelerin*, 98–139. Cambridge Massachusetts: Harvard University Press.

Ruggie, J. (1982). International regimes, transactions, and change: Embedded liberalism in the postwar economic order. *International Organization, 36,* 379–415.

Shenk, T. (2013). The Long Shadow of Mont Pèlerin. *Dissent Magazine*.

Stone, D. (2014). *Goodbye to all that?—the story of Europe since 1945*. Oxford: Oxford University Press.

Streeck, W. (2011). The crises of democratic capitalism. *New Left Review., II,* 5–29.

Tribe, K. (1995). *Strategies of economic order—german economic discourse, 1750–1950*. Cambridge: Cambridge University Press.
White, R. J. (1950). Review. *The Economic Journal, 60*, 575–577.
Winegarten, R. (2011). *Germaine de Staël & Benjamin Constant—A Dual Biography*. New Haven and London: Yale University Press.

Chapter 8
The Second Week

"PROFESSOR BRANDT: The Mont Pelerin Society?

Dr. POPPER: That is meaningless"

Excerpt from the very last discussion of the Mont Pelerin Society meeting. Subheading: "What should be the TITLE OF THE ORGANISATION?" (1947)

This chapter will look at the second week of sessions, which had not been pre-programmed by Hayek in advance. The analysis of the dual argument from Part I is also instructive in this chapter, as it will become clear that a recurring topic in many sessions was the problem of agreeing on principles for how to use states in order to support and protect the mechanisms of markets. Mises continued to insist that all "interventionism" was negative, thus frustrating the efforts of Hayek and the other participants, who wanted to move beyond laissez-faire. Mises was given support by some of the American think tank employees, and in a key intervention, Loren Miller would argue that the neoliberals themselves were guilty of proposing a planned economy. The discussions on wages, trade unions and poverty also revealed some of the profoundly right-wing sensibilities of this group of thinkers. This shows the extent to which neoliberalism was not a form of social liberalism, even if they did discuss ways of using the state.

The programme for the second week was as follows:

Monday, April 7th:
Afternoon: Contracyclical Measures, Full Employment and Monetary Reform

Tuesday, April 8th:
Morning: Wage Policy and Trade Unions
Evening: Taxation, Poverty and Income Distribution

Wednesday, April 9th:
Morning: Agricultural Policy
Afternoon: Discussion of Organisation of permanent body

O. Innset, *Reinventing Liberalism*, Springer Studies in the History of Economic Thought,
https://doi.org/10.1007/978-3-030-38885-0_8

Evening: The Present Political Crisis

Thursday, April 10th:
Discussion and adoption of "Memorandum of Association" of the Mont Pelerin Society

In addition to analysing these sessions, this chapter looks at the series of discussions which were held throughout the week regarding a public statement and the future of the organization. As indicated in the epigraph, the attendees struggled to agree on a name for their organization, and as we will see, the later history of neoliberalism abounds with confusion over which label to attach to the intellectual creed and political project emanating from Mont Pèlerin. This chapter will also be used to summarize the whole conference with some key quantitative and qualitative analysis of the discussions.

Economic Policy

The three first sessions of the second week all focused on issues directly concerned with economics and economic policy. The Monday afternoon session on Contracyclical Measures, Full Employment and Monetary Reform incorporated no less than three large sets of issues within economics grouped together into one discussion. This format led to a fragmented discussion, in which the attendees also disagreed as to whether or not the issues were even connected or needed to be discussed separately, and if so in which order. These issues were certainly amongst those which had most occupied the economists among the conference attendees in the 1930s; therefore, many of them had extensive experience and differing views on many of the subjects. It is often observed that Hayek turned away from "pure" economics shortly after his Austrian Business Cycle Theory had been heavily criticized by Keynes' close associate Piero Sraffa in a review of *Prices and Production* in 1931; he subsequently "failed" to respond to Keynes' *General Theory* in 1936 (Caldwell 2004, 179–181; Wapshott 2011, 110–123). Hayek did not speak in the discussion, and neither did Mises. Instead the discussion was dominated by American economists and by Lionel Robbins, who was highly influenced by Austrian economics but had made a turn towards Keynesianism in recent years.

George Stigler introduced the session, and the Austrian-inspired Norwegian economist Trygve Hoff was in the chair.[1] Stigler foresaw a large split between the American and Continental economists, as the USA was concerned with full employment, and the continent with reconstruction. He asked the conference attendees if they could all agree that the first step should be to bring all money-making institutions under the control of the state. In the following discussion, Frank D. Graham wanted to discuss a proposal of a commodity reserve money system, which he had put forward in his 1942 book *Social Goals and Economic Institutions*, another book

[1]Liberaal Archief, Mont Pelerin Society, Box 1, "Mont Pèlerin 1947".

from this period which put forward the dual argument (Graham 1942). After some discussion between the Americans and Lionel Robbins, Wilhelm Röpke became impatient and asked why the problem was even being discussed. According to him unemployment was a much more serious question, and one on which the group was divided. Some saw full employment as one of the essential prerequisites of the time, whereas others thought that the influence of Keynes and his whole school had been dangerous. Röpke himself had called *The General Theory* "little short of satanic" in a letter to Robbins in 1936, so it was not hard to imagine which side of this divide he came down on.[2] Röpke favoured what he called a rational business cycle policy in order to control the boom, and only use Keynesian measures if there was a risk of a secondary depression after the boom had run its course. This was Röpke's own version of the Austrian business cycle theory, in which he suggested that Keynesian measures might actually be appropriate, but only if a recession was so severe as to run the risk of turning into what he called a secondary depression. In Röpke's synthesis, the effectiveness of Keynesian policy measures was admitted, but there was also a claim in there that the main reason for slumps to occur in the first place was due to government intervention creating perverse incentives (Hardhaug Olsen 2015, 146–162). Röpke then claimed that the problem of instability was due to a highly institutionalized, "proletarianized" society. After lengthy interventions by the likes of Hazlitt, Graham and Robbins, Röpke proclaimed that even if he believed in most of Keynes, he would hesitate to say so publicly. Against Robbins, Röpke argued that the great problem was not deflation, but inflation. Milton Friedman was the last to speak in the discussion, telling the other attendees that by examining the monetary system, it might be possible to get the whole house in order. Friedman spoke highly of the need for systems that are automatically active in terms of stimuli, and said everyone ought to consider getting the fundamental framework in order.

Stigler and Friedman's interventions pointed towards the *monetarism* developed in the 1950s and 60s by the Chicago School, which contended that monetary as opposed to fiscal policy ought to be the preferred method to achieve economic policy goals. Readers will note the fundamental neoliberal acknowledgment that the state needs to play a constructive role in creating a modern society as very much present in the general idea of monetarism. Stigler's suggestion that money-making institutions be put under the control of the state was in no way anti-state. As with neoliberalism in general, monetarism as a particular aspect of neoliberalism refers to a *different way of using the* state, and Stigler insisted that government had to work in a framework of law, and that the results of fiscal policy through contracyclical measures were still uncertain. In 1969, Friedman would publish the essay collection *The Optimum Quantity of Money*, giving rise to the so-called "Friedman-rule" in monetary economics, which consists of setting the nominal interest rate at zero (Friedman 2005). Friedman's comments at the 1947 Mont Pelerin Society meeting may be one of the first expositions of the monetarism which would make Friedman so famous and bring neoliberalism its breakthrough some twenty-five years later (Jones 2012, 215–273).

[2]London School of Economics Library and Archives, Lionel Robins Collection, Box 128.

Frank D. Graham was in the chair for the next morning's session on Wage Policy & Trade Unions.[3] The introduction was held by Fritz Machlup, who claimed that wage determination, trade unions and certain state legislation regarding trade unions were the main serious obstacles to the working of a free order in the US. He referred to how John Stuart Mill had considered legislation against trade unions as government interference, due to Labour's natural disadvantage in bargaining; thus the question again centred on what sort of state actions could be considered as interference in the market order and which state actions were important to maintain it. Like so many of the early neoliberals, Machlup used the language of "monopoly power" when referring to the perceived problems of labour organization. His view was that the size of unions should be restricted either geographically or with respect to one single plant, in order to exclude combination between the different unions. The growth of working-class organization and cooperation between unions in different sectors throughout whole nations was an irrational and dangerous development for Machlup: a rather clear example of early neoliberalism as a defence of property and power relations.

A critical note against Machlup's uncompromising attitude was sounded by William Rappard. He argued in favour of educating trade union leaders and members into a conception of solidarity of both employers' and employees' interests, in order to adapt them to "the needs of the modern society". After an intervention by Maurice Allais, Henri de Lovinfosse said that there was now a tendency to discuss firms' interests with the workers themselves. According to him, the interests of employers and employees often converged, and both realized it. He went on to state that "labourers" naturally aspired to be a privileged class, but since they were in the majority this would not be possible, as privilege could only apply to a minority. According to him, labourers realized this. Labourers had also started becoming more aware of the relation between prices and costs, he thought, adding that workers often came to see the advantages of cooperation. Lovinfosse the industrialist had himself often found that workers were far from disinclined to serve the consumers by cooperating; something which applied not only in the production of consumers' goods, but also in the production of producers' goods.

Some of the attendees agreed with this, but Frank Knight spoke up against what he saw as an idyllic picture of solidarity, which he thought was inimical to the free society and a free economic order. He said that the existence of such an order would imply orderliness and stability, something he claimed was an untrue portrayal of the very dynamics of modern society. A more standard laissez-faire position was then advocated by Orval Watts from the Foundation of Economic Education, who claimed that the problem of cycles had largely been caused by government. According to him, the maldistribution of labour in Great Britain was due to wage controls and unemployment relief. Had there been a free market for goods and services, there would have been greater speed in removing maldistribution. Stanley Dennison chimed in, claiming that neutralizing the "violence" of the trade unions on the picket line would go a long way towards solving what he called the "labour problem"

[3]Liberaal Archief, Mont Pelerin Society, Box 1 (Mont Pèlerin 1947).

and removing the obstacles of mobility. John Davenport then proclaimed that in the US, "the tower of labour power had erupted". He joined those who said that anti trust laws should be used against the unions. He also agreed with Machlup that one should bring back the concept of a company union or a plant union. John Jewkes then argued that the success of the British wage policy during the war was largely due to the understanding and restraining influence of union leaders, which he thought had been continued after the end of the war. According to him there had been a revolution in England, and the working classes had come into power. In the main, however, he thought that people were taking the long view about wage increases, largely due to what he referred to as excellent union leadership.

Machlup was then allowed to sum up the discussion at the beginning of the evening session, grouping together the opinions of professors Rappard, Polanyi and Jewkes. They had claimed that the unions were there to stay, and that one should hope they would be restrained from making excessive demands, and also attempt to educate union leaders and members. Machlup argued that this position was romantic, and that he could not see how a labour union with the power to keep its members from starvation would actually let them starve. This had been a session in which the class-based politics of many of the attendees were quite apparent, and Machlup seemed to suggest breaking up unions. There were some attempts at overcoming this, but the way in which organized labour was largely treated as a profound problem makes it quite clear why the proposed moniker of "left-wing liberalism" was so easily dismissed at the Walter Lippmann Colloquium some nine years earlier. An interesting aspect of their discussions is how organized labour was conceptualized as "monopolies", in the same way as large corporations had been in previous sessions. I noted earlier how the neoliberals came to criticize socialism and laissez-faire in a similar way, since they were both held to be arrangements that frustrated the work of markets. In a similar fashion, the early neoliberals criticized both labour unions and large corporations as institutions that corrupted the work of the market mechanism. This points to how the focus on markets as mediators of modernity was an innovation which lead to new types of right-wing liberalism, profoundly different from the old-fashioned notion of laissez-faire.

After Machlup's summary, the attendees moved on to a closely related theme, that of taxation, poverty and income distribution. Ludwig von Mises was in the chair, and Milton Friedman, who had suggested the topic, held the introduction.[4] He linked the session directly to the previous one by first stating that there was a desire to eliminate poverty, and that measures to break up unions could only succeed if the liberals could offer policies to combat the evils that unions were designed to counteract. It was the problem of poverty that lay beneath many of the lines of intervention that had been discussed, he said, even though he also argued that poverty had in many cases been caused by policy interventions in the first place. But even with completely free access to different employments and capital, Friedman ventured, there would still be the problem of poverty for what he called "sub-marginal workers". He asserted that "Men are not born equal", and further claimed that in a large country, the sub-marginal

[4]Liberaal Archief, Mont Pelerin Society, Box 1, "Mont Pèlerin 1947".

workers would not be evenly distributed throughout the population. He claimed as a definite fact that there were people unable to earn even a minimum income in the market place, and that others would have to pay for this help. No democratic society would tolerate people starving to death if there was food with which to feed them, he said, and this was the reason for progressive taxation. Friedman differed between two kinds of techniques for this: one being a set of general techniques of the national minimum type, and the other being poor law techniques where every case was judged on its merits. Friedman claimed that if they had been starting from scratch there would be a case for the second type, but as there was too much of the poor law type already, any additional measures should be of the first type. Friedman proposed maintaining the types of progressive income tax currently in force, but with the addition of progressive, *negative* taxation below the exemption limit. This would mean that if a man earned nothing, he would be given something by the state. The advantages of this would be that it gave an incentive to get additional income, and that it would make clear how much society would have to pay for the poor. He underlined that this was meant as a substitute and not as an addition to present social policy in the form of unemployment relief, old age pensions and so on. He finished by saying that progressive taxation had gone too far in affecting incentives in the USA, but that it seemed "fantastic" to try and prevent other countries to use it at all. He thought it would be easier to persuade them to use his policy and to be restrained in the use of progressive taxation.

In the following discussion, Friedrich Hayek intervened by noting that Friedman had an ideal of eliminating poverty, but asked what he meant by poverty, and how far he could extend the idea from rich countries to poor countries. He made it clear that he doubted whether he would put the phrase "eliminating poverty" on his programme as a liberal, while still noting that it was just impracticable not to make *some* provisions for the poor. He was, however, doubtful whether a certain money income from the state would be the right means. Instead he suggested a voluntary labour service, in which anyone who could not find employment could do so at just under market rates and under "semi-military conditions". He said that the freedom not to work was a luxury which the poor country could not afford, and suggested the slogan "Duty to work under direction". He added that one could refuse to enter this service if preferring to exist "on a pittance". The discussion continued, during which Karl Popper took the floor to point out that Professor Friedman's idea was an attractive alternative to socialism, whereas Professor Hayek's was not. Why should the poor "get it in the neck" both ways? he asked, at which point Hayek commented that as long as it was less attractive to work for the government than for the market, then the essential was already there. From his position as chair, Mises then intervened to say that there were high rates of allowances in the USA, and asked if they should not discuss the problem of poverty all over the world. Speaking rhetorically, Mises wondered why the Chinese and Japanese should not ask for this alleviation to be international.

Milton Friedman, to his credit, actually did come up with a plan for poverty relief. It was based on a rather elitist idea of there being such a thing as "sub-marginal" people, without the skills needed for survival in a modern world. The way he presented it to his fellow neoliberals suggested also that the most important reason for alleviating poverty was to facilitate the break up of unions. Nonetheless, it was a proposal for how to deal with social problems, and to this day Friedman is cited as one of several people on the political right who are or have been supportive of the idea of a Universal Basic Income (UBI) (Thornhill and Atkins 2016). Hayek and Mises were less than impressed, however, and both questioned whether fighting poverty had anything to do with liberalism at all. Hayek instead suggested "semi-military" employment for the poor, because it would be "impractical" to simply do nothing in relation to problems of poverty. The more socially oriented Popper defended Friedman's scheme as an attractive alternative to socialism, whereas both Hayek and Mises suggested that the fact that people were even worse off in poor countries should be enough to give up the idea of alleviating poverty in the West. These were intellectual arguments, but it is hard not to conclude yet again that the social composition of this group contributed to the way in which they discussed labour unions and taxation, things they mainly saw as problems. The notion that early neoliberalism was a form of social liberalism (Audier 2012; Nordbakken 2017) holds up especially poorly when compared with the content of these discussions. Alleviation of poverty was not high on the agenda in this group, and when it was discussed in a short session, it was in rather elitist terms and met with strong criticism.

Agricultural Policy

Wednesday, April 9th, the second last day of the conference and the last with ordinary sessions, included a session suggested by Michael Polanyi entitled "The Present Political Crisis", and also Karl Brandt's suggested session on "Agricultural Policy". In the first session, the neoliberals mainly discussed the possibility of nuclear war, a topic not particularly pertinent for this analysis of early neoliberal thought. Perhaps surprisingly, however, the latter session on agricultural policy was to include something of a key moment of the conference. Karl Brandt was himself an expert on agriculture, and as we have seen, the ordoliberals, in general, and Röpke, in particular, were deeply interested in agriculture and rural life, as they sought to tackle the problems of modernity in a way that would let people lead more traditional ways of life (Zmirak 2001, 163–207). Leonard Read of the Foundation for Economic Education was in the chair, and Brandt opened the discussion by claiming that agricultural policy was one of the testing grounds of the liberal philosophy. According to him, farmers more than any other class held a key position, and only Marxists thought the proletariat should hold such a position. Brandt informed the audience that the price of rye had begun to fall in Germany, a trend which had lead the farmers to call for state intervention to raise prices; in the USA, Hoover had had the same policies as Roosevelt with price assurance since 1933, with a limitation of agricultural production through quotas and then price-raising. Brandt claimed that agriculture made two chief claims, for equality and security. He claimed that equality would lead to nothing less than the end of freedom, but he did think that a minimum of security would be compatible with a liberal society. It might, however, distort the whole economic system and was therefore very dangerous. This was the crux of the matter, not only in terms of agricultural policy, but also for the neoliberal project of somehow intervening in markets in order to save them from intervention.

Brandt pointed to how the competitive economy had a procedure of reward and penalty, so that by loss and bankruptcy those who fail were eliminated. By and large people accepted this, said Brandt, but this ethic was thought to be wrong when even the best farmers failed to make profits. He explained how the credit structure in agriculture was very rigid, making it hard to make adjustments without thousands of families losing their livelihood. The time measure for adjustments of scale in agriculture was years, so the prevention of collapse had to begin at the start of an upswing. Brandt therefore thought that in the special case of agriculture, it should be possible to ask for state regulatory supervision of mortgages, all the while emphasizing that he was strictly against any impediments of the rights of creditors in any other way. In this way, farmers would pay increased interest rates in the boom and lower interest rates in the slump, which would diminish the bad effects of the rigidities of the credit structure.

Once again the question was one of arguing against "interventions" and for "liberal values", while at the same time claiming that certain policies *were* necessary and somehow also defendable within their liberal framework. Brandt underlined again that he did not want "artificial" profits for agriculture with quotas and restrictions. Much like Friedman's ideas of automatic systems, Brandt was trying to make a plan with the feature of automatism. This would leave the market entirely free, he claimed, but where the government, remote from the market, was prepared to underwrite a minimum level of income based upon commodity prices. Brandt finished the outline of his proposal by stating that winning the farmers back to the idea of a free economy seemed very important to him; apparently, this had to be done by inserting some measures into this "free" economy, so that it would not be so utterly difficult for them.

In the discussion that followed, Aaron Director was quick to tie the issue of agricultural policy to other discussions held the same week, by referring to the hesitation expressed the preceding night on the subject of minimum incomes. Unlike Brandt, Director seemed to think of farmers in the same way he thought of workers, and he claimed that the challenge to democracy in the US came from these groups organized on occupational lines, and that the pressure of these "minority groups" was only increasing. According to him, fluctuations in the economy as a whole affected agriculture and not the other way around, so that if the problem of general oscillations could be solved, there would be no problem of agriculture at all. Wilhelm Röpke, who as we have mentioned was known for his traditionalism and romanticizing of agricultural life, said there was a tendency to look at agriculture as any other industry. He claimed that more and more liberals were coming to believe the opposite that agriculture was "a way of life". He proclaimed to no longer be so interested in agriculture as such, but rather in the social life of the family farm. This had led him to think that it would be wise to have units smaller than would otherwise be rational for normal business standards. Through a family farm system, one would avoid the "proletarian nomads of industrialization", he thought. Röpke then pointed to a general tension in right wing thought, when he stated that liberals wanted to do justice to the social way of life of the farmer, while at the same time not wanting to associate himself with reactionary policies. He stated that it was the family farm which provided the optimum form of agricultural production in industrial countries, and according to Röpke this required land policies, credit policies and policies of succession and tenure. He thus agreed fundamentally with Brandt.

Loren Miller then returned to the previous days' discussion on tolerable and minimum standards, asking Brandt how he would define these. He asked why not *everyone* should be insured against the vicissitudes of the markets if farmers could be. A key moment arrived, when Miller finished his intervention by asking rhetorically what the total sum of all the interventions which had been suggested during the conference really would be. Would it not be a planned economy? he asked. It appeared as if the think tank man from New York had stumbled upon the basic contradiction of the dual argument.

Things were heating up now, and Karl Brandt exclaimed that the essence of a liberal economy was not to construct a 100% logical machine purely because the Nazis had done so. With this he seemed to suggest that neoliberals should be pragmatic and accept *some* state intervention when it could be considered expedient. After a lengthy intervention by Robbins, Hayek took the floor and said that he, like Loren Miller, was alarmed at the aspect of considering problems one by one, which indeed was the way in which the second week of non-pre-programmed sessions had been going. He stated that the primary task should be to clear out their minds on what principles they would like to see applied if they had a free hand, and to make it clear what concessions they considered to be politically expedient at the present moment. According to Hayek, it was already a definite ethical judgement to say that everyone in a particular country ought to be entitled to a minimum standard; and also to say that people getting into agriculture, aware of all the risks, ought to be relieved of these.

Then it was William Rappard's turn and he said that he couldn't help but feel that it was no accident that the subject of agriculture had been kept towards the end. According to Rappard, agriculture was *the* great challenge to economic liberalism, and he argued that they could not apply liberalism to agriculture simply for doctrinaire reasons. Frank D. Graham said he shared Miller's alarm, but could not follow his completely simplistic policy. According to Graham there was a need for a definition of aims, because there was a conflict of loyalties at the basis of the assembly's difficulties. "Do we make liberalism our supreme aim or our unique aim?" he asked, opting for the first himself. He made the example of perfectly free migration, saying that this would be simplistically liberal, because "transfers" from what he called a "super-Malthusian situation" would bring down the rest of the world. He asked rhetorically if the liberals would want freedom above everything if it meant freedom for all to be miserable. He insisted that freedom was not the only value on which they should lay importance, and that they were not ready to concede that all who were "sub-marginal" on a "free basis" should be allowed to die. According to him, allowing freedom to individuals would not lead to them providing themselves with insurance, so he was therefore in favour of some forms of social insurance.

Unsurprisingly, Mises disagreed, and a rather confusing discussion followed. Yet again, the different topics of discussion were blended together, as the issue of whether or not to give some special insurances to farmers was turned into a general discussion of what sorts of interventions would be needed to make a liberal society work and whether alleviating poverty was a goal of liberalism. These debates are highly interesting, as they show the degree to which the neoliberals wanted to move beyond a laissez-faire approach to liberalism, but also how they struggled somewhat to defend the interventions they thought were necessary. Like many others, Frank Graham argued that the notion of "freedom" could not be put above everything else. The example he chose was what would happen if people were allowed to migrate freely from poorer countries; something which again points to the not so social nature of early neoliberalism, especially considering how so many of the attendees had themselves become migrants in the preceding years. Yet Graham did favour some sort of social insurance, since he was not "ready to concede" that all who were "submarginal" should be "allowed to die". Yet again he was turned on by Mises, who disagreed with *any* form of social provision.

Loren Miller's intervention will stand as a summary of not only the divergence between different attendees of the conference, but also of the clear tension within the dual argument, as posed by Hayek and most of the other neoliberals. Miller asked whether the total sum of all the interventions that had been suggested during the conference would not be "a planned economy", thus making crystal clear the conceptual difficulties involved in the neoliberal project of saving the market order from state action *by* state action. Hayek's response is also telling, as he agreed that the approach of going through issues one by one and discussing types of intervention that would preserve liberalism was not proving fruitful. As was clear from the first week of sessions, he had wanted to discuss the general principles of "planning for competition", before attempting to apply those to special cases. Since that discussion instead derailed into a discussion about whether or not to use the state at all, it could be argued that the discussions at the conference did little to advance the ideas of neoliberalism, as they had been put forward in the years between the Lippmann Colloquium and the Mont Pèlerin conference.

Statement of Aims

The Statement of Aims which was produced at Mont Pèlerin is, to this day, the only official statement ever published by the Mont Pelerin Society. Discussions regarding its outline had already begun towards the end of the first week, when a committee led and appointed by Hayek presented their draft to the rest of the conference. The committee members chosen by Hayek were John Jewkes, Walter Eucken, Henry Gideonse, Carl Iversen and Henry Hazlitt. Their first draft is reproduced here:

A group of students of society met at Mont Pèlerin, Switzerland on April 1 to 10, 1947 to discuss the foundations for the preservation of a free society. For fruitful collaboration in working out these principles they feel that means for maintaining closer contact should be maintained among all those who share in substance the following convictions:

1. Individual freedom can be preserved only in a society in which an effective competitive market is the main agency for the direction of economic activity. Only the decentralization of control through private property in the means of production can prevent those concentrations of power which threaten individual freedom.
2. The freedom of the consumer in choosing what he shall buy, the freedom of the producer in choosing what he shall make, and the freedom of the worker in choosing his occupation and his place of employment, are essential not merely for the sake of freedom itself, but for efficiency in production. Such a system of freedom is essential if we are to maximize output in terms of individual satisfactions. Departure from these individual liberties leads to the production not only of fewer goods and services but of the wrong goods and services. We cannot enrich ourselves merely by consenting to be slaves.
3. All rational men believe in planning for the future. But this involves the right of each individual to plan his own life. He is deprived of this right when he is forced to surrender his own initiative, will and liberty to the requirements of a central direction of the use of economic resources.
4. The decline of competitive markets and the movement towards totalitarian control of society are not inevitable. They are the result mainly of mistaken beliefs about the appropriate means for securing a free and prosperous society and of the policies based on these beliefs.
5. The preservation of an effective competitive order depends upon a proper legal and institutional framework. The existing frameworks must be considerably modified to make the operation of competition more efficient and beneficial. The precise character of the legal and institutional framework within which competition will work most effectively and which will supplement the working of competition is an urgent problem on which continued exchange of views is required.
6. As far as possible government activity should be limited by the rule of law. Government action can be made predictable only when it is bound by fixed rules. Tasks which require that authorities be given discretionary powers should therefore be reduced to the indispensable minimum. But it must be recognized that each extension of the power of the state gradually erodes the minimum basis for the maintenance of a free society. In general an automatic mechanism of adjustment, even where it functions imperfectly, is preferable to any which depends on "conscious" direction by governmental agencies.
7. The changes in current opinion which are responsible for the trend toward totalitarianism are not confined to economic doctrines. They are part of a movement of ideas which finds expression also in the field of morals and philosophy and in the interpretation of history. Those who wish to resist the encroachments on individual liberty must direct their attention to these wider ideas as well as those in the strictly economic field.
8. Any free society presupposes, in particular, a widely accepted moral code. The principles of this moral code should govern collective no less than private action.
9. Among the most dangerous of the intellectual errors which lead to the destruction of a free society are the historical fatalism which believes in our power to discover laws of historical development which we must obey, and the historical relativism which denies all absolute moral standards and tends to justify any political means by the purposes at which it aims.

10. Political pressures have brought new and serious threats to the freedom of thought and science. Complete intellectual freedom is so essential to the fulfilment of all our aims that no consideration of social expediency must ever be allowed to impair it.[5]

Hayek's influence on this document is very clear. The first six out of ten bullet points, by far the most elaborate ones, all relate to the issues he raised in his opening address and in the first session on "'Free Enterprise' or Competitive Order". They all relate to the dual argument in how they combine ideas from the socialist calculation debates about markets as mediators of modernity, with an implicit attack on laissez-faire through vague formulations about the need to modify existing frameworks in order to achieve a competitive society. The last four points relate vaguely to questions of morals and historiography—all issues discussed in the first week of sessions, as programmed by Hayek. The economic issues raised in the three first sessions of the second week, agricultural policies and geopolitical questions, are all completely absent. This tells us something about what mattered most for Hayek, who was the main organizer of the event. He kept trying to steer the meeting and the organization they were founding onto the dual argument-track. The most important purpose in reinventing liberalism, according to him, was to develop policies for the active use of state power in the service of markets and liberalism. Many of the attendees were on board with this, while others either disagreed or were easily distracted by other issues they found to be even more pressing.

If we look closer at the bullet points, the first four points attack economic planning. The first point proclaims "competitive markets" as the guarantor of freedom, hinting at the attack on laissez-faire without spelling it out, and then affirming "private property in the means of production" as the only way to achieve this. The second and third points both relate to how economic planning deprives both consumers and producers of various freedoms; and the fourth point affirms that the movement towards planning is not inevitable, but based on "mistaken beliefs". It is only in the fifth point that the second part of the dual argument, the attack on laissez-faire, is presented, and it is stated that existing frameworks must be "considerably modified" in order for competition to be more efficient and beneficial.

The statement was meant to be distributed externally, and as in their various pre-1947 publications, the attack on economic planning is given more prominence than the attack on laissez-faire, even though we have seen that their internal discussions focused more on the other plank of the dual argument. This points to the importance of studying this first meeting closely in order to understand the importance of the attack on laissez-faire for the neoliberal project. In the sixth point, the idea of the "rule of law" is brought in, in an attempt to reconcile the two aspects of the dual argument; it is stated that "automatic adjustments" would be preferable to conscious direction of the economy. The eighth point mentions a moral code; the ninth repeats the notion from point four about historical fatalism and the movement towards planning as an "intellectual error"; and the last point mentions intellectual freedom.

[5] Liberaal Archief, Mont Pelerin Society, Box 1 (Mont Pèlerin 1947).

In the discussion that followed the presentation of the draft, Frank Graham put further emphasis on the less understood part of the dual argument by saying it would be good to further recognize that they did not want a "planless" system. Milton Friedman said it needed to be added that liberalism had a humanitarian aim and was a progressive philosophy; Lionel Robbins said he thought the draft would be more effective if the larger cultural and moral issues were put first, and the economic one later on. There was much criticism of various aspects of the statement from the likes of Maurice Allais, Bertrand de Jouvenel, Frank Knight and Erich Eyck. Responding to this criticism, Hayek referred back to the discussion on "'Free Enterprise' or Competitive Order", stating that on the issue of concentration of economic power there could be no chance of agreement, so they simply kept it out of the statement. This was not strictly true, as paragraph 5 made it clear that a competitive order needed a legal and institutional framework and that this had to be modified. However, the paragraph left the question of which sorts of modifications open, and the fact that no agreement was reached on this and that most of the discussions had been on whether or not it was right for liberals to modify state frameworks for markets at all, could be seen as something of a setback for Hayek. On the other hand, the fact that they even discussed it, and that Hayek, the ordoliberals, Lionel Robbins, Aaron Director, Frank Graham and several of the other writers who had peddled the dual argument before the conference were even able to raise the issue, and to frame the discussion in this way, could also be seen as a major step on the road to neoliberal politics. They were bringing forth a new form of right-wing liberalism, which sought to go beyond laissez-faire.

Henry Hazlitt, who had also been on the committee, added that the committee members had had to limit expression of their own opinions and try to deal with the presumed opinion of the meeting. This was hardly true, as the whole statement dealt only with issues from the first three sessions in a meeting which so far had consisted of seven sessions and still had four to come. Hayek was then disparaged by further criticism from Lionel Robbins, and said it was extremely difficult to put beliefs into a very short statement. He asked if they were wasting their time and if the meeting perhaps did not want a statement at all. Lionel Robbins was asked to outline a new statement and agreed to do so after breakfast the following day. Hayek insisted that some things had to be absolutely essential, and that this was *property*. This was an important admission from the *primus motor* of the society. Robbins then asked how there could be adequate liberty in a society with only one property owner and one employer, a rhetorical question meant to outline the problems of holding up property as the essential aspect of liberty. Maurice Allais then stated, controversially within this context, that control by democracy was better than state planning, and that it had not yet been proven that competitive controls were impossible under collective ownership. Allais obviously did not share the analysis of Mises and Hayek, who had made it clear in the socialist calculation debates that the problem with state planning was precisely its supposed democratic nature. Röpke remarked dryly that he thought Professor Allais had proved with his comment that private property had to be retained. This pointed to another conflict within the conference: where attendees like Mises and Miller appeared to be to the "right" of Hayek and the main thrust of neoliberalism by disagreeing with any form of state intervention at all, attendees like Allais, Rappard, Tingsten and Iversen seemed to be to the "left" of that, arguing that Keynesianism and democratic planning was perhaps not as bad as it was made out to be. I am putting "right" and "left" in inverted commas, because part of the argument of this book lies in showing that right and left on the political spectrum are not reducible to questions of whether or not, or how much, to use the state. This book shows that the early neoliberals were both profoundly "right wing" in their politics, but that they also wanted to use the state actively and that these two things are not mutually exclusive. Nonetheless, it was clear that the main ideas of neoliberalism were challenged from different angles at the first meeting of the Mont Pelerin Society.

Lionel Robbins presented his new draft for a statement of aims on the Tuesday of the second week. It is reproduced here:

> A group of economists, historians, philosophers and other students of public affairs from Europe and the United States met at Mont Pelerin, Switzerland, from April 1st to 10th 1947 to discuss the crisis of our times. This group, being desirous of perpetuating its existence for promoting further intercourse and for inviting the collaboration of other like minded persons, has agreed upon the following statement of aims.
>
> The central values of our civilization are in danger. Over large stretches of the earth's surface the essential conditions of human dignity and freedom have already disappeared. In others they are under constant menace from the development of current tendencies of policy. The position of the individual and the voluntary group are progressively undermined by extensions of arbitrary power. Even that most precious possession of Western Man, freedom of thought and expression, is threatened by the spread of creeds which claiming the privilege of tolerance when in the position of a minority, seek only to establish a position of power in which they can suppress and obliterate all view but their own.
>
> The group holds that these developments have been fostered by the growth of a view of history which denies all absolute moral standards and by the growth of theories which question the desirability of the rule of law. It holds further that they have been fostered by a decline of belief in private property and the competitive market; for without the diffused power and initiative associated with these institutions it is difficult to imagine a society in which freedom may be effectively preserved.
>
> Believing that what is essentially an ideological movement must be met by intellectual argument and the reassertion of valid ideals, the group, having made a preliminary exploration of the ground, is of the opinion that further study is desirable *inter alias* in regard to the following matters:
>
> (1) The analysis and explanation of the nature of the present crisis so as to bring home to others its essential moral and economic origins.
>
> (2) The redefinition of the functions of the state so as to distinguish more clearly between the totalitarian and the liberal order.
>
> (3) Methods of reestablishing the rule of law and of assuring its development in such manner that individuals and groups are not in a position to encroach upon the freedom of others and private rights are not allowed to become a basis of predatory power.
>
> (4) The possibility of establishing minimum standards by means not inimical to initiative and the functioning of the market.
>
> (5) Methods of combatting the misuse of history for the furtherance of creeds hostile to liberty.

(6) The problem of the creation of an international order conducive to the safeguarding of peace and liberty and permitting the establishment of harmonious international economic relations.

The group does not aspire to conduct propaganda. It seeks to establish no meticulous and hampering orthodoxy. It aligns itself with no particular party. Its object is solely, by facilitating the exchange of views among minds inspired by certain ideals and broad conceptions held in common, to contribute to the preservation and improvement of the free society.[6]

In many ways, Lionel Robbins was the perfect man to write the statement of aims. He was deeply inspired by Mises and Austrian economics; on the other hand, his views had softened during the war years, and he was able to see things also from the perspectives of more moderate conference attendees, like Rappard, Allais, Tingsten and Iversen. Hayek wanted to unite a very conservative approach to property and redistribution with a new approach to using the state for what he defined as liberal ends. The ordoliberals, the Chicago economists and someone like Frank Graham followed him in this more or less to the letter, whereas his old mentor Mises remained highly sceptical of the others' enthusiasm for using the state as a tool to create a functioning market society. Others agreed with Hayek on the importance of the state, but went much further in a "Keynesian" or "new liberal" direction in wanting to use the state to "fix capitalism".

Robbins was able to unite all these strands in a statement of aims with many words, but not an awful lot of substance. He did go into redefining the functions of the state in bullet point two (in many ways the first point since bullet point number one simply stated that they wanted to study contemporary problems). This point was softened, however, in the following sentence where it was stated that the redefinition of the state had to be done in order to distinguish more clearly between a totalitarian and a liberal order, something to which it would be difficult for anyone to object. Even so, it was established in this statement that the redefining of the functions of the state was the prime goal of the Mont Pelerin Society. Another mention of the rule of law as a guiding principle for liberal economic planning was then noted, before the fourth bullet point alluded to social questions, but made clear that the establishment of minimum means could not be "inimical to initiative and the functioning of the market". The last two bullet points mentioned the misuse of history and the need for an international order. The discussion of the statement of aims that followed was not recorded, but after some amendments (the quoted statement is the finished product), it was approved by everyone except Maurice Allais. Further discussion was devoted to the question of the form of the organization of the permanent body, and a sub-committee was set up to prepare a draft memorandum of association for submission to the meeting on Wednesday afternoon.

Thursday, the 10th of April was the last day of the conference, and it had only one short session to discuss both the memorandum, based on the above statement of aims that had been agreed upon the previous day, and the name of the organization being founded. Wilhelm Röpke opened the proceedings by stating that the word "liberal" was associated with different things in different countries, asking whether it would

---

[6]Liberaal Archief, Mont Pelerin Society, Box 1 (Mont Pèlerin, 1947).

not be better to replace it with the phrase "philosophy of freedom". Bertrand de Jouvenel asked why the committee had refrained from calling the society the Acton-Tocqueville Society, as Hayek had originally suggested. Hayek answered briefly it was because "some" had objected. After some discussion, Hayek decided to reiterate that his suggestion remained to call it the Acton-Tocqueville Society, with the subtitle of "an international academy of political philosophy"; however, Frank Knight argued that neither Acton nor Tocqueville stood for anything economic. Ludwig von Mises claimed that using that name would be a political mistake with regard to Tocqueville, as he had held a position under Napoleon. Aaron Director suggested "The Adam Smith-Tocqueville Society", but William Rappard noted that both Acton and Tocqueville were Catholics and noblemen. Milton Friedman said it would be incongruous to name the society after people when it should be named after principles. Lionel Robbins suggested "The Protagonist Society"; Karl Popper suggested "The Periclean Society". "International Society for the Study of Freedom in Society" and "International Academy for the study of the requisites of a free society" were also put on the table. Finally, Karl Brandt suggested "The Mont Pelerin Society", to which Karl Popper responded: "That is meaningless".

Summary

The above is in fact the very last entry in the minutes of the first meeting of the Mont Pelerin Society. The attendees had covered a wide variety of topics in their discussions, from religion and unions to agriculture and nuclear war, but as should be clear, they returned time and again to the issue of how to use the state for liberal ends. Thirty-seven intellectuals meeting for ten days were bound to discuss a variety of different issues, but it was obvious that this diversity of issues, especially prevalent in the second week of the conference, annoyed Hayek, the main convenor of the conference. He had programmed the first week in order to steer the participants towards serious discussions on the future of liberalism, and a collective effort at working out of the contradictions involved in the dual argument. The conference was opened by his own introduction and the session on "Free Enterprise" or Competitive Order, which he made absolutely clear was the most important one. Hayek also took a great interest in the politics of history, and Dieter Plehwe has noted that the neoliberals "recognized the paramount importance in political action of rewriting history…" (Mirowski and Plehwe 2009, 26). Wanting to steer liberalism in a more conservative direction, Hayek was also deeply interested in the question of uniting liberalism and Christianity, something which was also reflected in their excursion to the cathedral of Einsiedeln for Easter. These issues were not Hayek's speciality, but we can assume that he recognized their importance and wanted input from others, especially from non-economists. With the dual argument it was different, and Hayek's lengthy introductions and interventions on these issues show us that he very much wanted to make others understand the importance of developing principles for a liberal state policy in the service of market mechanisms. To a certain extent, he was successful, but the conference also drifted somehow off track, and we can see from the proceedings that Hayek got progressively less involved as the discussions panned out onto a variety of specific topics, instead of discussing the general question of liberal state intervention.

A key moment of the conference was thus on Wednesday, 8th of April when Loren Miller came upon what he saw as a basic contradiction in the dual argument, and asked if the interventions suggested at the conference did not amount to a form of planned economy. Despite their attacks on social liberalism and economic planning, the vast majority of neoliberals also understood that laissez-faire would not save the day either. The bigger question looming was then how to define which state actions were to be considered "interventions" that distorted the "spontaneous" work of the market mechanism; and which state actions could be considered to be supportive of, and even foundational for the working of said mechanism. Hayek intended to steer the meeting in the direction of these questions, and as we saw, he responded to Miller in the agricultural session by saying he too was alarmed at the aspect of considering problems one by one. The primary task of the conference as he saw it was to clear out the neoliberals' minds on what *principles* they would like to see applied if they had a free hand, and also to make it clear which concessions they considered to be politically expedient at that present moment.

The divergence of views between some of the conference attendees meant that the discussion on exactly how neoliberals could claim the market order as largely self-regulating, but still endorse a strong state with active economic policies, did not always proceed in the way Hayek had hoped. Towards the end of the very first session, Aaron Director, along with key figures like Lionel Robbin and Walter Eucken, agreed completely with Hayek's exposé on the problems of laissez-faire. Director commented that they would never come anywhere in defining what the rules of the game should be if they did not even know whether there should be any rules at all. On one side was Mises, who in several discussions refused to budge from a laissez-faire position. He saw the dual argument as a contradiction in terms, and he criticized the other neoliberals' proposals for liberal state actions a great number of times. Some of the American think-tankers, like Loren Miller and Felix Morley, would support Mises, whereas other attendees, like Frank D. Graham, would attack Mises outright and criticize him with very harsh words. As I have noted earlier, Mises views set him apart from the other neoliberals, but due to his status as mentor to Hayek and a great inspiration to people like Lionel Robbins and the ordoliberals, he held a privileged position in the group and was named a member of the executive committee.

Interestingly, this was not the case with those who diverged from the dual argument in the other direction. Herbert Tingsten spoke of the need for a "reasonable liberalism" which was not averse to state monopolies; Carl Iversen suggested that state monopolies could in fact be liberal, and Maurice Allais speculated that a planned economy could still be competitive. In spite of their allegiance to liberalism, these attendees found that their views on state planning were out of tune with the rest of the neoliberals. Allais claimed that state planning lead to totalitarianism, but still wanted to find ways of using the state to support the market order, not to replace it. It is reasonable to assume that Morley was not the only one among the American think tank attendees who supported Mises' non-compromising stance, and in a letter to Morley on 26 January 1948, Leonard Read wrote that he had few hopes for the Mont Pelerin Society, and made retrospective references to the discussion on the statement:

> Ideologically, even with the initial group hand-picked by Hayek, with the exception of a dozen, it ranged all the way from state-interventionists to one who was an all-and-out-socialist. It doesn't appear to me to have quite the element of liberalism in it that would make its expansion something to be ardently desired. The attempt to write a statement was actually funny. It was as though it was being done by socialists who like to label themselves liberal.[7]

It is not clear who Read was referring to as the all-and-out-socialist, but it is quite possible he meant Allais, who had been the only one who did not vote to support the statement of aims. Indeed, not long after the meeting at Mont Pèlerin, Allais wrote an article in the journal *Féderation*, in which he argued for a "competitive socialism". He wrote: "le planisme central n'est pas un doctrine de gauche pas plus que la concurrence n´est spécifiquement une doctrine de droite" (central planning is no more a doctrine of the left than competition is specifically a doctrine of the right).[8] This was very much a minority view, however, and both in his introduction and in a later discussion, Hayek iterated that the most central point in their endeavours was the belief in *private property*. Thus unlike what Tingsten, Iversen and Allais might have thought, the reinvention of liberalism would not be about acknowledging the need for redistribution or democratization of the economic sphere, but about finding new ways to fight this growing threat. In the discussion on unions, these divisions arose again when Iversen, Allais and others who did not share in the outright contempt towards labour organization exhibited by members like Machlup, Knight and Graham were derided as romantic and naïve.

The fragmentary nature of both the conference as a whole and indeed even of single discussions could lead us to think that Hayek failed somewhat. Then again, anyone who has been to a meeting or conference with more than a couple of people who are perfectly in tune with each other knows that these sorts of events are almost always somewhat disappointing. Participants in discussions can have widely different perspectives and often talk past one another. The mere fact that the meeting took place, that an organization was formed and that the dual argument was the attempted frame for the Hayek's reinvention of liberalism is an extremely relevant point if we want to understand early neoliberalism.

---

[7] Hoover Library and Archives, "Mont Pelerin Society", Box 29, Folder 4, "Hunold—Morley".

[8] Rubenstein Library and Archives, Maurice Allais Collection, Folder 39 (P) "Fédération, août—septembre 1947—31–32".

Speaking Time

The Mont Pelerin Society was Hayek's brainchild. As we saw in Chap. 3 through the correspondence between Hayek and Lippmann in 1937, Hayek had already been one of the key players in the organization of the Walter Lippmann Colloquium in 1938, nine years earlier. During his extensive travels in the US after the publication of *The Road to Serfdom* in 1944, he was actively promoting the idea of an organization of right-wing intellectuals to develop and spread a neoliberal creed. In the meeting itself, it could be argued that Hayek kept a somewhat low profile, always insisting that the society was what the members would make it out to be and that he did not have time to take on more responsibilities himself. Still, he was by far the most active participant at the meeting, making a total of 24 interventions (including his opening address and the introduction to the session on "'Free Enterprise' or Competitive Order?"). Just behind him were Lionel Robbins with 21 interventions and Milton Friedman with 18 (see Fig. 8.1).

The reader will remember that Hayek only programmed the first week of sessions, and that the second week's agenda was decided upon by the conference attendees. It is obvious that Hayek was less interested in this part of the conference, and he also spoke comparatively less, making only 8 interventions, which still put him in "fourth place" in the second week of proceedings, behind Milton Friedman with 14 interventions; Lionel Robbins with 12; and Karl Brandt with 10 (see Fig. 8.2). It was in the first week, then, that Hayek dominated the meeting, making 16 interventions, with the second highest number being reached by Lionel Robbins with 9 (see Fig. 8.1).

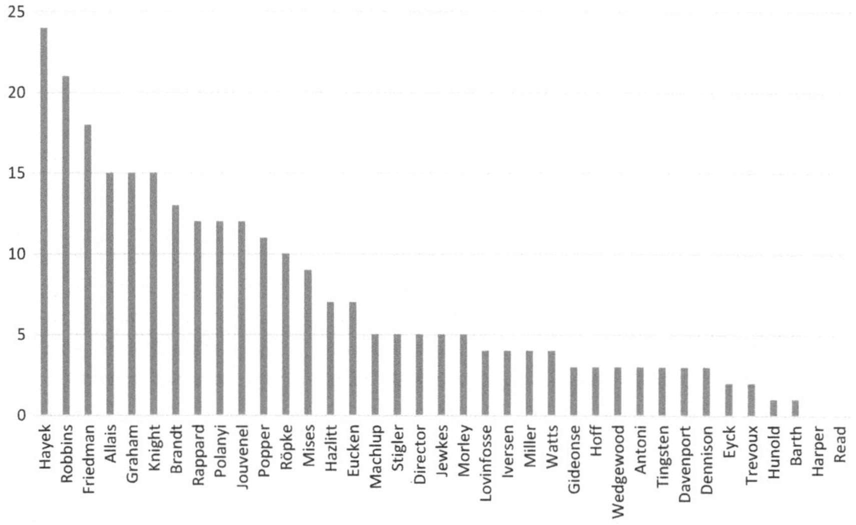

Fig. 8.1 Number of interventions in total

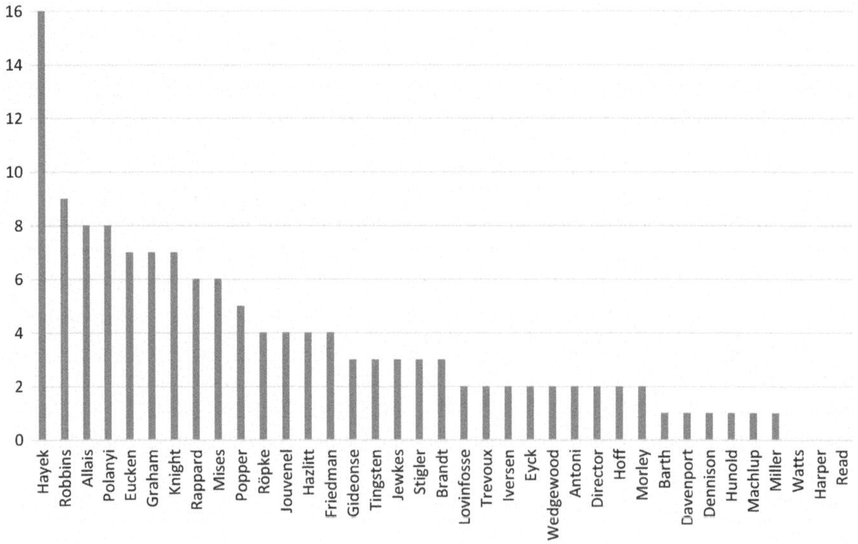

Fig. 8.2 Number of interventions in the first week

Of course, not all interventions were the same length, Friedman's, for instance, were often very short. Hayek, on the other hand, spoke at length in a great number of his many interventions. If we break down total speaking time of the conference as lines covered in the minutes,[9] Hayek spoke for a staggering 41,4% of the time during the first week of the meeting. William Rappard came closest with 6,9%. This way of measuring gives special credence to those who gave introductions, and as mentioned in the footnote it is a far from perfect method. It does, however, say something about the dominance of Hayek at the first Mont Pelerin Society meeting, especially during the first week that he himself had programmed (Figs. 8.3 and 8.4).

A Neoliberal Cadre

It did not take long for the conference attendees to start writing to each other after returning from Mont Pèlerin to their respective home bases. Leonard Read and the other members of the Foundation for Economic Education must have taken a costly

[9]A method which is far from perfect for several reasons, but still tells us *something*. Some of the pages of the minutes are in smaller print than others, and some parts of the discussions were only transcribed by Dorothy Hahn in keywords. Other pages of the minutes of the discussion are lost, and this is also the case with a couple of the introductions, in which case I have counted an average number of lines per introduction into the speaking time of those holding introductions that did not hand in manuscripts (Carlo Antoni, Bertrand de Jouvenel, Walter Eucken).

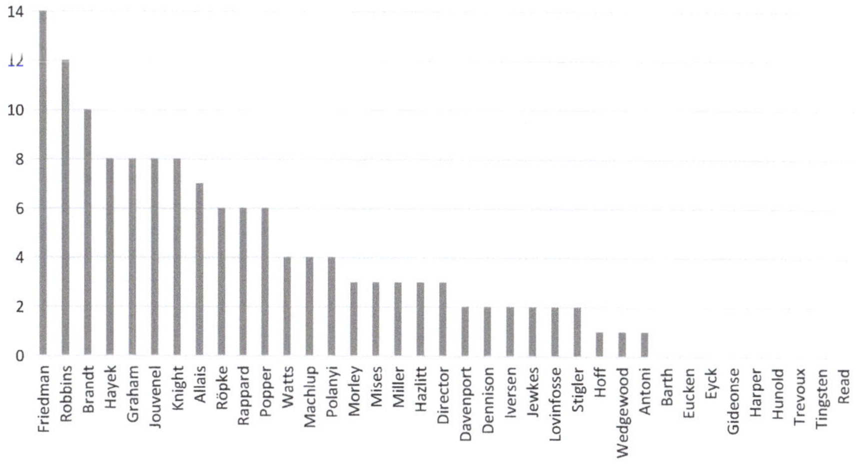

Fig. 8.3 Number of interventions in the second week

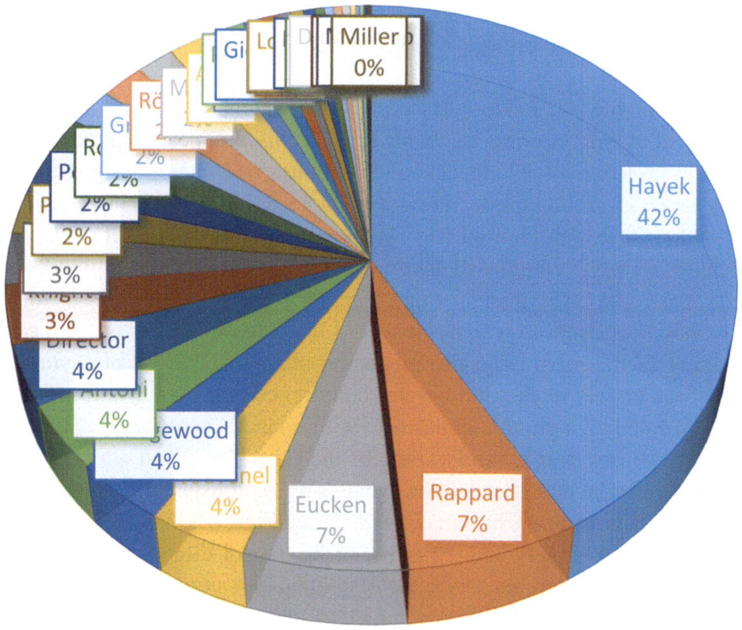

Fig. 8.4 Percentage of total speaking time

international flight to make it back to the US, because by April 14 Read had already written to Hunold:

> It seems rather remarkable that all of us from the Foundation staff, who attended the conference at Mont Pelerin, were at our desks this Monday morning—particularly when leaving you Thursday and spending a day in Geneva and another in Paris. This accomplishment in travel, a carry-over from the liberal economy of the past, is everywhere threatened with extinction. It could not be brought into being with today's socialistic practices. All of this gave a meaning to the Mont Pelerin meeting. Added to this was your gracious hospitality and the inspiration that comes from knowing you personally. I am certain we can be mutually helpful in our common purposes.[10]

Neither Read nor Hunold[11] spoke during the plenary sessions of the conference, but they were both very important behind the scenes. Read attached a memorandum from The Foundation for Economic Education, addressed to "Liberals of the British Isles and the Continent of Europe", in order for Hunold to distribute it to all those who had attended the conference. Read put his staff and their resources at the disposal of Mont Pelerin Society members in order to purchase and send books that were difficult to obtain in Europe due to post-war exchange controls. The Foundation for Economic Education exists to this day, and amongst many other activities they finance the work of several Austrian and libertarian scholars on the history of economic thought that this book quotes.

Michael Polanyi wrote to Hunold from his office at the University of Manchester on the 19th of April, in order to thank him for his kindness: "Quite apart from several additions to my knowledge and understanding of contemporary affairs, I have received a new background for my thoughts which will be lasting in its effects", wrote Polanyi, adding that both Hunold and Hayek ought to be thanked for founding the Mont Pelerin Society, "which will serve as a guidance to liberal thought".[12] It was obvious to the conference attendees that Hunold was organizationally as important as Hayek, but since Hunold was not involved in discussions, this is not clear from our treatment of the minutes in the preceding chapters. Polanyi also emphasized the friendships he had made, and several conference attendees would go on to do the same. Hunold had a photo album made with financial contributions from Henry Hazlitt, Felix Morley and possibly some of the other American attendees, and he circulated it to all who had attended the event. It was enthusiastically received by the European delegates around Christmas 1948,[13] (see Figs. 8.5, 8.6, 8.7, 8.8 and 8.9).

The Mont Pelerin Society was registered in the state of Illinois in November 1947 by Aaron Director. In October 1948, the first "members circular and booklet of the Mont Pelerin Society" was printed and mailed to all the society's members by Hayek. The first page listed the officers of the society, with Hayek as president and Eucken, Jewkes, Knight, Rappard and Jaques Rueff as vice presidents. Rueff had not been

---

[10]Hoover Library and Archives, "Mont Pelerin Society", Box 29, Folder 5, "Hunold-Read".

[11]Hunold made one remark in the first session regarding the use of English as the conference language.

[12]Hoover Library and Archives, "Mont Pelerin Society", Box 29, Folder 4, "Hunold—Polanyi".

[13]Hoover Library and Archives, "Mont Pelerin Society", Box 29, Folder 3, "Hunold—Hazlitt".

Fig. 8.5 Hayek in the chair, Dorothy Hahn keeping the minutes

Fig. 8.6 The meeting room at Hotel du Parc

Fig. 8.7 Mises to the right—Karl Popper behind him

present at the first meeting, but had taken an active part in the Walter Lippmann Colloquium in 1938. Secretaries were listed as Albert Hunold and Aaron Director. A C.O. Hardy, who held a senior position at the Brookings Institution in Washington D.C., was listed as treasurer. Under "other members of the council" were listed Carlo Antoni, Henry Gideonse, Carl Iversen, Ludwig von Mises, Lionel Robbins and Wilhelm Röpke. The only other entry in the booklet was a list of members, which now ran to a full 121 people. It seems that recruitment had been the thing occupying

Fig. 8.8 Lively discussions

Fig. 8.9 Excursion, to Chateau Coppet or Schwyz (All pictures from the album found in London School of Economics Library and Archives, Lionel Robbins Collection, Box 10, Folder 2.)

Hayek and the rest of the council, and in this very first circular, the exclusive group of 37 people who had gathered for the original meeting were only marked by an asterisk next to their name in the members' list. The new additions are too many to mention and go beyond the scope of this book, but notable inclusions were the economists Ronald Coase, Constantino Bresciani-Turroni, Gottfried Haberler and Eli Drekschler; Anthony Fischer who would start the Institute of Economic Affairs; Max Eastman of the Readers' Digest; Harold Luhnow of the William Volker fund; Ludwig Erhard, the Spanish politician Salvador de Madariaga; and "His Excellency Luigi Einaudi", president of the Italian Republic.[14]

Some of the members who had not yet written books or articles expounding the dual argument went on to do so. Henry Hazlitt's book *Will Dollars Save the World?*, published later in 1947, would be described by the Mises Institute as "a blockbuster argument against the idea of putting post-war Europe on the US dole". In a letter to Hazlitt on the occasion of receiving his book, Hunold wrote:

> It is a great pleasure to me to see how the broad views of the personalities of the Mont Pelerin conference are getting more and more influence in the USA and also here on the continent (…).[15]

Another example is John Jewkes, who opened his 1948 book *Ordeal by Planning* with the following statement:

> Everything I have to say here, and indeed much more, is to be found in Professor Hayek's masterly *Road to Serfdom*. Every planner who believes in reason as the guide in social organisation should read or re-read that book now and honestly ask himself whether events are or are not following the course against which Professor Hayek warned us four years ago. (Jewkes 1948, ix)

Jewkes paraphrased many of the insights developed during the socialist calculation debates to make a strong critique of "economic planning":

> For central planning ultimately turns every individual into a cipher and every economic decision into blind fumbling, destroys the incentives though which economic progress arises, renders the economic system as unstable as the whims of the few who ultimately control it and creates a system of wirepulling and privileges in which economic justice ceases to have any meaning. (Jewkes 1948, 8)

Yet, when one knows what to look for, it is clear that *Ordeal by Planning*, in spite of its central message as an attack on the Labour government's economic policies, did not advocate laissez-faire. Instead, Jewkes made implicit reference to the discussions on monopoly held at the 1947 meeting, by referring to the state's "legitimate function of controlling monopoly…" (Jewkes 1948, 24). Jewkes wrote:

> It is just as much a normal part of the function of the State to curb monopoly as to formulate and enforce traffic rules (…) some practices should be definitely proscribed, others should be kept under constant surveillance. A Government research body should be engaged continuously in the study of changes in industrial organisation so that the public may be kept informed of those changes, and industries given proper and timely warning of practices which threaten the free economy. (Jewkes 1948, 55)

---

[14] Hoover Library and Archives, "Mont Pelerin Society, Box 1, Folder 1, "Booklets".

[15] Hoover Library and Archives, "Mont Pelerin Society", Box 29, Folder 3, "Hunold—Hazlitt".

It is well known that Winston Churchill invoked ideas from *The Road to Serfdom* in his unsuccessful bid for re-election in 1945, by claiming that Labour would have to fall back on some form of Gestapo in order to carry out their economic programme (Ebenstein 2003, 131). Jewkes, however, had read Hayek carefully enough to understand the dual argument, and in his critique of Clement Atlee's nationalization policies he was careful to add that "in Great Britain certainly there is much that the State could do to revivify the competitive process" (Jewkes 1948, 56).

The neoliberal movement was now well under way. In articles written for Felix Morley's US-based conservative weekly *Human Events*, Bertrand de Jouvenel, who in *Du Pouvoir* had only attacked economic planning and democracy as leading to totalitarianism, went on to criticize *both* state intervention and laissez-faire, thus completing the dual argument (Knegt 2015, 226). Included as a new member was another Frenchman, René Courtin, editor of *Le Monde*, who in a letter to Hunold dated 2 December 1948 wrote "je suis persuadé que nous avons là la seule possibilité de créer une cadre pour le néolibéralisme" (I am convinced that we have a unique possibility to create a cadre for neoliberalism).[16]

The neoliberal cadre Courtin was referring to was the Mont Pelerin Society, whose membership had tripled in one year. The next available membership list in the archives is from 1956 and shows that the membership had doubled since its initial tripling, and now stood at some 195 members.[17] This last section of Chap. 8 has analysed the very first meeting of the Mont Pelerin Society in 1947, aided by the analysis in the previous section of the dual argument as foundational for their intellectual and political project. The conclusion will now make some considerations as to how this analysis can be helpful in judging the influence of these thinkers in the years after 1947 and up until the present moment.

Primary Sources

Hoover Institution Library and Archives, Stanford University, Palo Alto, California, USA:
Mont Pelerin Society Collection

Yale University Library, New Haven, Connecticut, USA:
Walter Lippmann Collection

Het Liberaal Archief, Gent, Belgium
Mont Pelerin Society Collection

Rubenstein Library and Archives, Duke University, Durham, North Carolina, USA:
Maurice Allais Papers

[16] Hoover Institution Library and Archives, "Mont Pelerin Society, Box 29, Folder 1, "Hunold—Courtin".

[17] Hoover Institution Library and Archives, "Mont Pelerin Society, Box 1, Folder 1, "Booklets".

London School of Economics Special Collections, London, UK:
Lionel Robbins Collection.

Secondary Literature

Audier, S. (2012). *Néo-Libéralisme(s)*. Paris: Grasset.
Caldwell, B. (2004). *Hayek's challenge: Intellectual biography of F.A. Hayek*. Chicago: University of Chicago Press.
Ebenstein, A. O. (2003). *Friedrich Hayek: A biography*. Chicago: University of Chicago Press.
Friedman, M. (2005). *The optimum quantity of money*. Piscataway, New Jersey: Transaction Publishers.
Graham, F. D. (1942). *Social goals and economic institutions*. Princeton, New Jersey: Princeton University Press.
Hardhaug Olsen, A. (2015). *Keynes + Hayek*. Oslo: Civita.
Jewkes, J. (1948). *Ordeal by planning*. London: Macmillian and Co., Limited.
Jones, D. S. (2012). *Masters of the universe: Hayek, friedman, and the birth of neoliberal politics*. Princeton: Princeton University Press.
Knegt, D. F. (2015). *A new order for france and europe? bertrand de jouvenel and alfred fabre-luce between liberalism, fascism and europeanism (1930–1954)*. Florence: European Unviersity Institute.
Mirowski, P., & Plehwe, D. (Eds.). (2009). *The road from mont pèlerin: The making of the neoliberal thought collective*. Cambridge, Mass: Harvard University Press.
Nordbakken, L. P. (2017). *Liberale tenkere for vår tid*. Oslo: Civita.
Thornhill, J., & Atkins, R. (2016). Universal basic income: Money for nothing. *Financial Times*, May 26.
Wapshott, N. (2011). *Keynes hayek: The clash that defined modern economics* (1st ed.). New York: W.W. Norton & Co.
Zmirak, J. (2001). *Wilhelm Röpke—Swiss localist, global economist*. Wilmington, Delaware: ISI Books.

Chapter 9
Conclusions: What Is Neoliberalism?

> Not without admiration, we have to concede that neoliberal intellectuals struggled through to a deeper understanding of the political and organizational character of modern knowledge and science than did their counterparts on the left, and therefore presents a worthy challenge to everyone interested in the archaeology of knowledge. (Mirowski 2013, 49)
>
> Philip Mirowski, *Never Let A Serious Crisis Go To Waste* (2013)

When the attendees of the Mont Pèlerin conference left Hotel du Parc on the 10th of April 1947, what we may call the history of neoliberalism had only just begun. Many would even argue that it wouldn't fully begin until at least 25 years later, when various developments in the economic history of the world seemed to coincide with the gradual acceptance of ideas emanating from the Mont Pelerin Society. In this conclusion, I will attempt to show how my study of early neoliberal thought can contribute to a better understanding of neoliberal ideas today. Rather than see neoliberalism as a set of now outdated economic policies regarding deregulation and "free markets", I argue that it should be seen as something more fundamental: A broad political philosophy encompassing many diverging strands, which have influenced politics and society in a variety of ways, all based on the original neoliberal conception of markets as mediators of modernity.

This notion of markets as mediators of modernity gave rise to the dual argument: a unifying and foundational claim put forward by a variety of early neoliberal intellectuals in the years leading up to 1947. On the one hand, they claimed that economic planning lead to totalitarianism; on the other hand, they argued against laissez-faire and for a strong state.[1] At the first Mont Pelerin Society meeting in 1947, Ludwig von Mises and Loren Miller claimed that this was contradictory. Mises and Miller thus failed to grasp and get on board with the novelty of neoliberalism. Stuck in their laissez-faire views, they thought government activity and a strong state would

[1]The concept of totalitarianism was largely abandoned by neoliberals after 1947, as totalitarianism theory became a more unified school of thought, more related to so-called "Cold War liberalism" (Müller 2008).

O. Innset, *Reinventing Liberalism*, Springer Studies in the History of Economic Thought,
https://doi.org/10.1007/978-3-030-38885-0_9

always mean social liberal interference with markets. Hayek, the ordoliberals and economists like Robbins, Director and Graham arguably took the notion of markets as mediators of modernity more seriously. They concluded that in a modern world, modern states would have to be put to use to protect and spread these mechanisms. This was their main innovation, and the resistance of someone like Mises shows what a leap it was for right-wing liberalism to consider active government policies and a strong state. The reasons of the neoliberals for opening this conceptual space were not that they were social liberals who wanted to use the state for redistributive purposes and tasks they believed should lie outside of the domain of markets. Their cautious embrace of states was not due to a mistrust in markets, but rather the opposite. I believe that this is a key insight offered by the analysis of this book: neoliberalism was neither laissez-faire nor social liberalism. Neoliberals wanted to use the state, not because they didn't believe in markets, but precisely the opposite: since they believed so deeply that markets were the bedrock of civilization and had to be the basis of a modern society, it made perfect sense for them to start considering how to best use modern states in their service.

Even so, neoliberalism has been understood both as laissez-faire liberalism and more recently as a form of social liberalism. The latter interpretation has begun to arise in publications by scholars connected to the Mont Pelerin Society (Nordbakken 2017), but is also present in the work of Serge Audier (Audier 2012), who see some of the social topics of the Lippmann Colloquium as indicative of neoliberalism as a third way between socialism and laissez-faire. In certain ways, the case of France is the most confusing one, not only due to the slightly more social liberal bent of the Lippmann Colloquium, which was held in France. The French tradition of planning would make French neoliberalism somewhat more Keynesian and social than was the case in other countries (Denord 2007). Nonetheless, my study of early neoliberal thought has shown very clearly that neoliberalism was an attack on the ideas of social liberalism. In the case of Hayek and other conference attendees like Director and Eucken, there was a strongly held conviction that liberalism had lost its way by becoming more socially oriented.

What is more common than the idea that neoliberalism was a form of social liberalism is the opposite mistake: the notion that it was a revival of laissez-faire liberalism. We have noted that David Harvey's standard work *A Brief History of Neoliberalism* makes this assumption (Harvey 2005), and in journalism, public debate and even academia it is very widespread. Scholars specializing on neoliberalism have arguably moved passed this notion by now, but a historian like Angus Burgin, who is certainly aware of the nuances of early neoliberal thought, nonetheless calls neoliberalism a reinvention of "free markets". Bernhard Harcourt, author of the influential book *The Illusion of Free Markets*, refers to what he calls "the American paradox of laissez-faire and mass punishment" as an apt description of neoliberalism (Harcourt 2011). How neoliberalism came to be perceived as closely connected to, or even a revival of laissez-faire when it was an explicit attack on it, is really no great mystery. Those at the 1947 meeting who criticized Hayek and the core group of neoliberals from a social liberal position would more or less disappear from the group after 1947, and were certainly not influential in any way. This group includes Maurice Allais, Herbert Tingsten and Carl Iversen. Conversely, Ludwig Mises, who arguably criticized the neoliberals in much harsher language at the Mont Pèlerin meeting, but from a laissez-faire position, was made a director of the society. Neoliberalism built on the elitist, anti-democratic strand of liberalism that James L. Richardson argues mutated into laissez-faire liberalism in the 1800s, and it was therefore in many ways its heir. Moreover, the neoliberal argument for a strong state to spread and support markets was also built on an invisible-hand rhetoric of organic growth, which Hayek called "spontaneous order". The idea of a market order automatically regulated by an "invisible hand" is a powerful secular reworking of the concept of providence, and it has held great appeal among various conservative thinkers for centuries (Hirschman 1991). The metaphor indicates that the status quo is the result of a logic beyond the control of mere humans; it should come as no surprise that it has often been popular amongst those who find themselves comparatively well off under current social arrangements. As Chap. 5 showed very clearly, the members of the Mont Pelerin Society were certainly members of a privileged elite, and as such would be prone to defend the general outline of the capitalist society in which they found themselves. Razeen Sally, scholar of economics and international relations and current member of the Mont Pelerin Society, has claimed that this notion of *order* is in fact what characterizes what he calls "classical liberalism" (Sally 1998, 5). The latter was a term used by Hayek, and it seems to be an amalgam connecting earlier ideas from the cannon of what Richardson calls "elitist liberalism" with more recent neoliberalism. Liberalism was long seen to be a product of the nineteenth century, and perceived to be more socially and democratically oriented than what is now the case (Bell 2014, 700). This is what the early neoliberals sought to change, and understood relationally to other political projects existing at the time, early neoliberalism was profoundly right wing. So much so that a key question becomes what really separates it from conservatism.

Hayek himself attempted to answer that question in a presidential address to the Mont Pelerin Society in 1957, later reprinted as a post-script to *The Constitution of Liberty* (1960) under the title "Why I Am Not A Conservative". There he stated that "though there is a need for a 'brake on the vehicle of progress', I personally cannot be content with simply helping to apply the brake. What the liberal must ask, first of all, is not how fast or how far we should move, but where we should move" (Hayek 1972, 398). Corey Robin argues that this general understanding of conservatism as merely a moderating force is misleading. According to Robin, conservatism has always been an activist, counterrevolutionary creed, born out of the experience of having power and privilege, and seeing it threatened (Robin 2011, 28–35). Robin considers Hayek a conservative and implies that conservatism is always a form of reaction. Erwin Dekker concedes that many Viennese thinkers would not have been very offended by the term "reactionary", but argues that "edification and therapeutic knowledge captures better what we are after" (Dekker 2016, 158). Regardless of whether we want to use terms like conservative or reactionary to label Hayek's thinking, Robin's analysis can be useful for understanding neoliberalism as a movement placed squarely on the political right. The foundational attack on laissez-faire, exhibited in the writings of, for instance, Lippmann, Hayek, Röpke and Robbins, and backed up in discussion by, for instance, Eucken, Director and Graham, signalled that neoliberalism was to be something different from the perceived passivity of nineteenth-century laissez-faire liberalism, but it did not signal a turn towards social liberalism. According to Hayek, the main point of the conference at Mont Pèlerin was precisely to rid liberalism of the dogma of laissez-faire and find ways of using states to create the conditions for a market society, without falling into the constructivist trap of social liberalism. As we have seen, part of the challenge then lay in defining the boundaries of the mechanism and consequently to find which interventions created favourable conditions for market mechanisms, and avoid those which amounted to an interference with it. These subtle, yet highly important considerations were mainly reserved for internal meetings, and the paragraphs of published writing which alludes to them, remain obscure. This is why it has been so important to study the minutes of the first meeting of the Mont Pelerin Society in order to better understand what sort of project they were engaged in. Externally, however, the simple rhetoric of denouncing economic planning and praising the workings of the "free" market prevailed, and this was perceived by most as the main content of the ideology promoted by the Mont Pelerin Society. The French thinker, Raymond Aron, was amongst those who perceived Hayek in this way, even though Aron himself joined the Mont Pelerin Society for a few years in the 1950s (Aron 1939).

The Importance of Context

Another reason why neoliberalism has been understood as a return to laissez-faire liberalism, when it was in fact an attempt to steer right-wing liberalism away from the dogmas of laissez-faire, is that the content of neoliberal doctrine changed over time. Historians like Angus Burgin and Daniel Stedman Jones, who have studied early neoliberalism extensively, and thus found its anti-laissez-faire content, have been making this point for some time. There is certainly a case to be made for the idea that the neoliberal movement went through a sort of radicalization process in the 1970s, coinciding with what Angus Burgin dubs "the invention of Milton Friedman": his appointment as president of the Mont Pelerin Society in 1970 and his rise to fame as a major public intellectual in the USA (Burgin 2012, 152–186). In a letter to Friedman as early as 1960, Bertrand de Jouvenel claimed that the Mont Pelerin Society had "turned increasingly to a Manicheism according to which the State can do no good and private enterprise can do no wrong" (Burgin 2012, 150–151), so a change in orientation was perceived also by the society's members. In public especially, Friedman's message was a rather simple one of governments being good and markets being bad, and according to Burgin, Friedman developed "a rhetorical mode and popular profile that supplanted, and exceeded the Hayekian precedent" (Burgin 2012, 151). Friedman's simplifications, broadcast amongst other places in the television show *Free to Choose* which he made with his wife Rose Friedman (1910–2009) (née Director, sister of Aaron), were symptomatic of a broader shift between what has been known as the first and second generation of Chicago School economists. As we saw in Chap. 5, the discussion on how to use states for liberal ends centred mainly around the problem of monopolies. Apart from Mises, there was strong agreement that the rise of large corporations was a major problem with modern capitalism, which distorted the proper functioning of the price mechanism, and thus needed to be addressed by state action in the name of liberalism and competitive markets.

The degree to which this critique of corporations disappeared from the neoliberal agenda in later years is striking and has been studied to some extent by Robert Van Horn (Van Horn 2009; Van Horn and Klaes 2011). Led by founding MPS members like Milton Friedman and George Stigler, the second generation of Chicago economists turned the argument for strict competition laws on its head. They largely claimed that corporations could do no wrong, as any power they had was a result of market outcomes that ought not to be second—guessed by states and politicians. Mont Pelerin Society member Ronald Coase would later apply this principle also to the concept of externalities (Coase 1959). According to Van Horn and Edward Nik-Kah, the Chicago-based project known as The Free Market Study can be seen as a continuation of the project Hayek started at Mont Pelerin to define active, neoliberal economic policies (Nik-Kah and Van Horn 2016).

Gilles Cristoph has conceptualized the historical trajectory of neoliberal thought as a change in the object of regulation. In the beginning that is the object of study of this book, early neoliberal thinkers wanted to regulate markets, and our analysis has shown that they wanted to regulate them to secure better competition. In a way, they wanted to regulate markets to make sure they were more *market-like*, because the logic of competition was believed to be the essence of market mechanisms. As we have seen, however, it was realized that the active use of state power was necessary to achieve a competitive society based on markets. Cristoph argues that a change then took place with the rise of Public Choice theory, in which many neoliberals shifted their attention towards regulating states and the public sector, based on the same logic of competition (Cristoph 2013). Dardot and Laval suggest that a similar change has happened in Europe when they write of "the mutation of ordoliberalism". They argue that the original ordoliberal view of states as guarantors of markets, so important in the history of the European integration project, has morphed into a full-blown marketization of states. They claim that principles of market competition have been imposed both on the internal organization of states and in how nation states compete with other states on a global market (Dardot and Laval 2013, 193–215).

Compared to these ideas, the early neoliberals gathered at Mont Pèlerin do seem moderate, pragmatic and nuanced. They certainly wanted to regulate markets, while remaining liberal and true to the what they believed were the market mechanism's own logic of competition. The gist of their discussions focused on how to use the state to avoid monopolies and power concentrations. The trajectory of the many branches of neoliberal thought is difficult to follow as one after the initial meeting in 1947, but insofar as a general change is observable, I would argue that radicalization is a more suitable metaphor than mutation. The latter means to change into something quite different, whereas the former means going to the root or origin of something which is arguably what happened to neoliberalism. The work of historians like Burgin and Stedman Jones who argue the thesis that the ascent of Milton Friedman led to a radical, "Americanized" neoliberalism, suggests that we should see Hayek and the early neoliberals as "ambivalent" and with "notes of restraint" (Sloan Wilson 2015). I would argue that this is not necessarily the most fruitful way to understand the history of neoliberalism. This narrative runs the risk of attempting to understand the political thought of the past with the norms and vocabulary of the present. If early neoliberalism seems moderate to us today, it was no such thing in its own time: the ideas of the Mont Pelerin Society members were considered fringe and about as right wing as possible in the context of the immediate post-war years. It is indeed possible that the fact that they appear moderate from today's perspective says more about our own time than it does about the ideas in question.

My point is that later, more "extreme" versions of neoliberalism than the ones on display in the 1930s and 40s are not deviations from, but rather logical continuations of the pioneering efforts of early neoliberal intellectuals. I am not denying that the content of neoliberal doctrine changed somewhat, nor that Milton Friedman actually started using the term "laissez-faire" to describe his own views, merely that this should be seen not as a break with a more pragmatic past, but as continuity and adherence to a set of principles laid down by early neoliberals.

The key to this is to understand the context of the early neoliberals' supposed pragmatism. Their economic liberalism was on the defensive in 1947: they simply had to concede that the rise of corporations had led to major problems, and that capitalism was not at all working the way idealized liberal theories seemed to suggest. Indeed, some of the positions held by latter-day neoliberals would be almost unimaginable to the intellectuals gathered at Mont Pèlerin in 1947. Consider Hayek's statement in the session on "Free Enterprise or Competitive Order" regarding public services, where he said that some "services of this kind we must always expect the governments to provide <u>outside the market"</u> [Hayek's emphasis].[2] Contrast this with the widespread marketization of public services that has taken place all over the Western world in the past 20 years. In 1947, Public Choice theory had yet to be invented (mainly by James Buchanan, president of the Mont Pelerin Society from 1984–1986); but the important thing to realize is that these later developments could not have taken place without the pioneering efforts of the early neoliberals to start conceptualizing markets as mediators of modernity. The notion that a modern society can only function through market mechanisms is the core idea that allowed someone like Buchanan, in a very different context, to argue that public employees and even politicians had to be held in check by incentives and market-like structures (Doksheim and Kjøllesdal 2009; MacLean 2017). The same core idea which allowed Friedman, Stigler and other Chicago economists to backtrack on the 1947 meeting's ideas on anti-trust law, and claim that large corporations and market failures were arguably less dangerous than perceived failures by government (Van Horn and Klaes 2011).

[2]Liberaal Archief, "Mont Pèlerin Society", Box 1, Folder 1 "Mont Pèlerin, 1947".

Think Tanks

The Mont Pelerin Society exists to this day, and several of the scholars quoted as secondary sources in this book are or were members. The influence of this small, closed organization has been the subject of some scrutiny, especially by the numerous scholars loosely connected to the research network around Philip Mirowski and Dieter Plehwe (Mirowski and Plehwe 2009). One of the findings to emerge from this research is the close ties between the society, whose activities have usually been limited to annual conferences, and a much more active organization called the ATLAS Network (Djelic 2014). As mentioned in Chap. 1, this was founded in 1981 by Sir Antony Fisher, who was invited to Mont Pèlerin in 1947. The ATLAS network is today an umbrella organization for close to 500 think tanks in next to 100 countries. Fisher began his foray into the ever-expanding world of think tanks by founding the Institute for Economic Affairs (IEA) in London in 1955. He had made a fortune in farming caged chickens and, after reading *The Road to Serfdom* (the condensed version), decided he wanted to use his money and energy to spread the ideas of neoliberalism (Cockett 1995). Fisher approached Hayek in 1945, who told him that going into politics, as he had originally intended to, might not be the most efficient way to influence society. Fisher wrote: "He [Hayek] explained that the decisive influence in the great battle of ideas and policy was wielded by the intellectuals whom he characterised as 'second-hand dealers in ideas'" (Frost 2008, 10). Hayek would use this latter phrase and elaborate upon this strategy for achieving social change in his 1949 essay "The Intellectuals and Socialism". More important than running for office, according to him, was to slowly influence intellectuals and opinion makers so that politicians wielding power would eventually do so in a society where neoliberal ideas were available as alternatives, or even dominant and seen as common sense (Hayek 1949). Hayek claimed to be inspired by the social democrats in the Fabian Society, which for some time before the Second World War exerted great influence over British politics, and he advised Fisher to visit Leonard Read and the other Mont Pelerin Society members at the Foundation for Economic Education in 1952.

The IEA has been widely credited with laying the foundations for and actively promoting the rise of Margaret Thatcher to the UK prime ministership in 1979. Two years after that, Fisher set up ATLAS to be a "think tank that creates think tanks" (Meagher 2009, 94). He contributed to the founding of the Fraser Institute in Canada; the Manhattan Institute and the Pacific Research Institute in the US; the Centre for Independent Studies in Australia and some 150 other think tanks all over the world. The most famous think tanks in the ATLAS Network are powerful organizations like the Heritage Foundation, Cato Institute and others among the over 150 registered outlets in the USA; as well as UK-based think tanks like the IEA and the Adam Smith Institute. ATLAS also has an overwhelming presence in Latin America and somewhat smaller contingents in Asia, Africa and Oceania. In Scandinavian countries, think tanks like Timbro (Sweden), CEPOS (Denmark) and Civita (Norway) have exercised tremendous influence over contemporary politics in the preceding decade, giving rise to right-wing governments with market-based reform programmes and setting the terms for public debate. The network also has a strong presence in post-Soviet states in Eastern Europe, and a more modest position in continental Western Europe. This network is perhaps the most important way in which the neoliberal ideas studied in this book have influenced the world, and it amounts to a new form of political organization which is yet to be fully understood by scholars.

The many changes that societies both in the Western world and the so-called developing world have gone through in the past four decades can surely not be attributed exclusively to the ideas and political practices of Friedrich Hayek, the Mont Pelerin Society and the ATLAS Foundation. Privatizations, trade liberalization, the abandonment of countercyclical fiscal policies, austerity, structural adjustment programme, financialization and other developments often labelled as part of a broader process of neoliberalization (Saad-Filho and Fine 2016) can also be explained through analyses of political economy that pay little attention to ideas. These narratives focus on various crises of the "embedded liberalism" (Ruggie 1982) and democratic capitalism of the post-war order, often falling back on a Marxian analysis of dwindling rates of profit (Streeck 2011) and, ultimately, class struggle (Duménil and Lévy 2004). This can then be joined to an analysis and critique of neoliberal thought, through a Gramscian hegemony-theoretical approach (Springer 2012), or by simply pointing to the fact that the Mont Pelerin Society and the vast network described above is lavishly financed by capital interests. It should be clear that analyses of the political economy of capitalism are necessary, and that they may very well tell us more about our current impasse than works of intellectual history. Reference only to the world of ideas and debates amongst intellectuals can never be sufficient to understand the many political changes in the wake of the collapse of the Bretton Woods system in 1971 (Innset 2020).

However, the ways in which we understand and imagine the economy are also of great importance to how we allow it to operate. Samuel Moyn has recently argued that "Intellectual history has never really reckoned with the implications of social theory". According to him, developments in post-Marxist social theory offer insights into the relationship between the social order and representations of it (Moyn 2014, 112). Moyn makes special reference to Cornelius Castoriadis' concept of a "social imaginary" and argues that "the most interesting work in the field of European intellectual history today is attempting a history of ideas as (constitutive) ideology" (Moyn 2014, 123). In so far as my analysis in this book can contribute to our understanding of the present, it is precisely in uncovering the roots of why we think the way we do about economics, politics and the social order as such. In the very first paragraph of Chap. 1, I asked what the relationship is between politics and the economy, and this book has shown that early neoliberalism very much amounted to a desire to keep democratic politics away from the economy. This was achieved with new ideas about how to use modern states to construct and support markets, but to also protect them from "interference". The foundational idea of markets as the mediators of modernity may, especially through the impressive work of neoliberal think tanks, have influenced common sense and what Foucault would have called "political rationalities" relating to the way we view the relationship between politics and the economy today. In conceptualizing neoliberalism purely as a set of policy proposals, we risk missing the deeper content of neoliberalism as a theory of modernity. I argue this can be better understood when we carefully analyse the historical context out of which it grew.

Conclusion

Economists (Reinert 2007; Quiggin 2010; Shaikh 2016) and political scientists (Blyth 2013; Ban 2016) have in past decades tended to define neoliberalism as an economic policy programme inspired by the thinking which has been the topic of this book. The research department of the IMF issued a report in 2016 entitled "Neoliberalism: Oversold?", in which the authors suggest that what they perceive to be "neoliberalism", namely, policies of increased competition and privatization in developing countries, had not had the beneficial effects they were once thought to have (Ostry et al. 2016). Similarly, Donald J. Trump's 2016 presidential bid is widely perceived to have been successful because of his campaign's appeal to people in areas affected by industrial closures, with a promise to withdraw from trade deals in order to raise employment figures (Epstein 2017). Policies of industrial protectionism would surely run counter to what in policy circles is considered "neoliberalism", and it brings back the questions asked by many after the 2008 financial crisis of whether neoliberalism is entering its final phase (Crouch 2011). This book's historicizing of early neoliberal thought as resting on a conceptualization of markets as mediators of modernity makes it clear that we should be under no such illusions.

The sociologist Will Davies has written that even if the economics of neoliberalism might be experiencing some setbacks, the real challenge is to come to terms with the *sociology of neoliberalism*. "At the root of the difficulty and meaning of neoliberalism is the way it straddles the terrain of sociology and economics", he writes, suggesting that: "One way of understanding it is as an effort to *anchor modernity in the market*" (Davies 2016). This is precisely what my study of early neoliberal thought has shown: neoliberalism is about much more than economic policies; it amounts to a theory of modernity. Wendy Brown has decried the reduction of "neoliberalism to a bundle of economic policies with inadvertent political and social consequences: they fail to address the *political rationality* that both organizes these policies and reaches beyond the market" (Brown 2005, 38). Foucault once defined a political rationality as « le conduire des conduites », which translates roughly as "the conduct of conducts" (Foucault 2000, 336). It is not defined by specific policies, but rather by how we think about politics even before policies are designed. In a sense, it concerns what we see as being *political* in the first place and what we mean by that adjective. The neoliberal notion of markets as mediators of modernity could be seen as the basis of such a political rationality.

We are used to thinking that the political turmoil and economic collapse of the interwar years gave birth to two, now largely defunct, political movements: communism and fascism. In this book, we have concerned ourselves with a third political movement that I argue should be understood as arising out of the very same context: neoliberalism. In some ways, neoliberalism is more comparable to fascism than communism is. I am not referring to the content of doctrines (Azar 2015), but merely to the indisputable fact that both neoliberalism and fascism can be understood contextually as generating much of their energy from reacting to socialism. Followers of Karl Polanyi have argued that fascism, communism and social liberalism/social democracy were different types of protective responses to the excesses of Utopian laissez-faire liberalism, and that neoliberalism should be understood as an updated response to the consequent success of the "embedded liberalism" of the post-war years (Polanyi-Levitt and Seccareccia 2016). This brings to mind the intellectual history methodology of the logic of questions and answers, introduced by R.G. Collingwood and redeveloped by Quentin Skinner. I have argued that the full meaning of neoliberal ideas is only brought home once we see it fundamentally as a theory of modernity: developed as a response to the interwar years' collapse of the liberal world order and the rise of socialism and social liberalism.

The neoliberals always considered socialism and indeed the whole workers' movement an intellectual error. In later writing, Hayek would claim that the main problem with socialism was that it was based on an ethical principle, altruism, which according to him could only work in a tribal society in which everyone knows everyone else personally. According to him, modern, intertwined societies could only work if organized as markets in which people act self-interestedly in competition with others. Unlike the caricature of neoliberalism we are often presented with, Hayek was well aware that people tend to act altruistically, but according to him, this was a problem in a modern, market-based society (Gamble 1996, 26–49). This sheds new light on Margaret Thatcher's famous quote "Economics is the method; the objective is to change the soul".

The neoliberal notion of markets as mediators of modernity is a powerful idea. It could be argued that it exercises a tremendous influence on contemporary political imaginaries, and that it makes neoliberalism a constitutive ideology of our time. This book has shown where these ideas came from, and hopefully contributed to a better understanding of them.

Primary Sources

Het Liberaal Archief, Gent, Belgium
Mont Pelerin Society Collection

Secondary Literature

Aron, R. (1939). Remarques sur L'Objectivité des sciences sociales. *Theoria, 5,* 161–194.

Audier, S. (2012). *Néo-Libéralisme(s)*. Paris: Grasset.

Azar, R. (2015). Neoliberalism, austerity, and authoritarianism. *New Politics, 15*.

Ban, C. (2016). *Ruling ideas–How global neoliberalism goes local*. Oxford: Oxford University Press.

Bell, D. (2014). What Is liberalism? *Political Theory, 42,* 682–715.

Blyth, M. (2013). *Austerity–The history of a dangerous idea*. Oxford: Oxford University Press.

Brown, W. (2005). *Edgework*. Princeton and Oxford: Princeton University Press.

Burgin, A. (2012). *The great persuasion: Reinventing free markets since the depression*. Cambridge, Mass: Harvard University Press.

Coase, R. (1959). The federal communications commission. *Journal of Law and Economics, 2,* 1–40.

Cockett, R. (1995). *Thinking the unthinkable: Think-tanks and the economic counter-revolution*. Waukegan, Illinois: Fontana Press.

Cristoph, G. (2013). *More neoliberalism to end neoliberalism? The historical trajectory of neoliberal thought and post-2008 political economy*. London: Kingston University.

Crouch, C. (2011). *The strange non-death of neo-liberalism*. New Jersey: Wiley.

Dardot, P., & Laval, Christian. (2013). *The new way of the world: On neoliberal society*. Brooklyn, NY: Verso.

Davies, W. (2016). The difficulty of neoliberalism. *Open Democracy*, June 1.

Dekker, E. (2016). *The viennese students of civilization–The meaning and context of Austrian economics reconsidered*. Cambridge: Cambridge University Press.

Denord, F. (2007). *Néo-libéralisme-Version française*. Paris: Demopolis.

Djelic, M. L. (2014). Spreading ideas to change the world–inventing and institutionalizing the neoliberal think tank. In *Political Affair: Bridging Markets and Politics*. Edward Elgar.

Doksheim, M., & Kjøllesdal, K. (2009). *Svikt! - en introduksjon til public choice*. Oslo: Civita.

Duménil, G., & Lévy, D. (2004). *Capital resurgent: Roots of the neoliberal revolution*. Cambridge Massachusetts: Harvard University Press.

Epstein, R. A. (2017). Trump vs. free trade. *Defining Ideas-A Hoover Institution Journal*, March 6.

Foucault, M. (2000). *Power*. New York: The New Press.

Frost, G. (2008). *Antony fisher-Champion of liberty*. London: Institute of Economic Affairs.

Gamble, A. (1996). *Hayek: The iron cage of liberty. Key contemporary thinkers*. Cambridge: Polity Press.

Harcourt, B. E. (2011). *The illusion of free markets: Punishment and the myth of natural order*. Cambridge, Mass: Harvard University Press.

Harvey, D. (2005). *A brief history of neoliberalism*. Oxford: Oxford University Press.

Hayek, F. (1949). Intellectuals and socialism. *The University of Chicago Law Review*.

Hayek, F. (1972). *The constitution of liberty*. Chicago: Gateway.

Hirschman, A. O. (1991). *The rhetoric of reaction: Perversity, futility, jeopardy*. Cambridge, Mass: Belknap Press of Harvard University Press.

Innset, O. (2020). *Nyliberalismens historie i Norge*. Oslo: Fagbokforlaget.

MacLean, N. (2017). *Democracy in Chains*. New York: Scribe Publications.

Meagher, R. (2009). *Right ideas: Discourse, framing and the conservative coalition*. New York: University of New York.

Mirowski, P. (2013). *Never let a serious crisis go to waste: How neoliberalism survived the financial meltdown*. London: Verso.

Mirowski, P., & Plehwe, D. (Eds.). (2009). *The road from mont pèlerin: The making of the neoliberal thought collective*. Cambridge, Mass: Harvard University Press.

Moyn, S. (2014). Imaginary intellectual history. In *Rethinking Modern European Intellectual History* (pp. 112–130). Oxford: Oxford University Press.

Müller, J. W. (2008). Fear and freedom: On cold war liberalism. *European Journal of Political Theory,* 45–64.
Nik-Kah, E., & Van Horn, R. (2016). The ascendancy of Chicago neoliberalism. In *The Handbook of Neoliberalism.* London: Routledge.
Nordbakken, L. P. (2017). *Liberale tenkere for vår tid.* Oslo: Civita.
Ostry, J., Prakash, L., & Furceri, D. (2016). Neoliberalism: Oversold? *Finance & Development 53.*
Polanyi-Levitt, K., & Seccareccia, M. (2016). Thoughts on Mirowski and Neoliberalism from a Polanyian Perspective. *Institute for New Economic Thinking.*
Quiggin, J. (2010). *Zombie economics-How dead ideas still walk among us.* New Jersey, United States: Princeton University Press.
Reinert, E. (2007). *How rich countries got rich and why poor countries stay poor.* London: Constable & Robinson.
Robin, C. (2011). *The reactionary mind: Conservatism from edmund burke to sarah palin.* New York: Oxford University Press.
Ruggie, J. (1982). International regimes, transactions, and change: Embedded liberalism in the postwar economic order. *International Organization, 36,* 379–415.
Saad-Filho, A., & Fine, B. (2016). Thirteen things you need to know about neolibrealism. *Critical Sociology, 1,* 1–22.
Sally, R. (1998). *Classical liberalism and international economic order.* London: Routledge.
Shaikh, A. (2016). *Capitalism–Competition, conflict, crises.* Oxford: Oxford University Press.
Springer, S. (2012). Neoliberalism as discourse: Between foucauldian political economy and marxian poststructuralism. *Critical Discourse Studies, 9,* 133–147.
Streeck, W. (2011). The Crises of democratic capitalism. *New Left Review, II,* 5–29.
Van Horn, R. (2009). Reinventing monopoly and the role of corporations: The roots of chicago law and economics. In *The Road from Mont Pelerin* (pp. 204–238). Cambridge Massachusetts: Harvard University Press.
Van Horn, R., & Klaes, M. (2011). Intevening in Laissez-faire Liberalism: Chicago's shift on patents. In *Building Chicago Economics* (pp. 180–208). Cambridge: Cambridge University Press.
Wilson, D. S. (2015). The road to ideology. How friedrich hayek became a monster. *Evonomics.*

Index

O. Innset, *Reinventing Liberalism*, Springer Studies in the History of Economic Thought,
https://doi.org/10.1007/978-3-030-38885-0

The manufacturer's authorised representative in the EU is Springer Nature Customer Service Centre GmbH, Europaplatz 3, 69115 Heidelberg, Germany. If you have any concerns regarding our products, please contact ProductSafety@springernature.com

Printed and bound by CPI Group (UK) Ltd, Croydon, CR0 4YY
30/09/2026
02225449-0003